P9-DNV-226

MOZZARELL
EXTRA VIRG
BALSAMIC,
OCACCIA

# Lidia's Italy in America

Lidia's family as newly arrived immigrants in 1958, standing in
North Bergen, New Jersey, with a view of the New York City skyline

# Lidia's Italy in America

## LIDIA MATTICCHIO BASTIANICH

*and Tanya Bastianich Manuali*

PHOTOGRAPHS BY HIRSHEIMER & HAMILTON
AND LIDIA MATTICCHIO BASTIANICH

ALFRED A. KNOPF  NEW YORK  2011

THIS IS A BORZOI BOOK
PUBLISHED BY ALFRED A. KNOPF

www.aaknopf.com

Food photography by Christopher Hirsheimer

Library of Congress Cataloging-in-Publication Data
Bastianich, Lidia.
Lidia's Italy in America / by Lidia Matticchio Bastianich and Tanya Bastianich
Manuali.—1st ed.
p.   cm.
ISBN 978-0-307-59567-6 (hardback)
1. Cooking, Italian.   2. Cooking—United States.   3. Italian American
families.   4. Cookbooks.   I. Manuali, Tanya Bastianich.   II. Title.
TX723.B3225 2011   641.5945—dc23   2011013581

Jacket photographs by Christopher Hirsheimer
Jacket design by Carol Carson

Manufactured in the United States of America
First Edition

This book is dedicated to all of the immigrants like my mother,
Erminia, who left behind their country and families to come
to America in search of a new life, in search of opportunity so their
families and children could have a life of freedom and a chance
at a better life. Their hard work, ingenuity, and courage have
helped to make America what it is today.

At the Andy Boy Farms in California, harvesting broccoli rabe

# Contents

## Zuppe

## Sandwiches and Pizza

## Salads

## Pasta

## Vegetables and Sides

## Seafood

## Meat

## Desserts

Harvesting radicchio in Salinas Valley, California

# Acknowledgments

There are so many people to thank when a book is complete. It is a collaboration of hard work, sharing ideas, guidance, and a lot of time spent together developing, testing, and ultimately tasting, and I want to thank all of my great team.

I thank Judith Jones for her ever sound advice and creative stimulation. We have worked together now on five winning cookbooks. I have learned much along the way and for this, I thank you. To Jessica Freeman-Slade, a new addition to my book work: thank you for your enthusiasm, for fresh perspectives, and for your incredibly thorough editing. And of course Ken Schneider, thank you for pulling it all so diligently together. Thanks to my kitchen cohort, Amy Stevenson, for her always dependable shopping, testing, and writing for the book as well as for being our culinary producer for the companion TV series.

For capturing my food through your lenses and making it all look beautiful, unending thanks go to Christopher Hirscheimer and Melissa Hamilton. For tying up all the efforts and hard work into a wonderful design, thank you to Carol Devine Carson and Kristen Bearse. A special thanks to my old friend Paul Bogaards and his team for their endless efforts in marketing and promoting my works.

Thanks to Robert Barnett and Deneen Howell from Williams Connelly (wc.com) for helping me when I needed assurance and security most. This book would not have happened without your guidance and counsel.

Where would I be without my family? They inspire my work and support me. Erminia, my mother, is a constant source of wise words for me. My two children, Tanya and Joseph, have paid me the greatest compliment, following in an industry that I love so dearly. I thank them for understanding their mother and allowing my passion to be infectious. Thank you to my daughter-in-law, Deanna, for taking care of my son and grandchildren. Thank you to my son-in-law, Corrado, for supporting my new business ventures with sound legal advice and good business sense. And not enough could be said about my love for my five little darlings: Olivia, Lorenzo, Miles, Ethan, and Julia. Thank you all for being the greatest family a mother could wish for.

Every successful woman has a strong team behind her, and leading my team is Shelly Burgess Nicotra. Her dedication to me and her intelligence is incomparable. Thank you, Shelly. To the young ladies in my office, Lauren Falk, Haley Salles, Meghan Liu, and Alexi Caputo, thank you for holding down the fort.

Hand in hand with my books, there are people I would like to thank for making my show on public television possible. Thank you to the American Public Television team for always doing a stellar job distributing my show. And thanks to the wonderful team at my presenting station, WGBH in Boston. Their enthusiasm is contagious and their professionalism is exemplary. My show would not be possible without my sponsors: Grana Padano, Colavita, and Perugina. I thank them for believing in what I do and for their support. Thank you also to the following companies for contributing: Le Creuset, OXO, Williams-Sonoma, LaFrieda Meats, Segafredo Coffee, Keil Brothers, San Pellegrino and Panna Waters, D'Artagnan, Baldor Foods, Bastianich wines, and Lidia's Pasta.

While I am on the road filming and researching, there is an army of people who work and make sure my businesses continue on as I would have them. For their dedication and hard work, thank you to the staff of Felidia, Becco, Del Posto, Lidia's Kansas City, Lidia's Pittsburgh, and Eataly.

A final thank you goes to all the Italian American immigrants and artisans who, during my travels, research, and filming, showed me their passion for all things Italian.

# L'America

I have written about Italian American food and given you recipes before, but it has become clear in my travels through the United States that there is so much more to tell about the Italian American experience. It is a story that is also about Italian immigration, and about the struggles of settling and finding a home, of feeding a family, of making a new life, and of building America. This is a country where immigrants of all cultures are welcomed, a land whose very fiber and strength is the diversity of its people, and putting food on the table for the family was, and still is, the quest of immigrants of every culture.

Starting with this question—how did immigrants put food on the table for their families?—I began my journey toward uncovering the Italian American story of food. Thousands of miles and many meals later, I share with you here some of the stories and facts, the triumphs and losses, the heroes, the artists, and the entrepreneurs I encountered. Along the way I have tasted and collected many recipes, and in this book the recipes tell the story of the Italian immigrant, from the earliest to their present-day descendants, now fourth- and fifth-generation Italian Americans.

Along the way I have visited many Little Italys: the North End in Boston, Mulberry Street and Arthur Avenue in New York, and North Beach in San Francisco, all of which are still vibrant with Italian culture and tradition. I went to Napa and Sonoma, where Italian winemaking gave birth to an entire industry, and where the Salinas Valley contains thousands of acres now growing broccoli rabe, radicchio, and artichokes, some of Italy's favorite vegetables. I learned about the birth of the canning industry in San Diego and Monterey, making the connection with the early immigrant fishermen, and I ate fig cookies at the feast of St. Joseph in New Orleans and Kansas City, reminding me that the Sicilians came here as immigrants in large numbers three generations ago. I stood with the fishermen of today in Rhode Island, Gloucester, and Baltimore, and paid tribute to those immigrants who braved these same waters to feed their families. And for every three places I visited, there were ten more that I missed due to lack of time. I wish I could have visited them all—perhaps someday I will.

I am certain that you will want to cook all of these delicious yet simple recipes I have collected. Food, after all, is the blueprint of who we are: the food of our culture gives us strength and identity as a group and as individuals. Along with their native language, Italian immigrants brought their native food to their new homes; it was a comfort and it gave them a sense of security. Language is often lost after the first generation, but the culture of the table and food remains. This book pays homage to the importance and the role food played in the adaptation of the Italian immigrants in America and how it has become part of what we consider Americana.

The Italian way of life—Italian customs, flavors, ingenuity, business savvy, and a tenacious will to survive—has left its mark on America. The Italian way has been weaved into and is an integral part of America today. I am one of those weavers, for I was blessed to be born Italian, and then I was blessed again when I was adopted by America. Now, I am connecting and weaving the two cultures together with the food that I cook and share with you. You have followed me on my journeys through my books: *La Cucina di Lidia, Lidia's Italian Table, Lidia's Italian-American Kitchen, Lidia's Family Table, Lidia's Italy,* and *Lidia Cooks from the Heart of Italy.* Now I am confident you will enjoy *Lidia's Italy in America* and take this very special and flavorful journey with me.

In *Lidia's Italian-American Kitchen* I introduced the large wave of immigrants who came from Italy to America, beginning in the 1880s and continuing well into the next century. America has been the largest single recipient of Italian immigrants in the world; however, the Italian love affair with America began much earlier. It was Italian explorers—Amerigo Vespucci in 1499, Giovanno Gaboto (whom most know as John Cabot) in 1497, and Giovanni da Verrazzano in 1524—who paved the way for the immigrants who would later arrive on these shores. Fledgling America had a friend in the Tuscan physician Filippo Mazzei, who fought alongside Thomas Jefferson during the American Revolution and advanced agricultural developments, including the cultivation of grapes for wine, on land adjacent to Jefferson's Monticello. America was already a big cauldron of different cultures and nationalities, but even in their early days in this country, Italians were making an impact.

As the country grew, Italian communities developed, and with them grew Italian markets, stores, and restaurants. The first Italian eating experience for most Americans was most likely in an immigrant home or in restaurants run by immigrants that cooked Italian American food. But for all their ingenuity, Italian immigrants could not bring all their resources over with them. The Promised Land did not offer plump, sweet San Marzano plum tomatoes or fresh Mediterranean herbs. So Italian cuisine underwent a transformation by adapting to whatever ingredients were available. Today many well-traveled Americans ask me, "Why is Italian food different in Italy?" I humbly respond, "Because that is the soil, the earth, and the regions where the people of Italy have been for millennia. The food they cook and eat reflects that *terroir,* climate, and history of the land. America is a different *terroir,* has different climates, and so the food has a different history. It is the memories and experience the Italian immigrants brought with them, coupled with the products they found, that developed into today's Italian American cuisine." Many dishes like Chicken Vesuvio, Veal Parmiciano, and Spaghetti and Meatballs are not dishes found in Italy but instead are new creations born in America. Italian flavors blossomed in the homes, the gardens, the specialty shops, and the hearts of Italian Americans. "Little Italys" began to sprout up all over the country, and they remain neighborhoods that uphold the Italian traditions to this day, in which Italian neighborhood feasts attract millions of Americans to enjoy delicacies such as *zeppole* and sausage and peppers. Some of these Little Italies are shrinking, and not much time is left to record the life and customs of the Italian immigrant, but traditions are still being kept alive.

But the story of Italian American cuisine does not end today, for food culture continues to evolve, and as our methods of transportation improve, the Italian cuisine in America is getting ever closer to the regional and contemporary cuisine in Italy. My personal quest since my opening of Felidia Ristorante in 1981 was to bring the regional cuisine of Italy to America. I began cooking the regional cuisine of Friuli-Venezia-Giulia and the little peninsula of Istria, where I hail from, and it soon became clear to me that the Italian American cuisine was not what my family was cooking. I did what came naturally when I opened Felidia: I cooked what we ate at home. But I needed the traditional Italian products, and life today is much easier now that many authentic Italian ingredients are available in the United States. But at a time when I could not get those ingredients, I managed to invent something new and delicious, just as my fellow Italian immigrants have done since their arrival in this country.

Like so many other nationalities that compose the mosaic we call America, Italians have been an integral part of the progression and development of this country. Traveling from coast to coast, I saw the Italian influence on food everywhere, from the ubiquitous pizza pie to gelato. Now more than ever, Italian influence, especially that on modern fashion, design, and culture, is evident in the United States. Five centuries ago, Italians landed on these shores. Over the last two centuries, they have grown from the working-class backbone that built infrastructure and developed the country's natural resources into successful entrepreneurs and leaders of industry. Today, this country's Italians are truly as American as apple pie, but they have also held on to the traditions of their heritage. It is this journey that I want you to take with me, and I am very proud to share this fantastic Italian American story with you.

# Lidia's Italy
# in America

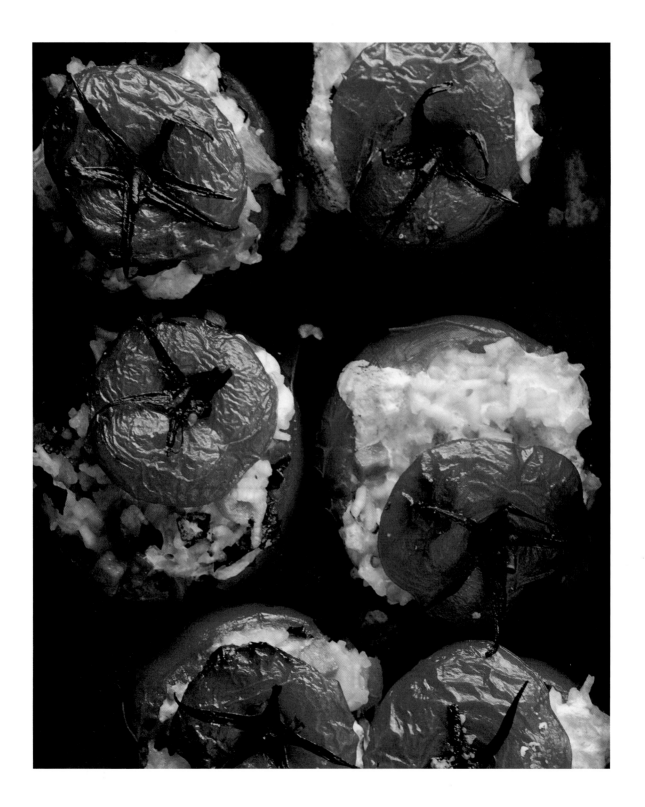

# Antipasti

# ❦ COLD ANTIPASTI

# Arthur Avenue—The Italian Heartbeat in the Bronx

The Belmont section of the Bronx became home to many Italian stonemasons and laborers. They worked in building the nearby New York Botanical Garden and the Bronx Zoo. Then, in the 1880s, the Germans and Irish began arriving in the area; they were followed by another wave of Italians in the 1890s. The land had originally been mostly farmland, a great portion owned by the Lorillard tobacco family. When they began to build streets in the area, Mrs. Lorillard asked that a street be named after the twenty-first president, Chester A. Arthur.

This is still the place to go in New York for all things Italian. Many people do weekend shopping, visit the covered market for freshly made Italian sausage, or stroll down the street to buy freshly pulled mozzarella or even a freshly rolled cigar. While many Little Italy neighborhoods across the country have become touristy or consist mainly of cafés and restaurants, Arthur Avenue has remained a neighborhood.

Our Lady of Mount Carmel Church is at the center of it all, and even Rafaello, the Italian shoemaker, is still busy fixing shoes. Mayor Fiorello La Guardia spearheaded the building of the Arthur Avenue Retail Market, and actors such as Chazz Palminteri and Joe Pesci grew up in this neighborhood. Many of my Italian American friends also grew up on Arthur Avenue, and inevitably, every time we meet, the conversation at some point turns to how wonderful their childhood was there, how they all knew each other, and how one was never without a meal. The neighbors fed you if your mother was late from work, and you were careful not to do anything wrong because you never knew which neighbor was watching you and would report back to Mom. One could go to a store and charge to Mom's account, and sometimes receive a free ice cream or fruit. The

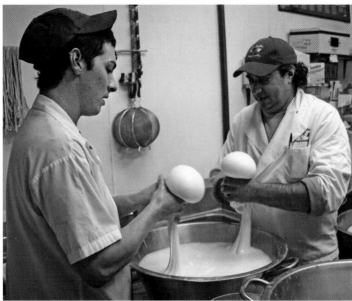

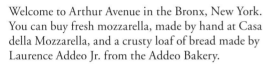

Welcome to Arthur Avenue in the Bronx, New York. You can buy fresh mozzarella, made by hand at Casa della Mozzarella, and a crusty loaf of bread made by Laurence Addeo Jr. from the Addeo Bakery.

Mike Greco at Mike's Deli in the Arthur Avenue Retail Market

conversations always led to food, but back then, just as today, the whole commercial life of Arthur Avenue is about food.

When I go to Arthur Avenue, I always pay a visit and get a sandwich at Mike's Deli, presided over by Mike Greco and his son David. Besides the long list of creatively named sandwiches, there is an endless array of cold cuts, marinated fish, olives, and even mozzarella, which is smoked by the back door every morning. When he is not hosting his Little Italy radio show, Mike is busy socializing at his deli in the Retail Market, or creating another great sandwich with a wild name. Just to name a few:

Big Vinny's Favorite   *Sopressata, ricotta salata & homemade roasted peppers . . ."If you're ever up the river . . ."*
The Godfather   *Oldani salami & imported provolone, "An offer that can't be refused"*
Herb's Sandwich   *Goat cheese with fresh tomato & roasted peppers or sun-dried tomatoes*
King David   *Sopressata with chunks of 4 year old parmigiano, roasted peppers & basil . . ."Fit for a king"*
Michelangelo   *Mozzarella & prosciutto, "A work of art"*
The Mussolini   *Capicola, shavings of fontinella cheese & anchovies*
The Politician   *Full of bologna—"except for Bloomberg, 'cause he's a leader"*
The Raging Bull   *Hot sopressata & sharp provolone, "A real knockout"*
Sophia Loren   *Swiss Lorraine & turkey for a beautiful figure*
Towering Inferno   *Smoked mozzarella & smoked prosciutto, "A real blaze"*
Virgin Mary   *Pure, white, fresh mozzarella . . ."It's a blessing"*
The Wanderer   *Sweet sopressata, homemade dry mozzarella, "You'll always wander back for this one"*

Next up after the Greco father-son team are Uncle Peter and nephew Mike at Peter's Meat Market, where you can get some of the best sausages in the area, made all day long in the back. In the display case up front are lots of offal, tripe, and rabbits. "Does all this sell?" I asked. "Here it never stopped," replied Peter. The economy of Italy is based on small family businesses, and on Arthur Avenue it is much the same.

No Italian meal is served without good crusty bread, and at the Addeo Bakery, the third generation, Laurence Addeo Jr. is still there every morning before the sun rises, busy kneading the bread. We arrived at 11 a.m., and almost all the bread was gone, but it was getting to be lunchtime, and Laurence was behind the stove cooking some mussels in what used to be the family kitchen and is still functional now. In Italy they call it *casa e bottega*—house and shop—it was all in one.

With a crusty loaf under the arm, we made our next stop at Casa della Mozzarella, where Orazio Carciotto pulls and stretches the curd for fresh mozzarella. In and around Napoli, where mozzarella is king, it is known that mozzarella is already not ideal two hours after it has been pulled, so Orazio is at it all day for his discriminating Italian American customers.

Down the street, you can have a few shucked oysters and clams on tables outside Randazzo's Fish Market, or go inside for a selection of glistening local and imported fish in season. The pictures of three generations hang on the wall, and the next generation is in training.

Sal is the fourth generation in his family to run Biancardi's Meat Market, where half of the store's ceiling is festooned with hanging salami, and counters are stacked with slabs of meat—beef, pork, and lamb. Some are butchered the American way, and some the European way, nuances that make a big difference when you come from Italy.

Owner Joe Randazzo, the third generation of his family to run Randazzo's Seafood

I always stop to say hello to my dear friends Rosa and Giancarlo Paciullo at Tino's Delicatessen. Sometimes on their days off they come to Felidia, but when they are cooking, I go and eat their delicious food on Arthur Avenue. They offer a great selection of antipasti, such as baked clams, eggplant rollatini, stuffed mushrooms, seasonal baked pastas, and lots of braised meats, which you can take out, or eat on the premises with Italian music playing in the background.

Roberto's has become an iconic restaurant on Arthur Avenue. Roberto Paciullo has achieved a great balance between the contemporary Italian food in Italy and the Italian American culinary culture here in America. A wonderful chef who runs both Roberto's and the Trattoria Zero Otto Nove, Roberto is a rather recent immigrant: he came from Salerno in 1960, one of eleven children, whose father was also a chef. One Italian word best captures Roberto—*simpatico,* which can only be translated as "extremely affable." He is very serious about his food and restaurants, but at the same time he tells wonderful stories about Salerno (not far from Naples), where he comes from, or about Arthur Avenue and its evolution, something about which Roberto is passionate. Many of his dishes reach back to his Salerno days and some are borrowed from his mom. All of them are delicious, and his restaurant is always full.

When I want to feel the Italian American spirit, when I want to smell the aroma of espresso wafting through the air, when I need Italian music to fill my soul, genuine Italian products to fill my basket, and a good Italian meal to enjoy, Arthur Avenue is where I go. It is what Italy in America was, and still is today. And as I travel throughout America searching for the Italian element—the flavor, essence, and feel in every bite I take—I realize ever more how much Italy has influenced America, and how generously America has welcomed the Italians.

# Squid Salad

*Insalata di Calamari*

Seafood salad is common in Italian American households, especially on Christmas Eve, La Vigilia, and almost always as an appetizer on menus in Italian American restaurants. As popular as the seafood salad is in the United States, in Italy one is more likely to find a simple salad like this version, containing one kind of seafood. What is most important in this recipe is not to overcook the calamari.

SERVES 6

Pour 2 inches of water into a large Dutch oven or pot and bring to a boil. Add the bay leaves and lemon peel, and continue to boil for a few minutes, until they release their aromas.

Set a colander or steamer over (but not touching) the water. Slip the calamari rings and tentacles into the colander or steamer, adjust the heat so the water is simmering, and cover. Cook until the calamari is just cooked through and has gone from opaque to translucent, about 6 to 7 minutes.

Combine the olives, celery, roasted pepper, salt, oregano, peperoncino, and lemon juice in a large bowl. When the calamari is done, add it to the bowl, drizzle with the olive oil, and toss. Sprinkle in the parsley, toss again, and serve warm or at room temperature.

3 fresh bay leaves

The whole peel and juice of 1 lemon

1½ pounds calamari bodies and tentacles, cleaned, bodies cut into ½-inch rings

1 cup pitted, slivered green olives

4 inner stalks celery, with leaves, sliced thin on the bias

1 cup roasted red-bell-pepper strips

½ teaspoon kosher salt

¼ teaspoon dried oregano

¼ teaspoon peperoncino flakes, or to taste

3 tablespoons extra-virgin olive oil

2 tablespoons chopped fresh Italian parsley

Clockwise from bottom left: Squid Salad, Smoked Sardine Salad, and Crab and Celery Salad

# Crab and Celery Salad

*Insalata di Granchio e Sedano*

When I ate my way through Baltimore, crabs were to be had in many ways. It was spring, and soft-shells were on every menu, as were crab cakes, crab cocktails, and crab salads. Most of the dishes had some version of tartar sauce, ketchup cocktail sauce, or rémoulade served with them.

I got a yearning for a crab salad Italian-style, so, without much ado, here is one that evokes a lobster salad they often make in Sardinia.

Mix the celery, eggs, tomatoes, and parsley together in a large bowl. Drizzle with the lemon juice and olive oil, seasoning with salt. Toss well, to coat the salad with the dressing. Add the crabmeat, and toss gently to combine, without breaking up the lumps of crab.

SERVES 4

1½ cups thin bias-cut inner stalks celery and leaves

2 large hard-boiled eggs, peeled and coarsely chopped

2 ripe medium tomatoes, seeded, cut into ½-inch pieces

3 tablespoons chopped fresh Italian parsley

3 tablespoons lemon juice

3 tablespoons extra-virgin olive oil

¾ teaspoon kosher salt

1 pound jumbo lump crabmeat, picked through for shells

A selection of fresh eggs at Antonelli Poultry in Providence, Rhode Island

# Salt Cod, Potato, and String Bean Salad

*Insalata di Baccalà, Patate, e Fagiolini*

Baccalà, or salt cod, has a long tradition on the Italian table, and since it traveled well, immigrants brought it with them to the New World, where they used it as barter as well as for cooking. (One need only notice how popular baccalà is in Caribbean cultures.) The Italian immigrants have made baccalà a big part of the Italian American table, especially around the holidays. This simple salad recipe will satisfy any baccalà nostalgia, holiday or no holiday.

SERVES 6

1 pound boneless baccalà fillet, soaked for 8 hours (enough time to get the salt out of the fish), changing the water 3 or 4 times

3 medium russet potatoes (about 1½ pounds)

1 pound green beans, trimmed

1 small red onion, thinly sliced

½ cup roasted red-pepper strips

½ teaspoon kosher salt

⅛ teaspoon peperoncino flakes, or to taste

¼ cup extra-virgin olive oil

3 tablespoons white-wine vinegar

Place the salt cod in a small saucepan, and add water to cover. Bring the water to a simmer, 1 to 2 minutes, just to refresh the cod and remove any last traces of saltiness. Drain, pat the cod dry, and set aside.

Slip the potatoes into a pot with water, cover, and bring to a simmer. Cook until tender; then remove the potatoes and let cool slightly. Peel and cut them into 1-inch chunks, and toss into a serving bowl.

In the meantime, bring a pot of salted water to a boil, and add the green beans. Boil until crisp-tender, about 6 minutes, drain, let cool, then add to the bowl with the potatoes.

Scatter the red onion and pepper into the serving bowl. Season with the salt and peperoncino flakes, drizzle with the olive oil and vinegar, and toss well.

Flake the cod in big chunks over the top of the bowl, and toss gently one more time, taking care not to break up the pieces of fish too much.

# Mozzarella and Tomato Salad

*Insalata Caprese*

Toss together the tomatoes, mozzarella, spinach, and salt in a large serving bowl.

Whisk together the oil and vinegar in a small bowl. Pour the dressing over the salad and toss well. Sprinkle with the oregano, and toss to combine.

SERVES 6

8 ripe medium tomatoes, cored, cut into 1-inch pieces

1 pound fresh mozzarella, cut into ½-inch cubes

4 packed cups coarsely chopped fresh baby spinach leaves

1½ teaspoons kosher salt

¼ cup extra-virgin olive oil

3 tablespoons red-wine vinegar

1 teaspoon dried oregano

The perfect pairing: a crisp, refreshing glass of Bastianich Rosato with freshly picked summer tomatoes

# San Diego and the Sardine Industry

When it was time for Tanya and me to go to San Diego, I was excited to research the sardine canneries and the history of the Italian immigrants who worked in them. I had visions of nets full of jumping, shimmering silver sardines being hoisted to shore, because I remembered how, as a child on the Adriatic, I would help my uncle Emilio, the fisherman of the family. I love sardines, and whenever I go back to Istria, one of my first stops is the fish market. I make sure I get there early in the morning, when the fishermen deliver their catch, and I look for *sardoni,* a cross between sardines and anchovies. For lunch I fry them lightly in olive oil, and eat them with a bowl of radicchio-zuccherino salad, a glass of Bastianich Vespa, and someone to share it; I am in heaven.

Pacific Coast sardines, on the other hand, are found from southeastern Alaska to Baja California, the Gulf of California, and also along the coasts of Peru and Chile. They form large schools (up to ten million fish) and are often associated with anchovy, hake, and mackerel. There is, technically, no fish called a sardine; the term "sardine" refers to various small fish that are all members of the herring family. Sardines are named after the Italian island of Sardinia, where they are abundant and very much part of the diet. The West Coast is a natural habitat for sardines, which migrate up and down the coast. They reach all the way up to Alaska and return back south for the mating season. A canning industry was built, ranging from San Diego up to Monterey, based on the migration of the sardines.

In the United States, fresh sardines are not used much, but canning them used to be a big industry. The sardine-canning industry peaked in the 1950s; now the San Diego canneries in Tuna Harbor Park are no longer operating. There is a calmness about this area, where a sculpture, *The Cannery Workers Tribute,* stands proudly in the Parque del Sol as a grateful reminder of all the immigrant workers who worked and made their home in this neighborhood upon arriving in America. In the beginning most of the workers were Sicilian or Ligurian immigrants, but slowly Asians became the new wave of immigrants and replaced the Italians in the canneries.

Tanya and I were hungry after our research, and opted to have lunch at Anthony's Fish Grotto, run by the Ghio family. Anthony Ghio, a hardworking Italian immigrant, eventually opened his own business, the Ghio Seafood Commissary. The Ghio family arrived in San Diego in 1912 and started right away in the fishing industry. What began as an eighteen-seat restaurant is now an enterprise that includes six restaurants and a flourishing wholesale and dockside processing company. The commissary thrived by cleverly displaying cases of fresh fish (and sauces to go with them). Inspired by her father's retail success, Catherine, also known as Mama Ghio, opened Anthony's Fish Grotto in 1946, which still remains one of San Diego's most successful restaurants. Tanya and I enjoyed a most delicious and unusual dish there, squid steak Milanese, which I'd never had before. It made perfect sense: a nice thick squid cutlet, lightly breaded, and sautéed in a little olive oil and butter with a squeeze of lemon juice added. *Delizioso!*

Another great Italian fish story is the Sardine Factory in Monterey, opened by Ted Balestreri and Bert Cutino in 1968. Ted and Bert have been committed to providing great service and local fresh products in their restaurant, especially fish. Their immigrant families came to the area as fishermen, and later as fish vendors and canners; their specialty was sardines. The area and its canning industry were immortalized by John Steinbeck in his novel *Cannery Row,* but Monterey's fishing industry was nearly abandoned by the late 1960s. However, Bert was confident. He was familiar with the area; as a young boy he used to take his father's catch to the canneries. Though he and Ted

The Sardine Factory in Monterey, California

Chef Bert Cutino, Ted Balestreri, and me at the Sardine Factory

started out as busboys, both aspired to open a fine-dining restaurant in Monterey. They started with one room in the abandoned cafeteria of a canning plant, and now own one of the iconic dining establishments in the country.

The Sardine Factory still serves sardines—smoked, then lightly marinated—with chopped egg, parsley, capers, lemon, and herbed croutons. They are not only delicious but good for you. As one of my good friends, the great food writer James Villas, put it in his essay "The Unsung Sardine": "Ounce for ounce, sardines provide more calcium and phosphorus than milk, more protein than steak, more potassium than bananas, and more iron than cooked spinach." Plus, sardines are a good source of omega-3 fatty acids.

# Smoked Sardine Salad

*Insalata di Sardine Affumicate*

This is a recipe from the Sardine Factory in Monterey, California. My longtime friends Ted Balestreri and Chef Bert Cutino smoke fresh sardines for this dish, but smoked canned sardines are delicious as well. However, I enjoy regular canned sardines packed in olive oil in this dish as well.

Toss the red onion, lemon slices, capers, chopped egg, and sardines in a large bowl. Drizzle the vinegar over the salad, sprinkle on the parsley, and toss gently to combine without further breaking up the sardine pieces.

Mound the salad on a platter, surrounded by the toasts.

SERVES 4

1 small red onion, thinly sliced

¼ lemon, peeled and very thinly sliced

2 tablespoons drained capers

1 large hard-boiled egg, quartered or roughly chopped

Two 3.7-ounce cans smoked sardines in olive oil, drained, cut into bite-sized pieces

1 tablespoon red-wine vinegar

1 tablespoon chopped fresh Italian parsley

Toast points or toasted ciabatta slices, for serving

Fresh sardines in Monterey, California

# Celery, Artichoke, and Mortadella Salad

## *Insalata di Sedano, Carciofi, e Mortadella*

In creating this recipe, I added the mortadella on the spur of the moment. I love raw artichoke salad, but have often prepared this salad with many other, different ingredients, such as raw mushrooms, or shavings of Grana Padano or Parmigiano-Reggiano. Recently I made a beautiful salad of small artichokes, crunchy celery, and some great imported mortadella, which I happened to have on hand. And so this salad was born: it certainly is based on tradition, but with my own touch. It has now become a family favorite for buffets, antipasto, or just for lunch.

SERVES 4 TO 6

8 baby artichokes (about 1 pound)

Juice of 2 lemons

4 inner stalks celery, with leaves, thinly sliced on the bias

4-ounce chunk Grana Padano or Parmigiano-Reggiano

3 tablespoons extra-virgin olive oil

½ teaspoon kosher salt

6-ounce piece mortadella, cut into matchsticks

Clean and prepare the artichokes as illustrated (see sidebar). Drain the artichoke slices from the water and set into a mixing bowl and toss with the juice of the remaining lemon.

Add the celery to the mixing bowl. On the coarse holes of a box grater, grate most of the cheese into the bowl, reserving a small piece for garnish. Drizzle the ingredients in the mixing bowl with the olive oil and season with salt. Toss well.

Now add the mortadella, and toss gently. Arrange the salad on a serving plate, grate the remaining cheese over the top, and serve.

---

### HOW TO CLEAN AND PREPARE ARTICHOKES

To clean eight baby artichokes and prevent them from oxidizing, fill a bowl with approximately one quart of cold water, and add the juice of one lemon, plus the squeezed-out lemon halves.

Peel and trim the stem of the first artichoke. Pull off any tough outer leaves and discard. Using a paring knife, trim away any tough parts around the base and stem of the artichoke. With a serrated knife, cut off the top third of the artichoke and discard.

If the recipe calls for sliced artichoke, halve the artichoke and slice very thin lengthwise (through the stem, either by hand or on a mandoline) or crosswise. Repeat this process with each of the remaining artichokes. As you finish with each artichoke, add it to the bowl of cold water and lemon juice, to keep it fresh.

If you are stuffing the artichokes: Once you have cut off the top third with a serrated knife, push the leaves out to expose the fuzzy purple choke. With a small spoon, scrape out the choke to expose the heart at the bottom of the artichoke. Put the prepared artichoke in the bowl of water and lemon juice to keep it fresh.

# 🍂 HOT ANTIPASTI

# Mozzarella in Texas

There is an old Italian saying: *Sei come il prezzemolo, da per tutto,* "You are like chopped parsley, all over the place." So it is for Italians who have settled all over the United States, including Texas. Italians are the sixth-largest ethnic group in Texas, but most of these Italians came in the last half of the twentieth century, as professionals and business workers attracted by opportunity and the booming job market. The prairie sky, wide and high, and the sage in bloom, like perfume, obviously attracted Italians deep in the heart of Texas.

The Gulf Coast was a principal center for Italian immigration, with many coming through the port of New Orleans, the Ellis Island of the South. Slowly they moved deeper into America. Many Sicilians settled in the lower Brazos Valley and in Galveston County; the Piedmontese preferred Montague County. The Modenese and Venetians worked in the coal mines at Thurber; the Lombards helped to construct the New York, Texas, Mexican Railway, called the "Macaroni Line." There were major Italian settlements in Houston and San Antonio.

Not only did the Italians bring their food culture with them to Texas, but Texans traveling abroad were falling ever more in love with Italian culture and its food. Paula Lambert, the founder of the Mozzarella Company in Dallas, was one of these Texans. During one of my visits to Dallas, Paula shared this story with me: "When I returned home after living in Italy, the thing I missed most was fresh mozzarella, and no one even knew what it was. So I decided to build a cheese factory and make mozzarella in Dallas, and since 1982 the Mozzarella Company has been in business." Now the Mozzarella Company produces over a quarter-million pounds of handmade cheese and sells all over the United States. And with the mozzarella, the Italian spirit continues to grow in Texas and other parts of America.

# Fried Mozzarella Skewers

## *Spiedini alla Romana*

This very tasty appetizer can also be a vegetarian meal. The Italian title says it's "Roman," but mozzarella and anchovies are a well-known combination in southern Italy. There are mozzarella-and-anchovy fritters; and zucchini flowers are stuffed with mozzarella and anchovies, then fried. In this recipe, the mozzarella is fried between layers of bread, and then topped with a puckery sauce of lemon, capers, and anchovy.

SERVES 4

2 tablespoons extra-virgin olive oil

5 garlic cloves, chopped

4 anchovy fillets

3 tablespoons drained tiny capers

2 tablespoons unsalted butter

½ cup dry white wine

3 tablespoons lemon juice

8 slices firm white bread, crusts removed

12 ounces fresh mozzarella, thinly sliced

All-purpose flour, for dredging

2 large eggs

2 tablespoons milk

Vegetable oil, for frying

1 tablespoon chopped fresh Italian parsley

NOTE  For extra flavor, I like to tuck a whole anchovy with the sliced mozzarella inside the sandwich. Try it!

Make the sauce: Pour the olive oil into a large skillet set over medium-high heat. When the olive oil is hot, add the chopped garlic. Cook and stir until garlic is sizzling and fragrant, taking care not to burn it. Add the anchovies and capers, and stir until capers dissolve into the oil. Add the butter and melt it, then pour in the white wine and lemon juice. Bring to a rapid simmer, and cook until reduced by half, about 6 to 7 minutes. Keep warm.

Lay four slices of bread on your work surface. Top with the sliced mozzarella, making sure the cheese does not extend over the edges of the bread, trimming to fit if necessary. Top with remaining bread, to make four sandwiches. Seal each sandwich at each corner with a toothpick (four picks per sandwich).

Spread flour on a rimmed plate. Beat eggs and milk together in a wide, shallow bowl. Heat about ½ inch vegetable oil in a skillet over medium heat; oil is ready when a crust of bread sizzles on contact.

Dredge sandwiches well in flour, making sure to coat all sides and tap off the excess. Soak the sandwiches on all sides in the egg, letting the excess egg drip back into the bowl. Carefully ease the sandwiches into the oil, and fry until they're golden brown on both sides and the cheese is melted, about 1 to 2 minutes per side. Remove the sandwiches, and drain well on paper towels. Remove the toothpicks and use a serrated knife to cut them in half on the diagonal.

Return the sauce to a simmer, and stir in the parsley. Spread the sauce on four serving plates, then top with a sandwich and serve hot.

Fried Mozzarella Skewers

# Fried Mozzarella Sticks

*Bastoncini di Mozzarella Fritta*

Fried mozzarella is a tasty dish that children especially like; it can be half fried in advance, then reheated in the oven when guests arrive. It is great finger food to be passed around at a party.

MAKES 16 STICKS

Vegetable oil, for frying

1-pound block low-moisture mozzarella cheese (lightly salted)

2 cups all-purpose flour, for dredging

2 cups fine dry bread crumbs

2 large eggs

Kosher salt

16 medium-sized fresh basil leaves, cut in half lengthwise (optional)

Warm marinara sauce (see page 108), for serving

Heat 1 inch of vegetable oil in a large skillet or wide, shallow pot to about 365 degrees F. (If you don't have an oil thermometer, drop a few bread crumbs in. If they sizzle but don't burn, the oil is ready.)

Cut the mozzarella into four slabs, then cut each slab into four pieces, to get sixteen sticks. Spread the flour and the bread crumbs on separate rimmed plates. Put the eggs in a shallow bowl, and lightly beat them. Season with salt.

If using the basil, dip the leaves in the beaten egg and let the excess drip off back into the bowl. Put a leaf on each of the mozzarella sticks, down the length of the stick, and press to adhere. Don't worry if the leaf doesn't stick completely; it will stay on once you begin the breading process.

Working a few at a time, dredge the mozzarella sticks first in flour, then in the beaten egg, then in the bread crumbs. Once they're breaded, dip them again one by one into the egg and bread crumbs, so that no cheese is visible.

When the oil is ready, drop half of the mozzarella sticks gently into the skillet. Fry until golden on all sides, about 3 to 4 minutes in all. Remove mozzarella sticks with a spider, or slotted spatula, to drain on paper towels. Season with salt. Repeat process with remaining mozzarella sticks. Serve warm, with marinara sauce for dipping.

# Rice Balls

*Arancini di Riso*

These tasty fried rice balls have been enjoyed in Italy for centuries. They are great when just out of the skillet, but are delicious at room temperature as well. They can be fried in advance, then reheated.

At our restaurant Del Posto in New York, the chef sends them out as a palate teaser.

Pour the chicken stock into a small pot, and warm over low heat. In a medium saucepan, heat the olive oil; when hot, add the onion and cook until softened, about 3 to 4 minutes. Add the ham or prosciutto and cook a few minutes, until the meat begins to render its fat.

Add the rice, and cook to coat the rice in the oil and fat. Pour in the wine, bring to a simmer, and cook until the wine is almost reduced away. Add 3 cups hot chicken stock and the salt; cover, and simmer until the chicken stock is absorbed by the rice, about 7 to 8 minutes. Add the remaining 2 cups stock, and cover. Cook until rice is al dente, about 6 to 7 minutes more. If any liquid remains, increase heat and cook until all is absorbed. Stir in the peas toward the end, and mix well, then spread the rice on a rimmed baking sheet to cool.

When the rice is cool, put it in a bowl and stir in the grated cheese and chopped basil. Scoop out about ⅓ cup rice, roll into a loose ball, then poke a cube of mozzarella into the center. Pat firmly, to form a tight ball around the cheese.

Spread the flour and bread crumbs on separate rimmed plates. Beat the eggs in a shallow bowl. Dredge the arancini in the flour, shaking off the excess. Dip them one by one in the beaten egg, letting the excess drip back into the bowl. Roll in the bread crumbs to coat.

Pour an inch of vegetable oil into a large, straight-sided skillet set over medium heat. When the tip of an arancino sizzles on contact with the hot oil, it is hot enough. Fry the rice balls in batches, taking care not to crowd the skillet, turning on all sides, until golden, about 3 minutes per batch. Drain on paper towels, and season with salt while still warm. Continue with the remaining arancini.

**MAKES ABOUT 2 DOZEN**

5 cups chicken stock (see page 40)

3 tablespoons extra-virgin olive oil

1 medium onion, finely chopped

1 cup finely diced ham or prosciutto (about 3 ounces)

2 cups Arborio rice

1 cup dry white wine

½ teaspoon kosher salt, plus more for seasoning

1 cup frozen peas, thawed

1 cup grated Grana Padano or Parmigiano-Reggiano

10 fresh basil leaves, chopped

4 ounces fresh mozzarella, cut in cubes (you'll need about 24 cubes)

1 cup all-purpose flour

2 cups fine dry bread crumbs

2 large eggs

Vegetable oil, for frying

# Stuffed Mushrooms

*Funghi Ripieni*

Italians stuff all kinds of vegetables, such as peppers, tomatoes, zucchini, and more. In America, white button mushrooms were plentiful and cheap, and delicious when stuffed, so the Italians added them to their stuffed vegetable list. Stuffed mushrooms of different varieties can now be found in Italian American homes and restaurants, from the simple button mushrooms to the large portobellos. All types make a delicious dish and satisfy today's vegetarian diners as well. I like mushrooms best stuffed simply with bread crumbs and cheese, but I have seen them stuffed with everything from crabmeat to shrimp to foie gras. Let your fancy guide you.

SERVES 6 TO 8
AS AN APPETIZER

Two 10-ounce packages large white stuffing mushrooms (about 24 mushrooms)

½ cup finely chopped scallions (about 4)

¼ cup finely chopped red bell pepper

¼ cup fine dry bread crumbs

6 tablespoons grated Grana Padano or Parmigiano-Reggiano

3 tablespoons chopped fresh Italian parsley

¾ teaspoon kosher salt

¼ cup extra-virgin olive oil

½ cup dry white wine

3 tablespoons unsalted butter, softened

Preheat oven to 425 degrees F. Remove the stems from the mushrooms (set the caps aside), and finely chop them. Put the stems in a large bowl, and add the scallions, bell pepper, bread crumbs, 3 tablespoons of the grated cheese, 2 tablespoons of the parsley, and half the salt. Stir in 2 tablespoons of the olive oil, to moisten all of the crumbs and make a fairly tight stuffing. Combine the white wine and ½ cup hot water in a small bowl, and season with the remaining salt.

Spread the butter all around the bottom of a 9-by-13-inch Pyrex baking dish. Fill the mushroom caps with the stuffing, and fit them in the baking dish. Sprinkle the remaining cheese over the mushrooms, and drizzle on the remaining olive oil. Pour the wine and water around the mushrooms in the baking dish.

Bake until the mushrooms are crisp on top but tender and the juices are bubbling underneath, about 30 to 40 minutes, depending on the size. If there is too much juice left in the baking dish, pour it into a small pan and reduce to thicken. Otherwise, stir the remaining parsley into the pan and serve sauce with the mushrooms.

# Fried Marinated Artichokes

*Carciofi Marinati e Fritti*

I have made fried artichokes many ways before, but I found this recipe at Liuzza's in New Orleans different and quite tasty. The interesting part is that the recipe is made with jarred or canned artichokes. The batter is light and fries up crispy, while the artichokes remain tender and tasty. This is an ideal recipe to serve when unexpected guests arrive and all you have is a can of artichoke hearts in the cupboard and a beer in the fridge.

Heat ½ inch vegetable oil in a deep skillet over medium heat.

Whisk together the flour and salt in a large bowl. Slowly pour in the beer, whisking to make a smooth batter. Whisk in the lemon zest.

Dredge the artichokes in the batter, and let the excess drip back into the bowl. When the oil is ready, fry the artichokes, in batches, until batter is crisp and golden, about 5 minutes per batch. Drain on paper towels, and season with salt. Serve hot, with rémoulade for dipping.

SERVES 6

Vegetable oil, for frying

1½ cups all-purpose flour

¼ teaspoon kosher salt, plus more for seasoning

12-ounce can lager-style beer (any light beer will do)

Finely grated zest of 1 lemon

Three 6-ounce jars artichoke hearts, drained well, patted dry, then quartered

Rémoulade, for serving (see page 204)

Fried artichokes at Liuzza's in New Orleans

# Asparagus Fritters

*Frittelle d'Asparagi*

I love asparagus and cook it many different ways, and on my visit with the Maugeri family, one of the oldest and largest family produce farms in New Jersey, I discovered this delicious recipe. I was told it is a family recipe handed down through three generations, and I am delighted they shared it with me so I can share it with you.

**MAKES 10 TO 12 FRITTERS**

2 bunches medium asparagus spears, peeled at the base (about 22 spears)

5 large eggs

½ cup grated Grana Padano or Parmigiano-Reggiano

½ small onion, finely chopped

¼ cup fine dry bread crumbs

2 tablespoons all-purpose flour

½ teaspoon kosher salt, plus more for seasoning

Vegetable oil, for frying

Bring a large pot of salted water to a boil. Add the asparagus spears, and cook until tender but not mushy, about 8 minutes. Drain, and rinse under cold water to cool them down. Drain and dry the spears, and cut into ½-inch pieces.

Whisk together the eggs, grated cheese, onion, bread crumbs, flour, and salt in a large bowl. Stir in the asparagus pieces.

Heat ½ inch vegetable oil in a large skillet over medium heat. (The oil is ready when a drop of batter sizzles on contact.) Drop ¼-cup rounds of the asparagus batter into the hot oil, flattening if necessary, to make flat cakes. Cook until golden on the underside, about 2 minutes, then flip, and fry until the fritters are cooked through, about 2 minutes more. Drain the fritters on paper towels, and season with salt.

# Clams Casino

*Vongole al Forno con Pancetta*

I first tasted this dish in an Italian American restaurant in the 1960s, and thereafter served it in my restaurants into the 1980s. In Italy, bacon and clams are not cooked together much, but I love this dish. It is an extraordinary combination of flavors—between the brininess of the clams, the sweetness of the roasted peppers, and the crispy pancetta or bacon taste that everybody loves. The dish has roots on the shore of Rhode Island, where it was created at the Little Casino hotel in Narragansett, early in the twentieth century.

SERVES 6 AS AN APPETIZER

36 littleneck clams

2 roasted red or yellow bell peppers, peeled and cut into 1-inch squares

6 ounces thinly sliced bacon or pancetta, cut into 1-inch squares

3 tablespoons unsalted butter

3 tablespoons chopped fresh Italian parsley

Dry white wine, as needed (see procedure)

Preheat oven to 450 degrees F.

Shuck the clams, leaving each clam in the half-shell and reserving the juices. Strain the juices through a cheesecloth into a bowl.

Place the clams on a rimmed baking sheet in one even layer. Top each clam with a pepper square, then with a bacon or pancetta square, and with a dab of butter, using all 3 tablespoons evenly. Sprinkle the chopped parsley on top. Pour the reserved shucking juices into a measuring cup, and add enough white wine to make 2 cups combined liquid. Pour the liquid into the bottom of the baking sheet.

Bake the clams, uncovered, until the bacon or pancetta is crispy and the clams are cooked all the way through, about 25 minutes. Serve on a platter, drizzled with baking juices.

Fresh littleneck clams on ice, ready for shucking

Baked Clams Oreganato and Clams Casino

# Baked Clams Oreganato

*Vongole Ripiene al Forno*

Rhode Island's Italian immigrants have made clam soup an integral part of the clam-shack cuisine. From Giovanni da Verrazano, the first Italian to visit Rhode Island, to the generations of today, the plentiful seafood of the Ocean State has been given an Italian twist. As I savored baked clams across the United States, in most cases the clams were chopped, but I like whole clams baked with bread crumbs in the shell. Small clams like littlenecks are the best.

Preheat oven to 425 degrees F.

Coarsely chop shucked clams, and put in a large bowl. Add the bread crumbs, bell pepper, parsley, oregano, and salt. Drizzle with 2 tablespoons olive oil, and toss with a fork to combine.

Stuff the reserved clamshells with the filling, and place on a rimmed baking sheet. Drizzle each clam with a little of the reserved clam juice, pouring any extra juice, along with the white wine, into the bottom of the pan. Drizzle the clams with 3 tablespoons olive oil, and drizzle the remaining tablespoon oil in the bottom of the pan with the juice and wine.

Bake until clams are lightly browned and crusty, about 15 to 20 minutes. To serve, set clams on plates with remaining sauce and a squeeze of fresh lemon juice for each.

SERVES 6

36 littleneck clams, shucked (reserve half of the shells for filling), juices reserved and strained

1½ cups fine dry bread crumbs

½ cup finely chopped red bell pepper

¼ cup finely chopped fresh Italian parsley

1 teaspoon dried oregano

½ teaspoon kosher salt

6 tablespoons extra-virgin olive oil

½ cup dry white wine

Lemon wedges, for serving (optional)

NOTE Another option—one I like very much— is not to chop the clams.

Shuck the clams, and leave each whole clam in a half-shell. Toss all the other ingredients separately, then cover the clams with a light coating of the mixture. Pat lightly, and continue as per recipe.

# Garlic Bread, Three Ways
## *Pane Strofinato all'Aglio*

In Italy, it is called bruschetta, *fett'unta,* and by various names in different regions, but the basic concept is that bread, fresh or old, is grilled or toasted and then brushed with olive oil and rubbed with fresh garlic. Toppings are optional, and surely seasonal. In the United States, this Italian custom took on different versions and became garlic bread. Garlic bread was an open loaf of Italian bread brushed with butter or oil and lots of chopped garlic, sprinkled with dry oregano, and grilled or baked. I recall liking the grilled and warm bread from my Italian American restaurant visits, but the garlic was always too much for me. I must say that now, in most restaurants, the grilling and toasting of bread has come full-circle, and bruschetta as well as garlic bread graces the table.

Here are three versions of the garlic bread made with the Italian American tradition in mind. Just keep a handle on the garlic.

SERVES 4

3 tablespoons extra-virgin olive oil

3 garlic cloves, crushed and peeled

12-inch loaf Italian bread without seeds

1 teaspoon dried oregano

Kosher salt, for seasoning

Combine the olive oil and garlic in a small bowl, and steep about 30 minutes, to let the flavors mingle.

Preheat the oven to 400 degrees F. Split the bread in half lengthwise, then cut in half crosswise, to make four pieces. Set the pieces, cut side up, on a baking sheet, and brush the bread with the flavored oil, rubbing with the garlic cloves and leaving them on top. Sprinkle with the dried oregano.

Bake until the bread is golden and crispy, about 4 to 5 minutes. Remove any large garlic pieces, and lightly season the bread with salt before serving.

GARLIC BREAD TOPPED WITH CHEESE
*(Pane Strofinato con Formaggio):* Substitute ¼ cup grated Grana Padano or Parmigiano-Reggiano for the oregano.

GARLIC BREAD RUBBED WITH TOMATOES
*(Pane Strofinato con Pomodoro):* Cut some ripe tomatoes crosswise in half. While the baked bread is still hot, rub cut surfaces of the bread with the tomato halves, until the bread has absorbed the tomato juices and the tomato pulp has rubbed onto the bread. Season lightly with salt, drizzle some extra-virgin olive oil on top, and serve immediately.

Freshly baked *taralli* can be found at Addeo & Sons Bakery on Arthur Avenue in the Bronx.

Betsy Devine of the flourishing cheese company Salvatore Bklyn

# Ricotta Frittata

*Frittata con Ricotta*

Frittata is the quintessential Italian meal. You can flavor it with anything you have on hand, and one of my favorite ways is adding dollops of fresh ricotta. Ricotta is a by-product of cheesemaking: after the curds for the cheese are drained from the whey, the whey is recooked with the addition of some milk, and soft ricotta curds slowly form. Ricotta is delicious, and Italians use it in just about any dish, from appetizer to pasta to soup to desserts, and, as here, in frittatas as well.

The Italian American immigrants continued this tradition of using ricotta, and it can be found in a lot of Italian American kitchens. Since it was also easy to have a couple of chickens on hand in the backyard, we always had some fresh eggs. When there is nothing else in the house except eggs, this is the meal to make.

Preheat the oven to 375 degrees F.

Heat the oil in a 10-inch nonstick skillet over medium heat. Slip in the onion and cook until softened, about 5 to 6 minutes. Push onion slices to one side of the skillet, and lay the tomato slices in one layer in the cleared space. Sear the tomato, turning once until the slices soften just at the edges, about 30 seconds per side. Remove the tomato to a plate, and let the onion continue to cook while you prepare the eggs.

Beat the eggs with the salt in a bowl. Stir in the basil and ¼ cup of the grated cheese until well mixed.

Spread the onion slices in an even layer in the bottom of the skillet. Pour the eggs on top, and let cook over medium-low heat until the eggs begin to set around the edges of the pan, about 2 to 3 minutes.

Arrange the tomato slices on top of the frittata and drop tablespoons of the ricotta between the tomato slices. Sprinkle all over with the remaining grated cheese. Bake the frittata until it is set all the way through and the top is golden, about 18 minutes. Let rest for a few minutes, then run a knife around the edge of the skillet and invert onto a plate or cutting board. Serve in wedges, warm or at room temperature.

SERVES 4 TO 6

3 tablespoons extra-virgin olive oil

1 large onion, sliced ¼ inch thick

1 large ripe tomato, sliced ½ inch thick

8 large eggs

½ teaspoon kosher salt

8 large basil leaves, shredded

½ cup grated Grana Padano or Parmigiano-Reggiano

6 tablespoons fresh ricotta, drained

# Sausage, Bread, and Pepper Frittata

*Frittata con Salsiccia e Peperoni*

From what I recall, frittata made with sausage, bread, and eggs was a dish my grandmother in Istria often prepared, whereas the addition of peppers was something more Italian American. It is nonetheless a delicious combination. This recipe makes a great lunch with some salad on the side.

SERVES 4 TO 6

3 tablespoons extra-virgin olive oil

8 ounces sweet Italian sausage, removed from casing (about 2 links)

1 large bunch scallions, cut into ½-inch pieces

½ teaspoon kosher salt

1 red bell pepper, cut into ½-inch strips

8 large eggs

¼ cup milk

1½ cups ½-inch bread cubes, from a day-old loaf of country bread

¼ cup grated Grana Padano or Parmigiano-Reggiano

Preheat oven to 375 degrees F. Heat the oil in a 10-inch nonstick skillet over medium heat. Cook the sausage, crumbling with the back of a wooden spoon, until the meat is no longer pink, about 3 to 4 minutes. Add the scallions, season with ¼ teaspoon salt, and cook, stirring, until the scallions begin to wilt, about 2 to 3 minutes. Toss in the bell pepper, and cook, stirring, until wilted but not completely limp, about 8 to 10 minutes.

Beat the eggs with the milk and remaining salt in a bowl. Let the bread cubes soak in the egg-milk mixture until moistened, about 2 to 3 minutes. Reduce heat under skillet to medium-low, then pour in the eggs and bread and let cook, without stirring, until the eggs begin to set around the edges of the pan, about 2 to 3 minutes.

Sprinkle all over the top with the grated cheese. Put the skillet in the oven, and bake until frittata is set all the way through and the top is golden, about 18 minutes. Let rest for a few minutes, then run a knife around the edge of the skillet and invert onto a plate or cutting board. Serve in wedges, warm or at room temperature.

Sausage, Bread, and Pepper Frittata

# Sonoma County: California Wine Country

Ever since I made my first trip to the California Wine Country in the seventies, I felt I could live there and be happy, except for one thing: it is too far from Italy. So I can understand why the Italian immigrants who began coming in the late nineteenth century felt at home there. California Wine Country, with its softly sloping hills, was surely a familiar landscape to the Italians. It was an ideal place to grow grapes, just like Piemonte and Chianti. The Italian Swiss Agricultural Colony, founded by Andrea Sbarboro in Sonoma County in 1881, was one of the first to grow grapes and open labor opportunities for newly arrived immigrants. Each worker was given room, board, and wages in return for working the land. They worked hard, hoping eventually to become independent farmers and winemakers. One such worker was Edoardo Seghesio, who came from Piemonte, Italy, in 1886 to work at the Italian Swiss Colony. Now, under the watchful eye of CEO Peter Seghesio, the fourth generation of the Seghesio family continues to produce and bottle wine.

Sitting with Ed Seghesio at the Seghesio Winery

One sunny April morning, Tanya and I drove up to the Seghesio Family Vineyards in Healdsburg. There was the bustle of people tasting as we entered the tasting room unannounced. One could not miss seeing, through the glass window, the barrels lined up in the *cantina,* but my eye caught the window of the curing room to the left, filled with hanging prosciutto and salami. I knew then, the traditions were alive and well in the Seghesio family.

I'd heard that Mamma Seghesio is often at the winery, and I wanted to meet her. Soon enough her son, Peter Seghesio,

The Italian Swiss Colony in Sonoma and the beautiful view of the budding vines in the early spring in the Seghesio vineyards—so reminiscent of Italy

came and told us that Grandma was at his son's piano recital (being a grandmother myself, I appreciated that). Peter was very welcoming and took us for a tour of the curing room, the cellar, and the upstairs kitchen, where the chef was preparing for the special wine-tasting lunch. The wine was delicious, and as we were saying our goodbyes under the pine trees, Mamma Rachel arrived, glowing from her grandson's recital, a charming woman, with family and business on her mind.

We drove off toward the northern part of Sonoma, and along the way we encountered many wineries with Italian names. Most of them were started by other Italian immigrants in the late nineteenth century: Simi, Foppiano, Vercelli, Passalacqua, Rafanelli, and Pedroncelli, just to name a few. Around one of the curves, under old oak trees, we found the old Olive Hill Cemetery, in which the tombstones are a lexicon of Italian names in Sonoma.

Cemeteries in Italy are considered places of reverence, reflection, and remembrance. So I reflect and revere the Italian immigrants who came before me, who planted and nurtured the Italian winemaking traditions, which now make this one of the largest industries in California, appreciated and enjoyed by the world.

Roman "Egg Drop" Soup and Wedding Soup

# Zuppe

# Chicken Stock

*Brodo di Pollo*

Free-range chickens, if you can find them, will make a superior stock. I also like the richness that turkey wings add to a chicken stock, so I use them all the time. You can save the chicken parts you need for stock over time, in a sealable bag or container to keep in the freezer, or perhaps your butcher can sell you what you need. Remove the livers from the giblet bag before making stock—livers will add a bitter flavor.

MAKES 4 QUARTS

3 pounds chicken and/or capon wings, backs, necks, and giblets (not including the liver), preferably from free-range or organically raised birds

1 pound turkey wings

8 quarts water

1 large onion (about ½ pound), cut in half

3 cups carrots, peeled and sliced 1 inch thick

3 stalks celery, cut crosswise into 4 pieces

6 garlic cloves

6 sprigs fresh Italian parsley

6 whole black peppercorns

Salt

Wash the chicken parts and turkey wings thoroughly under cold running water, and drain them well. Put them with the water in a large stockpot, and bring to a boil over high heat. Lower heat to medium, and boil for 1 hour. Skim off the surface foam and fat occasionally.

Meanwhile, place the onion, cut sides down, directly over an open flame, and cook until the cut surface is well browned, about 3 minutes. Move the onion halves with a pair of tongs as necessary to brown all over, evenly. (You may also brown the onion, cut sides down, in a heavy skillet over medium heat.)

Add to the pot all the remaining ingredients except the salt. Bring the pot to a boil again, occasionally skimming the fat and foam off the top. Lower the heat until the liquid is "perking"—one or two large bubbles rising to the surface at a time. Partially cover, and cook for 3 hours, adding salt to taste.

Strain the broth through a colander lined with a dampened kitchen towel or cheesecloth. If you want to use the stock immediately, you can remove much of the liquid fat floating on the surface by lightly dragging a folded paper towel over the surface. It will be easier to degrease the stock if you have time to chill it completely in the refrigerator. The fat will then rise to the surface and solidify, and can simply be lifted off. The stock can be refrigerated up to 4 days, or frozen up to 3 months. It will be easier to use if frozen in small (1-to-2-cup) containers. Once frozen, the stock can be removed from the containers and stored in sealable freezer bags, to be taken from the freezer as needed. You can also freeze stock directly in zip-lock plastic bags once it has cooled.

# Bread Pasta for Soup
*Passatelli*

Stale bread has never tasted so good, or been presented with such finesse, as in this dish—a delicious transformation, another fabulous way to use up yesterday's bread. Shaped into passatelli and combined with a good chicken stock, leftovers are transformed into an Italian classic.

Bring the chicken stock to a simmer in a soup pot.

Put the bread crumbs, cheese, salt, and nutmeg in an electric mixer fitted with the paddle attachment. Mix on low speed to combine the dry ingredients, then add the lemon zest. Increase the speed to medium, and add the eggs one at a time, continuing to mix until everything comes together to form a thick dough.

To make the passatelli, switch to the meat-grinder mixer attachment with the largest-holed die (or set up a countertop meat grinder). Push the dough through the grinder, cutting with a knife into 2-to-3-inch strands as they come out the other end of the grinder. Lay strands on a baking sheet lined with parchment, and continue until all of the dough is used.

Once all the dough is used, drop the passatelli into the simmering stock, and stir. Simmer until the strands are cooked through, about 1 to 2 minutes. Ladle out bowls of passatelli and broth, passing more grated cheese for serving.

SERVES 8

2 quarts chicken stock (see preceding recipe)

1 cup fine dry bread crumbs

½ cup grated Grana Padano or Parmigiano-Reggiano, plus more for serving

½ teaspoon kosher salt

¼ teaspoon freshly grated nutmeg

Finely grated zest of 1 lemon

2 large eggs

# Roman "Egg Drop" Soup

*Stracciatella alla Romana*

*Stracciare* means "to rip to shreds" in Italian, and, indeed, that is how this soup looks after you've stirred some beaten eggs with some grated cheese into a good chicken broth. Once you have a good chicken broth, the rest is easy. *Stracciatella* is usually served with shredded spinach and beaten egg, but I recall having it with just egg and cheese when spinach was not in season. In the Italy that I grew up in, seasons made a difference, not only in how we dressed, but in what we ate. This is a great restorative soup, served in most Italian families.

SERVES 6

8 cups defatted homemade chicken stock (see page 40)

1¼ teaspoons kosher salt

4 packed cups shredded fresh spinach leaves

4 large eggs

⅓ cup grated Grana Padano or Parmigiano-Reggiano, plus more for serving

Freshly ground black pepper

Bring the stock to a simmer in a medium pot with 1 teaspoon salt. Once stock is simmering, add the spinach and cook until tender, about 3 minutes.

Whisk together the eggs, grated cheese, remaining ¼ teaspoon salt, and freshly ground black pepper to taste in a medium bowl.

When the spinach is tender, add about a third of the egg mixture to the soup, continuously whisking, to make shreds of eggs. Add remaining eggs in two more batches, letting the soup return to a boil between additions. Once all of the eggs have been added, bring the soup to a final boil, and use the whisk to break up any large clusters of eggs. Serve the soup with the additional grated cheese.

# Vegetable Soup

*Minestrone*

Every region of Italy has its version of minestrone. The Italian American version seems always to have diced carrots, celery, potatoes, beans, and cabbage, rendering it distinct, with a touch of sour aftertaste. Variations include vegetables that were readily available in the small gardens Italian immigrants kept in their backyards or window boxes. Italian Americans love their minestrone so much that in 1949, Progresso Quality Foods began selling minestrone, as well as *pasta e fagioli,* in cans as a convenience food. At first the soup was available only in Italian American markets, but soon enough it hit mainstream America.

Combine pancetta, garlic, and 2 tablespoons olive oil in a food processor, and pulse to make a fine-textured paste or *pestata*. Heat the remaining olive oil in a large pot over medium-high heat. When the oil is hot, scrape in the *pestata*. Cook, stirring, until *pestata* renders its fat, about 4 minutes.

Add the onion, and cook until it begins to soften, about 3 minutes. Toss in the potatoes, and cook until they begin to stick to the bottom of the pan, another 3 minutes. Push aside the vegetables to make a dry "hot spot" in the center of the pan, and plop the tomato paste into that space, toasting it on all sides for a minute or two. Return the vegetables to the center of the pan, and stir the toasted paste into them. Pour in the water, along with the bay leaves, carrot, celery, and soaked cannellini. Bring to a rapid simmer, and cook until the beans are almost tender, about 40 minutes. Add the zucchini, cabbage, chard, and salt. Cover, and cook until beans and vegetables are tender and soup is flavorful, about 45 minutes more.

Meanwhile, bring a large pot of salted water to a boil and cook the ditalini al dente. Just before serving, scoop up the ditalini and add to the soup.

## MAKES ABOUT 4 QUARTS

3 ounces pancetta or bacon, cut into pieces

4 garlic cloves, crushed and peeled

4 tablespoons extra-virgin olive oil

1 medium onion, chopped

2 medium russet potatoes, peeled, cut into ½-inch chunks (about 12 ounces)

2 tablespoons tomato paste

6 quarts water

2 fresh bay leaves

1 large carrot, chopped

1 stalk celery, chopped

1 cup dried cannellini beans, soaked overnight and drained

1 large zucchini, chopped

1 small head Savoy cabbage, cored, shredded (about 8 cups)

1 bunch Swiss chard, shredded

2 tablespoons salt

8 ounces ditalini

# Escarole and White Bean Soup
## *Zuppa di Scarola e Cannellini*

Escarole is in the chicory family, the bitter dark-green vegetables that Italians love. Escarole played such a big role in the cooking of Italian Americans because it seemed to be one of the few chicory vegetables available here in the States. It is a very versatile and inexpensive vegetable as well: easy to grow, resilient to cooler weather, and giving a large yield per head. The outer leaves can be used in soups, braised with garlic and oil, or stuffed; the tender center white leaves are great for salads. This is an Italian recipe, but the ingredients are adapted to include the local ingredient kale, much loved and eaten in the States.

MAKES 4 QUARTS

6 quarts water

1 pound dried cannellini beans, soaked overnight and drained

4 fresh bay leaves

3 tablespoons extra-virgin olive oil

1½-pound head green kale or *cavolo nero,* tough stems removed, leaves washed and coarsely shredded

12-ounce head escarole, tough stems removed, leaves washed and coarsely shredded

2 tablespoons kosher salt, plus more as needed

FOR FINISHING
½ cup extra-virgin olive oil, plus more for serving

10 garlic cloves, sliced

7 whole dried peperoncini

Grated Grana Padano or Parmigiano-Reggiano, for serving

Boil the 6 quarts water with the drained beans and the bay leaves in a large soup pot. Adjust the heat to a rapid simmer, pour in the olive oil, and cook partially covered until the beans are halfway cooked, about 30 minutes. Add the kale, and cook uncovered for an additional 15 minutes. Add the escarole and 2 tablespoons salt, and cook until the beans and greens are tender and the soup has reduced to about 4 quarts, another 20 to 30 minutes.

To finish the soup: Heat the ½ cup olive oil in a skillet over medium-low heat. Toss in the garlic and peperoncini and cook, stirring occasionally, until garlic is golden and fragrant, about 2 to 3 minutes. (Do not let the garlic or peperoncini burn.) Carefully add a few ladles of soup to the skillet, let simmer a minute or two, then pour the contents of the skillet back into the soup pot.

Taste for salt, return the soup to a simmer, and cook another 10 minutes, to blend the flavors. Remove the peperoncini. Serve with a drizzle of olive oil and grated cheese.

# Artichoke Soup

*Zuppa di Carciofi e Patate*

I got this recipe from Guido Pezzini, the patriarch at Pezzini Farms in Castroville, California, who claims that just about every dish his mother cooked included artichokes in some form. This soup is one of his favorites. The Pezzinis are a delightful and caring family, with Sean, the grandson, as the next generation in training.

Clean and prepare the artichokes as detailed on page 18. Put artichokes in a serving bowl and toss with the lemon juice.

Heat the olive oil in a soup pot over medium-high heat. Add the potatoes, and cook until they begin to stick to the bottom of the pot, about 5 minutes. Add the leeks and shallots, and cook until softened, about 10 minutes.

Sprinkle in the garlic, thyme, bay leaf, salt, and peperoncino. Cook until the garlic is fragrant, about 1 to 2 minutes. Pour in the water and bring to a boil. Add the prepped, drained artichokes, and bring the soup to a rapid simmering. Cook, uncovered, until potatoes and artichokes are tender and the potatoes have broken down to thicken the soup, about 1½ hours.

Stir in the chopped parsley, and serve the soup with grated cheese.

**MAKES 4 QUARTS**

5 medium (or 10 baby) artichokes

Juice of 1 lemon

⅔ cup extra-virgin olive oil

1¾ pounds russet potatoes, peeled and cut into ½-inch cubes

2 leeks, white and pale-green parts, sliced, washed well (about 4 cups)

3 shallots, chopped (about ½ cup)

6 garlic cloves, chopped

1 tablespoon fresh thyme leaves

1 fresh bay leaf

1 tablespoon kosher salt

⅛ teaspoon peperoncino flakes

4 quarts cold water

2 tablespoons chopped fresh Italian parsley

Grated Grana Padano or Parmigiano-Reggiano, for serving

Inspecting the nine different sizes of artichokes grown at Pezzini Farms in Castroville, California

# Cauliflower Soup

*Zuppa di Cavolfiori*

I love soups, and I love cauliflower, and who doesn't like pancetta? This is a delicious soup, and, yes, you can serve it as is, or you can add some cooked white or brown rice. Get yourself some crusty bread, a glass of Chianti Classico or Morellino (the other Tuscan red), and enjoy.

MAKES ABOUT 2½ QUARTS

¼ cup extra-virgin olive oil, plus more for drizzling

2 ounces pancetta, cut into ¼-inch dice

1 medium onion, finely chopped

1 large carrot, cut into ¼-inch dice

4 quarts cold water

1 tablespoon plus 1 teaspoon kosher salt

1 large head cauliflower, cut into small florets

1 cup brown lentils, rinsed

Grated Grana Padano or Parmigiano-Reggiano, for serving

Heat the olive oil in a large soup pot set over medium heat, and toss in the pancetta. Cook and stir until the pancetta renders its fat, about 4 to 5 minutes. Add the onion and carrot, cooking until they begin to soften, about 5 minutes. Pour in the water, and add 1 tablespoon of the salt. Partially cover, bring to a rapid simmer, and cook to develop the flavors, about 25 minutes.

Add the cauliflower and lentils, and bring again to a rapid simmer. Cook, uncovered, until the cauliflower has broken down and the lentils are tender, about 40 minutes. Season with remaining salt.

Serve soup in bowls, with a drizzle of olive oil and some grated cheese.

# Wedding Soup

*Zuppa Maritata*

This soup has weathered well among the generations of the Italian immigrant families that have cooked it. As I travel through America and look for the flavors and recipes the Italian immigrants brought with them, this recipe is almost always remembered fondly. It is still cooked with nostalgia and reverence, and at holidays, particularly in the homes of immigrants from southern Italy. It is a dish usually served when the whole family is at the table. Even if the "marriage" mostly likely refers to the marriage of the ingredients, the soup is also thought to give strength to a newly married couple for their wedding night.

Pulse the onion, garlic, celery, carrot, basil, peperoncino, and 1 tablespoon salt in a food processor, making a fine-textured paste or *pestata*. Heat a large skillet over medium-high heat, and add the olive oil. When the oil is hot, scrape in the *pestata*. Cook, stirring, until the *pestata* dries out and begins to stick to the bottom of the pan, about 10 minutes. Pour in the water and bring to a rapid simmer. Cover, and cook 20 minutes; then add the fennel, zucchini, and 1 tablespoon of salt.

Cover again, and let the soup cook at a rapid simmer for another 20 minutes. Add the escarole (or escarole and spinach). Uncover, and cook until all of the greens are tender and the soup has reduced by about a third, 30 to 40 minutes.

Make the meatballs: Combine the ground pork, ground beef, bread crumbs, grated cheese, parsley, egg, and the remaining salt in a large bowl. Mix well with your hands, and form into 1-inch meatballs. Place meatballs on a sheet tray.

When the greens are tender and the soup has reduced, gently add the meatballs. Cook until they are cooked through, about 20 minutes more. Serve soup with more grated cheese and a drizzle of olive oil.

MAKES ABOUT 5 QUARTS

1 medium onion, roughly chopped

4 garlic cloves, peeled

2 stalks celery, roughly chopped

1 medium carrot, roughly chopped

10 large fresh basil leaves

½ teaspoon peperoncino flakes

2 tablespoons plus ½ teaspoon kosher salt

6 tablespoons extra-virgin olive oil

7 quarts cold water

1 large fennel bulb, cored, finely chopped, plus some chopped fronds

1 pound zucchini, cut into ½-inch chunks

1 large head escarole, coarsely shredded (or half escarole, half spinach)

1 pound ground pork

1 pound ground beef

1 cup fine dry bread crumbs

1 cup grated Grana Padano

⅓ cup chopped fresh Italian parsley

1 large egg, beaten

# Pasta with Lentils
## *Pasta e Lenticchie*

Legumes are a big part of the culinary tradition in Italy, and they found a place in Italian American homes as well. Almost every Italian American I spoke with wanted to share a memory of his or her favorite lentil dish. Legumes, especially lentils, deliver a lot of flavor, plus nutritional and economical value, and everyone could afford them. The immigrants ate them a lot, and they are still a favorite in Italian American kitchens. Pasta and beans, *pasta e fagioli*—or, as Italian Americans call it, *pasta fazool*—is a traditional meatless Italian dish, although it usually refers to white beans, such as cannellini or borlotti. *Pasta fazool* probably came from Neapolitan immigrants, derived from the Neapolitan word for beans, *fazul*.

The recipe below is a soup consisting of lentils and pasta, but you can turn it into a dry pasta dish instead of a soup by adding only 5 to 6 cups of water. Or even make the lentils as a vegetable dish by eliminating the 4 cups of water and omitting the ditalini. The pancetta is added for flavor, but to make the soup vegetarian, omit the pancetta and start with the onion.

MAKES ABOUT 3½ QUARTS

2 tablespoons extra-virgin olive oil, plus more for drizzling

6 ounces pancetta

1 medium onion, chopped

1 stalk celery, chopped

1 large carrot, peeled and shredded

2 fresh bay leaves

1 cup canned San Marzano whole tomatoes, hand-crushed

2 cups brown lentils, rinsed and drained

8 cups water

1 tablespoon kosher salt

8 ounces ditalini

Grated Grana Padano or Parmigiano-Reggiano, for serving

Pour 2 tablespoons olive oil into a large Dutch oven and heat over medium heat. Cut the pancetta into ¼-inch strips and add them. Cook until they begin to render fat, about 3 to 4 minutes. Add the onion, celery, carrot, and bay leaves. Cook until wilted, about 5 minutes. Add crushed tomatoes and bring to a simmer. Cook until thickened, about 10 minutes.

Once it's thickened, add lentils, water, and the tablespoon of salt. Bring to a simmer, cover, and cook until lentils are just tender, about 30 minutes.

Add the ditalini, and cook, covered, until pasta is al dente, about 8 minutes. Serve with a drizzle of olive oil and some grated cheese.

# Pasta and Beans

*Pasta e Fagioli*

Known as *pasta fazool* in the Italian American community, this is the cornerstone of Italian soup-making. This recipe traveled easily from Italy along with the early immigrants. Beans and the other ingredients were easy to find, and the technique they used was just like back home. An inexpensive, nutritious soup, it cooked by itself while the woman of the house did her chores.

Some options to vary this soup would be to purée part or all of the beans after they have been cooked, and before you add the pasta. This is the version kids love, and it is also used in restaurants for a seemingly elegant touch, although I like to bite into my beans. I also substitute rice or barley for the pasta, a common practice in the north of Italy, where rice is abundant.

Soak the cannellini beans overnight and drain.

Pulse the bacon, garlic, and rosemary in a mini–food processor to make a fine-textured paste or *pestata*.

Heat 3 tablespoons olive oil over medium heat in a large soup pot. Add the *pestata,* and cook until bacon has rendered its fat, about 3 to 4 minutes. Meanwhile, make a second *pestata* (you don't have to wash the processor) by puréeing the onion and carrot. Add the second *pestata* to the pot, and cook, stirring occasionally, until it has dried out and starts to stick to the bottom of the pan, about 5 minutes.

Scrape the *pestata* to one side of the pan to clear a "hot spot," add the tomato paste, and let cook for a few minutes, until lightly toasted. Stir the tomato paste into the *pestata,* and add the drained beans, the potatoes, and the bay leaves. Pour in the water. Bring the soup to a boil, cover, and let cook at a strong simmer until beans and potatoes are tender, about 1 hour and 15 minutes, uncovering to reduce liquid about halfway through the cooking time. Stir in the salt.

With a large wooden spoon, mash the remaining potatoes against the side of the pot to thicken the soup. Return soup to a boil, add the ditalini, and cook until pasta is al dente. Season to taste.

Serve soup with a drizzle of olive oil and some grated cheese.

### MAKES ABOUT 4 QUARTS

1 pound dried cannellini beans

4 ounces bacon

3 large garlic cloves, peeled

Needles from 1 sprig fresh rosemary (about 1 tablespoon)

3 tablespoons extra virgin olive oil, plus more for serving

1 medium onion, chopped

1 medium carrot, chopped

2 tablespoons tomato paste

2 pounds russet potatoes (about 6 to 8 potatoes), peeled

2 fresh bay leaves

6 quarts cold water

2 tablespoons kosher salt

1 pound ditalini pasta

Freshly ground black pepper

Grated Grana Padano or Parmigiano-Reggiano, for serving

# Philadelphia

Italians have been part of the life of Philadelphia since colonial times. Italian immigration to Philadelphia was one of the earliest waves, and in the mid-eighteenth century consisted mainly of intellectuals, artists, and entrepreneurs. William Penn had visited Italy, and, believing in religious freedom, he welcomed the Italians, allowing them and other European immigrants to practice Catholicism. In 1753, Benjamin Franklin offered instruction in Italian at the Philadelphia College. In 1779, Filippo Mazzei came to Philadelphia, a friend of Thomas Jefferson. Mazzei had written "All men are by nature equally free and independent" in a letter to Jefferson a few years before 1776, which was said to have deeply influenced Jefferson as he was drafting the Declaration of Independence. In the late nineteenth century, many wealthy Italians left Italy for political reasons and came to Philadelphia, followed by blue-collar workers looking for work and opportunity.

Not far from the waterfront, where most blue-collar immigrants lived, the 9th Street market was and still is a bustling place. The market was once the very essence of the Italian neighborhood of Philadelphia, and every product reflected the Italian heritage. Now waves of immigrants from other countries have made the produce stands their own.

I go to Philadelphia often and for many different reasons, but whenever I go to South Philadelphia for a cheese steak and some shopping, I stop and visit my friend Mariella Giovannucci at Fante's Kitchen Wares Shop. Mariella hails from Friuli, the same region I come from, and is a rather recent immigrant to Philadelphia, having arrived with her family in the 1960s. Luigi Fante and his father, Domenico Fante, founded the store in 1906 and made the whole family part of the operation for generations. In 1981, the family retired and Mariella (then the acting general manager) and her family acquired the store. Under its new direction, Fante's became even more focused on goods for the preparation and service of food, carrying items difficult to find elsewhere in the United States. Positioned in the middle of a bustling market, it is always busy.

Not too far from Fante's and the market, near Triangle Park, there is Pat's and Geno's, known for their cheese steaks and for their ongoing rivalry regarding who has the best cheese steak. Pat and Harry Olivieri are often credited with inventing the sandwich. The two stores are situated across the street from each other, and even the locals cannot agree on whose is the best sandwich. But last time I went to the market, we stopped by George's, on 9th Street, and I had a tripe sandwich while Tanya ate a cheese steak. Mom Olga was serving, while her son Mark was at the griddle. Both sandwiches were very good.

While walking down 9th Street, one can only imagine the bustle of the immigrants shopping for the foods that reminded them of home, such as in D'Angelo Brothers Meat Market, where one can still buy boar, venison, and rabbit. Claudio Specialty Food Shop and Di Bruno Brothers' cheese shop rival any Italian market in the varieties of cheese, salumi, and other Italian products.

You can find bread as good as it can get at L. Sarcone & Son bakery. On the day Tanya and I were there, the family's daughter Lynne was behind the counter—it is a

Mark cooks up some beef for the Philly cheese steaks at
George's Sandwich Shop in Philadelphia.

Sal, the owner (above), and Fred Landis (below)
at Claudio Specialty Foods on Ninth Street
in Philadelphia

Lou Sarcone, the second generation running L. Sarcone & Son bakery in Philadelphia

second-generation business, and Dad still mans the enormous brick ovens that hold six hundred loaves of bread. No matter how much they can make, the bread is usually sold out by 11 a.m. If you come in any later, you will most likely hear from the elderly salesladies, "Where have you been all morning? The bread is all sold out."

Next to the Sarcone bakery is Ralph's Italian Restaurant, opened in 1900 by Francesco Dispigno. It claims to be the oldest Italian restaurant in America still run by the same family. Now Eddie and Jimmy Rubino run it, still in the family. The menu is Italian American, and Tanya and I had chicken Trombino (see page 249), chicken Sorrento, baked clams, manicotti, and spumoni.

But Philadelphia is also known for its winning contemporary Italian restaurants, such as the one run by my friend Marc Vetri, Vetri at 1312 Spruce Street, one of the best contemporary Italian restaurants in the country, along with his restaurants Osteria and the newly opened Amis Trattoria. Of Italian descent, Marc began his culinary training at his Sicilian grandmother's side in South Philly, then went on to the source and trained in Bergamo, Italy, only to return to Philadelphia to bring his bold contemporary sensibility to classic Italian cooking.

The vibrancy of Italian culture, whether on the table or in daily life, continues to be an integral part of the Philadelphia way.

Soft-Shell Crab Sandwich

# Sandwiches
# and Pizza

# Soft-Shell Crab Sandwich

*Panino con Moleche Fritte*

When in season, soft-shell crabs are a big seller in all of our restaurants. People just love them. We make a light batter, fry them nice and crisp, and set them over a salad for our guests.

During one of my trips to Baltimore, I wanted to go visit Crisfield Seafood in Silver Spring, Maryland, known for its soft-shell crab sandwich. The experience was good: the soft-shell crab, nice and crispy, was the best part; the sesame bun and the coleslaw were the usual suspects. In this recipe I've added my own twist to the bread and ingredients. Get a good semolina roll, and top the crabs with an arugula-and-egg salad, an Italian American solution. If you want to serve this as a salad, double the salad and dressing and omit the rolls. Serve crabs on top of the greens, with dressing dolloped on the side.

**MAKES 4 SANDWICHES**

1 head garlic

½ cup extra-virgin olive oil, plus more for drizzling

2 large hard-boiled eggs, whites and yolks separated, whites finely chopped

2 tablespoons grainy mustard

3 tablespoons lemon juice

1 teaspoon drained horseradish

½ teaspoon kosher salt

Vegetable oil, for frying

Fine yellow cornmeal, for dredging

4 soft-shell crabs, cleaned (by the fishmonger; if you want to do it yourself, see note below)

4 ounces baby arugula

4 seeded semolina rolls, split and lightly toasted

Preheat oven to 375 degrees F. Place the head of garlic on a square of foil, drizzle with olive oil, and wrap the foil to seal. Roast in oven until the garlic is tender throughout, about 30 to 40 minutes, depending on the size of the garlic head. Let cool, then squeeze garlic cloves into the work bowl of a mini–food processor.

To make the dressing, pour 6 tablespoons olive oil, hard-boiled egg yolks, mustard, 2 tablespoons lemon juice, the horseradish, and ¼ teaspoon of the salt into the food processor. Process to make a smooth dressing, scraping down the sides of the work bowl as needed. Set dressing aside while you cook the crabs.

For the crabs: Heat ¼ inch vegetable oil in a large skillet over medium heat. Spread cornmeal on a plate. With a little water still clinging to the rinsed, cleaned crabs, dredge in the cornmeal, tapping off the excess. Add the crabs to skillet, and cook until browned and crisp on one side, about 3 to 4 minutes. (Be careful—the water in the crabs may cause the oil to splatter.) Turn, and cook until crabs are cooked

> NOTE  If you want to clean the soft-shells yourself, snip off the tip of the face with scissors, then cut out the spongy gills inside the sides of the bodies.

through and crisp on the outside, about 3 to 4 minutes more. Drain crabs on a paper-towel-lined plate.

To serve, put arugula and chopped egg whites in a large bowl, and toss with the remaining 2 tablespoons olive oil, 1 tablespoon lemon juice, and ¼ teaspoon salt. Spread most of the dressing on the bottom of the rolls. Top with a crab and the arugula salad. Spread remaining dressing on the inside of the tops of the rolls, make sandwiches, and serve while the crabs are still hot.

Inside Crisfield Seafood Restaurant in Silver Spring, Maryland

Joe Di Pasquale and Lidia at Di Pasquale's Marketplace in Baltimore

# Italian American Civic Club Sandwich

*Panino del Club Civico Italo-Americano*

I had this sandwich in Baltimore, in a small, quaint mom-and-pop shop in Little Italy. Turkey is not too popular in Italy. After all, it was brought back to Europe after the discovery of America, and in Italy chicken and rabbits ruled the roost, along with other courtyard animals. In America, though, the turkey is the celebrated and celebratory animal, the one that fed famished early explorers coming to America. Well, this is a great sandwich to make on the days following Thanksgiving—or anytime, for that matter. The condiment and the greens are the Italian part, and the turkey is the American part—the perfect Italian American civic club sandwich.

Whisk together the mayonnaise and pesto in a small bowl. Cook pancetta in a large skillet over medium heat as you would bacon, until crisp, about 4 to 5 minutes. Drain on paper towels. Add turkey slices to the same skillet, and cook, turning, until just warmed through, about 1 to 2 minutes.

Assemble sandwiches: Spread 2 slices bread with half of the mayonnaise. Top each with a handful of arugula. Top with the pancetta and turkey, then the sliced tomatoes. Top with the remaining arugula. Spread remaining mayo on remaining bread slices, and place on top of the arugula. Cut sandwiches in half with a serrated knife, and serve.

MAKES 2 SANDWICHES

1½ tablespoons mayonnaise

1 tablespoon Basil Pistachio Pesto (see page 110), or other basil pesto

4 ounces pancetta, thinly sliced

4 ounces turkey, sliced

4 thick slices country bread, lightly toasted

2 cups baby arugula

1 tomato, sliced

# Salumeria Panino

*Panino della Salumeria*

Salumeria Italiana is the place to go in the North End of Boston to buy Italian specialty foods. The store is small but meticulously furnished with some of the best of Italian imported and domestic products. For nearly five decades, the Martignetti family has upheld the time-honored tradition.

It was early on a rainy morning when Tanya and I, camera and notepad in hand, paid a visit to the Salumeria. The workers were beginning to set up the products and sandwich of the day, getting ready for lunch. The resident *salumiere,* a timid elderly gentleman, repeatedly skirted the lens of our camera, but we did get some really good close-ups of the Salumeria panino of the day. No one was willing to share the recipe, either, so here is my rendition of what we saw and tasted; it is simple and simply delicious. Don't miss out on visiting Paul Revere's house, almost around the corner!

### MAKES 4 SANDWICHES

Four 4-to-5-inch squares rosemary focaccia (if you want to make your own, see the recipe in *La Cucina di Lidia,* page 229)

4 ripe plum tomatoes, sliced ½ inch thick

1 pound fresh mozzarella, cut into 16 slices

12 fresh basil leaves, shredded

2 tablespoons good-quality balsamic vinegar

2 tablespoons extra-virgin olive oil

¼ teaspoon kosher salt

8 to 10 ounces prosciutto, sliced (about 12 slices in all)

Preheat oven to 300 degrees F. Slice focaccia in half crosswise, and put on a baking sheet. Warm in the oven while you prepare the sandwich filling.

Gently toss together the plum tomatoes, mozzarella, basil, vinegar, oil, and salt in a bowl.

Put the bottom half of each piece of focaccia on your work surface, and layer sandwiches as follows. Drizzle focaccia with some of the juices from the tomato mixture. Layer with a slice of prosciutto, then layer with the slices of tomatoes. Follow with another slice of prosciutto, then the slices of mozzarella, then the remaining prosciutto. Drizzle cut sides of the tops of the focaccia with remaining juices from the tomato bowl, and set atop the sandwiches. Cut in half and serve.

# New Orleans

When one thinks of the cultural history of New Orleans, one thinks French immediately, and it was with the Louisiana Purchase that the United States bought from the French the territory that included today's Louisiana. And no one doubts that Creole, the local cuisine, grew out of the customs of the people who settled there—Spanish, French, and African.

But maybe less known is that New Orleans was the largest initial port of entry for Italians, and today one finds much Italian influence, especially Sicilian, in the city's food. Some of the first Italians living in Louisiana prior to the late nineteenth- and early twentieth-century Sicilian mass migration were from northern Italy, mainly Torino, Milan, Genova, Naples, Malta, and Sardinia. Between 1850 and 1870, the U.S. Census Bureau estimates, there were more Italians in New Orleans than in any other U.S. city. Almost a hundred thousand Sicilian immigrants settled in New Orleans between 1898 and 1929. They sailed from Palermo and landed in New Orleans: the trip was much cheaper than going to the expensive North, New York City.

Many Sicilian immigrants to New Orleans were peasants escaping poverty in their homeland. Once arrived, they worked the docks and sugar plantations. Sicilians occupied the declining French Quarter of New Orleans, often called Little Sicily or Little Palermo. Italian immigrants lived in close-knit communities, and even though over a century has passed and they are completely integrated into the American fabric, some traditions have held strong. One such tradition in New Orleans is the Feast of St. Joseph (March 19, Father's Day in Italy). Three-tiered food altars are built, dedicated to St. Joseph, a tradition that came from Sicily. The altars, featuring statues of St. Joseph, candles, and flowers, are supposed to be completely funded by donations of those that visit and pray to them. Preparations begin weeks in advance; many of the ladies make cookies, especially fig cookies, in the church-hall basements. Bread, cannoli, and seafood and vegetable dishes can also be found on the altars, but no meat, because the feast day almost always falls during Lent.

Another Italian tradition that is alive in New Orleans is the muffuletta sandwich, and Central Grocery in the French Quarter claims to be the re-creator of this Sicilian sandwich, stuffed with salami, capicola, mortadella, provolone, and Emmenthaler

The dining room at Liuzza's in New Orleans

(Swiss cheese), topped with a juicy olive salad that includes celery, cauliflower, and carrots all marinated together for over twenty-four hours. The bread absorbs the juicy condiments of the olive salad, the vegetables are crunchy, and the layers of meat and cheese make this such a great sandwich that, last time we went to Central Grocery to eat one, there were cordons keeping the crowd in line.

Another three-generation Italian stronghold in New Orleans is Liuzza's, where we had spaghetti with shrimp and artichokes, and spaghetti with eggplant St. John, which was very reminiscent of *pasta alla Norma*. In Sicily, *pasta alla Norma,* topped with fried eggplant, is dressed with tomato sauce, whereas in Liuzza's the sauce was cream-based. I guess, in these pasta dishes in New Orleans, the creamy French met the green Italians on the plate. At Liuzza's we also had a delicious rendition of crispy fried artichokes, which recipe I share with you in this book. Chef Annea Honoré came out and sat with us, and we had a wonderful conversation about pasta and the fried artichokes.

For dessert, Angelo Brocato's was the place to visit, and, sure enough, granddaughter and grandmother were behind the counter selling, and filling cannoli to order, a very Italian sight indeed. The pasticceria looked and smelled Italian. At the few tables in the middle of the room, mothers came in to sit, pushing their children in strollers. The mothers had coffee; the children had ice cream, and took home some cannoli, which were stuffed to order. We chose spumoni, a three-colored and -flavored ice-cream slice, and a tortoni, an amaretto-cookie-topped ice-cream cup. These renditions of Italian ice creams were popular in the 1970s, when I opened my first restaurant, Buonavia, and I wanted to try them. One rarely finds them on the menu in New York, but here in New Orleans they were selling like hotcakes. The two desserts that I really liked were the cappuccino ice-cream cake, like a frozen cappuccino, and the torroncino, a hazelnut-and-almond semifreddo.

Chef Annea Honoré of Liuzza's

I love going to New Orleans; the spirit, the rhythm, and the food of the city move me. I go as often as I can, for, after the devastation of Hurricane Katrina, the city truly needs all of us now. While I am there, I visit with the Brennan family at the Commander's Palace and a longtime friend, the matriarch, Ella Brennan. Of course I kick it up a notch with Emeril when I find him in town, but even if I am not with my friends, I feel as if I belong in this city that loves good food and the good life, just like Italy.

# Muffuletta Sandwich

*Panino Muffuletta*

There are many versions of the muffuletta sandwich around New Orleans, but it seems that Central Grocery in the French Quarter is the place to go. The store is charming enough, but at the back counter, seated on a stool with a muffuletta sandwich in front of you, is where you want to be. We sat down across from a man who told us he'd had his first muffuletta sandwich here fifty years ago and came back regularly for more. Next to him were a couple who have been coming to Central Grocery to enjoy the muffuletta sandwich for more than forty years.

We ordered one without any hesitation. The large hamburger bun–like bread was soaked significantly with the olive-oil dressing of the olive salad; then layers and layers of the salad and the cold cuts were added. The sandwich was cut in four and wrapped in parchment paper. It was ten in the morning, one would say time for breakfast, but the two of us savored the muffuletta sandwich as did all the other customers.

MAKES I SANDWICH

OLIVE SALAD—VERSION I

1 cup sliced marinated artichoke hearts

½ cup shredded carrot

½ cup shredded inner stalks celery

½ cup finely chopped pitted green olives

½ cup finely chopped roasted red peppers

½ cup seeded, finely chopped pickled Tuscan peperoncini

½ cup pitted chopped kalamata olives

½ cup sliced pickled cocktail onions

¼ cup drained tiny capers in brine

2 tablespoons red-wine vinegar

The famous Central Grocery in New Orleans

To prepare either version of the olive salad, mix all the ingredients in a bowl. Cover, and refrigerate several hours or overnight, to let the flavors develop. This makes more salad than you need for one 8-inch sandwich. Extra olive salad will keep for a week or more and can be used in salads, sandwiches, etc.

FOR THE MUFFULETTA

    8-inch round muffuletta bread, split open
    2 ounces provolone, sliced
    2 ounces deli ham, sliced
    2 ounces capicola, sliced
    2 ounces mortadella, sliced
    2 ounces low-moisture mozzarella, sliced
    2 ounces Genoa salami, sliced

Lay the bottom of the muffuletta bread on a work surface, cut side up. Layer half of the cheeses and meats on the bread, then spread with ½ cup of the olive salad. Top with the remaining meats and cheeses. Finish with another ½ cup olive salad. Place top of bread on olive salad, and press down. Cut into four wedges.

3 anchovy fillets, chopped

2 teaspoons dried oregano

¼ teaspoon peperoncino flakes

OLIVE SALAD—VERSION 2

16-ounce container giardiniera (assorted pickled vegetables), drained and chopped

1 cup sliced marinated artichoke hearts

½ cup finely chopped pitted green olives

½ cup pitted chopped kalamata olives

¼ cup drained tiny capers in brine

2 tablespoons extra-virgin olive oil

3 anchovy fillets, chopped

2 teaspoons dried oregano

¼ teaspoon peperoncino flakes

My version of the Muffuletta Sandwich and a delicious Muffuletta Variation with Ricotta, Anchovies, and Olive Oil

# Muffuletta Variation with Ricotta, Anchovies, and Olive Oil

*Muffuletta alla Ricotta*

It seems that the muffuletta sandwich originated in Sicily, set on what most likely was flatbread sprinkled with sesame seeds. And since the Sicilians were the first mass wave of immigration to the port of New Orleans, it would seem that the soft sesame-seed bread of the muffuletta is an American cousin of the bread of the *pane ca' meusa* (spleen sandwich) still sold in Palermo markets today. This meatless rendition of the muffuletta was made on All Souls Day; the one with the cold cuts and salad is served on more festive days.

Lay the bottom halves of the muffuletta bread, cut side up, on a work surface. Spread each with half of the fresh ricotta, and line half of the anchovies over each top. Drizzle with olive oil, and top with the remaining tops of bread. Cut into four wedges.

MAKES 2 SANDWICHES

Two 8-inch rounds of muffuletta bread, split open

1½ cups fresh ricotta, drained

8 anchovy fillets, chopped

1 tablespoon extra-virgin olive oil

A lovely couple who have been coming to Central Grocery for forty years to enjoy the famous Muffuletta Sandwich

# Italian Beef Sandwich

*Panino di Carne di Manzo*

Chicago is the birthplace of this sandwich, and Al's "#1 Italian Beef Sandwich" claims to be the best. The last time I was there, there was a line, and the outside tables were full of people munching on the beef sandwich. However, I think the recipe below will give you a sandwich much closer to what the Italian American immigrants were and still are making for their families.

The Italian beef sandwich seems to have its roots in Italian weddings and celebrations as a frugal way to offer meat. The boneless beef rump, an otherwise tough piece of beef, when marinated, roasted, and cut into thin slices, and then topped with lots of Italian-style vegetables, went a long way served as a sandwich.

This recipe makes enough for a crowd, or you could halve the recipe and feed a smaller group. That will be a problem if you just want a sandwich for yourself, but I think the only true way to get this sandwich to be as good as it can be is to make it from a whole rump roast. You can always enjoy the leftovers later.

The sign outside Al's #1 Italian Beef in the heart of Chicago

Mix together 2 tablespoons salt, 2 teaspoons dried oregano, and the dried thyme in a small bowl. Rub the spice mixture all over the beef, and put the meat in a large resealable bag. Combine wine, 1 sliced onion, and the garlic, and pour this marinade over the meat. Seal tightly, and let marinate in the refrigerator from 4 hours to overnight.

Preheat oven to 350 degrees F. Remove the meat from the bag, and rub with 2 tablespoons of the olive oil. Place the meat and the marinade in a large pan, and roast, uncovered, until tender and the meat is pink in the middle, about 1½ hours, flipping the meat once during cooking. Remove, and let the meat rest 15 minutes before slicing, reserving the cooking juices in the pan. Slide the sliced rolls into the oven to toast slightly as the oven cools down.

Meanwhile, heat the remaining 4 tablespoons olive oil in a large skillet, and toss in the remaining onions and the celery. Sauté until the onions begin to soften, about 4 minutes. Season with the remaining salt and remaining dried oregano. Stir the bell peppers and the hot cherry peppers into the onions, and cover the skillet to cook, stirring occasionally, until the bell peppers are tender, about 8 to 10 minutes.

Slice the meat, against the grain, as thinly as possible. (Use a meat slicer if you have one.) When the peppers are tender, add the sliced meat to the skillet, along with any juices left in the roasting pan. Cook until the meat is just heated through, about 3 or 4 minutes. Serve meat with peppers and onions, on the toasted rolls.

2 tablespoons plus 1 teaspoon kosher salt

1 tablespoon dried oregano

2 teaspoons dried thyme

4½-pound boneless beef rump roast

2 cups dry red wine

4 medium onions, sliced ¼ inch thick

6 garlic cloves, crushed and peeled

6 tablespoons extra-virgin olive oil

Sixteen 6-inch sub rolls or lengths of Italian bread

4 stalks celery, sliced ½ inch thick on the bias

4 bell peppers (red and green), sliced ¾ inch thick

6 to 8 pickled hot cherry peppers, stemmed, seeded, and roughly chopped

# Gizmo Sandwich

*Panino Gizmo*

The gizmo, a glorified sloppy joe or Italian grinder, is Italian America on a sub roll. This is a great sandwich to make for a picnic or a party. Just make a big pot of the filling and keep piling it on the grilled bread. The filling can be reheated and even frozen—just be sure that it is wrapped tightly, so it won't get freezer flavor. The one I tasted was made with sausage and beef, but just crumpled sausages would be fine; even chopped turkey fits the bill.

MAKES 4 TO 6 SANDWICHES
*(depending on size you cut the bread)*

¼ cup extra-virgin olive oil

1 pound sweet Italian sausage without fennel seeds

1 pound ground beef

1 teaspoon kosher salt

1 medium fennel bulb, trimmed, cored, sliced ¼ inch thick

2 medium onions, sliced

3 garlic cloves, crushed and peeled

1 teaspoon dried oregano

1 red bell pepper, sliced ½ inch thick

1 green bell pepper, sliced ½ inch thick

2 loaves Italian bread

¾ cup marinara sauce, prepared or homemade (see page 108)

1½ cups shredded low-moisture mozzarella

Preheat oven to 400 degrees F. Heat oil in a large skillet over medium-high heat; when oil is hot, add the sausage, removed from its casing, and ground beef, and season with the salt. Cook the meat, breaking into small crumbles with the back of a spoon, until no longer pink, about 5 minutes.

Lower heat to medium, and add the fennel, onions, garlic, and oregano. Cook, stirring occasionally, until vegetables begin to soften, about 4 to 5 minutes. Cover, and let sweat a few minutes; then uncover and add peppers. Cover again, and cook until peppers are just beginning to soften but still have a little texture to them, about 5 minutes.

Split the bread and toast lightly. Cut it into four or six pieces, depending on the appetites of the people you are feeding. Spread the toasted bread out on a baking sheet. Top evenly with the meat and vegetables. Drizzle with the tomato sauce, and sprinkle with the shredded cheese. Bake in the oven until cheese is melted and bubbly, about 3 to 4 minutes. Serve hot.

# Primanti's Sandwich

*Panino alla Primanti*

Just down Smallman Street from our Lidia's restaurant, I have serious sandwich competition in Primanti's, a Pittsburgh institution. I am charmed by their incredibly oversized warm capicola sandwich stuffed with French fries and coleslaw. I am not sure where in the U.S.A. this tradition of stuffing a sandwich with French fries became Italian, but the sandwich was so tall that I could not open my mouth wide enough to get my first bite. Primanti's started as a sandwich pushcart, manned by Joe Primanti, in the Strip in the 1930s, selling sandwiches to truck drivers. One night, a trucker wanted to check if his load of frozen potatoes were good, so Joe Primanti cooked them up. Customers began asking for them, and to expedite the service they were added to the sandwich.

Toss together the cabbage, vinegar, olive oil, celery seed, salt, and sugar in a large bowl. Let the slaw sit and the flavors mingle while you make the fries.

Cut unpeeled potatoes into sticks about ¼ to ½ inch thick. Heat 1 inch of vegetable oil in a deep skillet over medium heat. The oil is ready when the tip of a potato really sizzles on contact. Carefully slide the potatoes into the oil to fry over moderate heat, turning occasionally with tongs, until crisp, golden brown, and cooked through, about 8 to 10 minutes. Don't let the fries brown too quickly! (They might remain raw on the inside and burned on the outside if they are cooked too fast.) Drain on paper towels, and season with salt.

Heat another large skillet over high heat. When the skillet is hot, sear the sliced capicola until crisped on both sides, about 1 minute per side. Remove skillet from heat, and make two stacks of capicola on a side plate, laying the sliced provolone on top, to get it started melting while you assemble the sandwiches.

To assemble, lay two slices of bread on your work surface. Top with the capicola and melted cheese. Top with the fries, slaw, and sliced tomatoes. Top with the remaining bread, cut in half, and serve immediately.

SERVES 2

3 cups very finely shredded Savoy cabbage

1 tablespoon cider vinegar

2 teaspoons extra-virgin olive oil

¼ teaspoon celery seed, crushed

¼ teaspoon kosher salt, plus more for seasoning

¼ teaspoon sugar

2 small russet potatoes

Vegetable oil, for frying

4 ounces capicola, sliced

4 ounces provolone, sliced

4 thick slices Italian bread (ideally, about 6 by 4 inches, not too crusty)

1 ripe tomato, sliced

# Veal Hamburger Parmiciano

*Parmigiana di Carne Macinata*

This is a unique rendition (and spelling) of veal parmigiana that I had in Rigazzi's, one of the oldest restaurants on The Hill in St. Louis. It exemplifies the frugality and the ingenuity of those early immigrants. Instead of expensive veal cutlets, they ground lesser, tougher cuts of veal, then shaped them and treated them like a veal cutlet; the result was delicious and tender! At Rigazzi's, it was the special of the day when we visited.

SERVES 4

3 cups marinara sauce (page 108)

1 pound ground veal

½ cup grated Grana Padano or Parmigiano-Reggiano

2 tablespoons chopped fresh Italian parsley

½ teaspoon kosher salt

All-purpose flour, for dredging

1 cup dry bread crumbs

2 large eggs

Vegetable oil, for frying

4 oblong Italian rolls, about 3 to 4 inches long, split open

8 large fresh basil leaves

8 ounces low-moisture mozzarella, thinly sliced

Preheat oven to 400 degrees F. Warm the marinara sauce in a small pot over low heat. Combine the veal, ¼ cup of the grated cheese, the parsley, and ¼ teaspoon of the salt in a small bowl. Mix with your hands, and shape into four oblong patties (that will fit on your rolls) about 1 inch thick. Spread the flour and bread crumbs on two shallow, rimmed plates, and beat the eggs with the remaining salt in a shallow bowl.

Pour ½ inch vegetable oil into a large skillet over medium heat. Dredge the patties in flour, shaking off the excess, then dip in the beaten egg, letting the excess drip back in the bowl. Press the patties into the bread crumbs to coat both sides. When the oil is hot, carefully slide the patties into the oil. Fry, turning once, until golden brown and just cooked through, about 8 to 10 minutes. (You will know the patties are cooked through when you press on one and no more juice comes out.) Drain the cooked patties on paper towels.

Lay the rolls open on a large baking sheet while still hot. Place a patty on the bottom half of each roll, and spread each patty with about ⅓ cup marinara, keeping the remaining marinara warm for serving.

Sprinkle remaining ¼ cup grated cheese over the marinara on the patties, then top each with 2 basil leaves. Evenly distribute the sliced mozzarella over the leaves. Bake until bread is toasted and cheese is melted and browned on top, about 10 minutes. Serve with additional warm marinara for dipping.

# Sausage and Broccoli Rabe Sandwich

*Panino con Salsicce e Rapini*

Sausage and broccoli rabe are a marriage destined to last. Often served with pasta, most commonly orecchiette, this recipe is for quick, easy, hearty sandwiches with some greens in them.

Heat olive oil in a large skillet over medium heat. When the oil is hot, add the sausage, and cook, breaking into small crumbles with the back of a wooden spoon, until sausage is browned, about 5 minutes.

Add the broccoli rabe, peperoncino, and salt, and stir. Cover, and cook, stirring occasionally, until the broccoli rabe is tender, about 6 to 8 minutes. Add a few tablespoons of water to the skillet if necessary.

Place Italian bread on plates, and top with the sausage and broccoli rabe. Serve hot.

MAKES TWO 6-INCH
SANDWICHES

3 tablespoons extra-virgin olive oil

¾ pound sweet Italian sausage without fennel seeds, removed from casing (about 3 sausages)

1 bunch broccoli rabe, trimmed, tough stems peeled

¼ teaspoon peperoncino flakes

¼ teaspoon kosher salt

Two 6-inch lengths Italian bread, split and lightly toasted

Chomping into my sandwich at Primanti's

# Sausage, Egg, and Peppers Breakfast Sub

*Panino con Frittata di Peperoni e Salsiccia*

Everybody can relate to a sausage-and-pepper submarine sandwich being Italian American, since it is served at every street fair in the Northeast. The use of peppers with sausages is not as prevalent in Italy as it is in the Italian American community here, but this is a delicious dish. Imagine turning it into breakfast, especially on a morning when you have a few extra mouths to feed. The recipe is easy to prepare, because the sausage is taken out of its casings and crumbled into the pan, and everything else is added to it. You just scramble it all together; do not worry about making a perfectly round frittata here.

MAKES TWO 6-INCH SUBS,
OR 4 SANDWICHES ON ROLLS

2 tablespoons extra-virgin olive oil

2 links sweet Italian sausage, removed from casing (about 8 ounces)

1 medium onion, thinly sliced

1 large red bell pepper, sliced ½ inch thick

¾ teaspoon kosher salt

4 large eggs

Two 6-inch lengths Italian bread, split and toasted, or 4 crusty rolls, split and toasted

Heat the oil in a large nonstick skillet over medium heat. When the oil is hot, cook the sausage, crumbling with a wooden spoon, until it is no longer pink, about 3 minutes. Add the onion and bell pepper, season with ½ teaspoon salt, cover, and cook until the vegetables are wilted and lightly caramelized, about 10 minutes.

Beat the eggs with the remaining salt in a small bowl. When the pepper and onion are wilted, pour the eggs into skillet and cook, stirring occasionally with a spatula, until just set but still a little wet, about 1 to 2 minutes. Remove from heat. (The eggs will finish cooking in the turned-off pan.)

Mound the frittata on the bread or rolls, and serve immediately.

# Asparagus, Egg, and Onion Sandwich

*Panino con Frittata di Asparagi e Cipolla*

This great and easy sandwich could serve you well for breakfast, lunch, or a picnic. Basically, it is scrambled eggs with onions and asparagus. I prefer thin asparagus for this dish, since I recall making it with wild asparagus that I would go and forage every spring with my grandmother. Here in the States, asparagus is farmed abundantly.

Wild asparagus is more bitter than the farmed variety, but I love any fresh asparagus. I sometimes use scallions instead of onions, including two-thirds of the green part of the scallion stalks as well.

Heat the oil in a large skillet over medium heat, and add the onion, asparagus, and ¼ cup water. Season with ¼ teaspoon of the salt, cover, and let simmer until the asparagus is tender, about 10 minutes, until the water has evaporated.

Beat eggs with the remaining salt. Pour the eggs into the skillet, and cook, stirring, until just beginning to set but still wet, about 1 minute. Sprinkle with the grated provola, then cover and cook until cheese melts, about 1 minute more. Uncover, stir to mix in the cheese, and serve on the toasted bread or rolls.

MAKES 2 HERO SANDWICHES, OR 4 SANDWICHES ON ROLLS

3 tablespoons extra-virgin olive oil

1 medium onion, thinly sliced

½ bunch asparagus, stems peeled and cut into 2-inch lengths

½ teaspoon kosher salt

4 large eggs

4 ounces mild provola, shredded

Two 6-inch lengths semolina bread, or 4 crusty rolls, lightly toasted

# Prosciutto, Scallion, and Egg Sandwich

*Panino con Frittata di Cipolotto e Prosciutto*

This sandwich was my grandfather's favorite sandwich for *merenda,* the midmorning snack. My grandmother would use the prosciutto scraps with bits and pieces of fat, and when there was no prosciutto, she would use pancetta.

MAKES 2 SANDWICHES

3 tablespoons extra-virgin olive oil

1 bunch scallions, cut into 1-inch pieces

2 ounces prosciutto, sliced, cut into thick shreds

4 large eggs

½ teaspoon kosher salt

Freshly ground black pepper

2 crusty rolls, lightly toasted

Heat the oil in a large skillet over medium heat. Scatter in the scallions, and let cook until softened, about 8 minutes. Add the prosciutto, and cook until crisp around the edges, about 1 to 2 minutes.

Beat the eggs with the salt, pour into the skillet, and cook until just set but still a little wet, about 2 minutes. Remove the skillet from heat, and season eggs with freshly ground black pepper. Serve on the toasted rolls.

# Pizza, Pizza, Everywhere

I had my first taste of pizza when I was twelve years old. My family took us to Rome to catch the plane at Ciampino Airport when we were immigrating to America, and I loved the thin crust of the Roman pizza. Little did I realize that I would someday encounter pizzerias in just about every neighborhood in America. Sometimes it seems today that pizza has become more American than Italian.

Naples is credited to be the birthplace of pizza as we know it today. The first pizzeria opened in 1830, the Antica Pizzeria Port'Alba, and it is still in business today, at Via Port'Alba 18. But flatbreads were enjoyed by the Phoenicians, Greeks, and Romans as well. Pizza was then and is now basically flour, water, and a natural leavening. The addition of tomatoes came only after the discovery of America; today anything goes on a pizza.

In my travels throughout Italy, I tasted many a pizza, but here are three of my favorite styles. I still love the Roman version, with a thin, crispy crust and minimal topping of tomatoes, mozzarella, and basil. For a different texture, there is the *pizza napoletana,*

Outside looking in at Lombardi's Pizza in Little Italy, New York City

which has a puffy, well-baked cornice and a juicier, wetter center, where the tomatoes and melted mozzarella run into each other as you fold it. Then there is the Sicilian *sfincione,* a thick rectangular pizza topped with tomatoes, oregano, and anchovies. The best *sfincione* is sold by street vendors at the local markets, hot off their carts. Overall, I still prefer Italian pizza, but I also love the Italian American phenomenon surrounding the dish.

Roman, Neapolitan, and Sicilian Italians vary in their preferences for pizza, and one can almost follow the different kind of pizzas made around America by looking at the regional Italian immigrants and where they settled. Pizza most likely came to America in the latter part of the nineteenth century. By then, Italians were becoming business-men and vendors, owning their own bakeries, stores, and restaurants. The first true American pizzeria was opened in 1905 by Gennaro Lombardi in New York City, at 53⅓ Spring Street. Today, Lombardi's is located at 32 Spring Street, and still produces a great pizza. It is a bustling business, and on any given day you can find a queue at peak hours. The place has checkered tablecloths, tiled floors, and tables lined up banquet-style along the wall in the back, forming a runway to the huge old pizza oven in the kitchen. And the pizza is delicious.

Sicilians must have been responsible for the Chicago-style pizza, in which the *sfincione* is transformed into deep-dish pizza baked with mounds of toppings. In St. Louis, they like their pizza superthin, on a crackerlike yeastless crust, using Provel cheese, a combination of Swiss, provolone, and white cheddar. I do not know where this mix of cheeses came from; I guess a lack of the traditional ingredients forced chefs to come up with a creative alternative. The New York–style pizza is served by the slice, and has a crust that is at the same time crispy and a bit chewy. It seems to be a combination of the Neapolitan and Roman pizzas, and has been prepared for convenient eating. In California, pizza crust is more like a vehicle for different, atypical toppings, usually of the healthier variety, such as mushrooms and avocado (I guess this is a return to the Greek and Phoenician tradition).

Pizza is easy to make, and a crowd pleaser in whichever form and with whatever toppings you choose.

St. Louis–style pizza, super thin and delicious (top); Joe Maugeri Jr. holding the just-harvested tomatoes at Maugeri Farms in southern New Jersey (below)

# Pizza Dough

*Impasto per la Pizza*

The most important element in making pizza or calzones is the dough. In this recipe, I give you instructions for making it all in one day. But usually I like to let my dough rise slowly in the refrigerator overnight: it develops much more complexity and flavor. This dough is good for calzones and focaccia as well.

**MAKES ENOUGH DOUGH FOR 2 PIZZAS OR A BATCH OF 18 SMALL CALZONES**

1 packet active dry yeast (2¼ teaspoons)

1 teaspoon sugar

6 cups all-purpose flour, plus more for the work surface

1 teaspoon kosher salt

Olive oil, for the bowl

To make the calzones, follow the recipe on p. 86. To make the focaccia: Once the pizza dough has risen, just press it into a large oiled pan, creating dimples with your fingers. The dough should be at least ½ inch thick when spread. Top it with some marinara sauce, a sprinkle of dried oregano, and a drizzle of extra-virgin olive oil. Bake in a 375-degree oven for about 30 minutes. The timing depends on the thickness.

Pour 2 cups warm water (between 90 and 110 degrees F) into a bowl. Stir in the yeast and sugar until dissolved; let sit until foamy, about 5 minutes.

To use an electric mixer: Combine the yeast mixture, flour, and salt in the mixer fitted with the paddle attachment. Mix on medium speed until the dough comes together. Switch to your dough-hook attachment. Increase speed to medium-high, and mix until the dough comes together into a smooth mass, about 2 to 3 minutes. The dough will not clear the sides of the work bowl at this point, but should not be too wet. Add a little more water or flour as necessary to get the right consistency. Scrape the dough onto a floured work surface and knead several times, until the dough comes together into a smooth ball.

To make the dough by hand: Pile the flour on a marble or wooden surface. Make a well in the center of the flour, then sprinkle in the salt and pour in the yeast mixture. Knead well until you've formed a mass of smooth dough.

Oil a large bowl, then turn the dough in the bowl until it is coated with the oil. Cover with plastic wrap, and let rise until doubled, about 1 to 1½ hours. Punch down the dough, and divide in half and let rise again.

The dough can be put in the refrigerator overnight (it will have a slower rise). Take the dough out of the refrigerator. If it is at a full rise, about double its initial size, then proceed in making the pizza. Otherwise, leave the bowl at room temperature until the dough rises fully.

# Pizza Margherita

Preheat oven to 450 degrees F. Place a pizza stone on a rack in the lower third of the oven.

Divide the dough in half, then form each half into a flat round and let it rest on top of your knuckles on both raised fists. Use your knuckles to pull out and stretch the round into a thin circle. Place the dough circle on your work surface, and press it out as thin as you can with your fingertips.

Place the dough circle on a flour-sprinkled pizza peel-paddle (or, if you do not have one, on the parchment-covered back of a baking sheet). Spread about half of the sauce on the dough, using just enough sauce to dot about half of the pizza's surface, leaving a lip around the edge. In the spaces where you haven't dotted sauce, lay half of the cheese. Drizzle with half of the olive oil. Slide the pizza off the pizza peel or the baking sheet with parchment onto the pizza stone.

Bake the pizza until the cheese is melted and bubbly and the crust is browned and crisp on the bottom, about 10 minutes. Remove from oven, and repeat with remaining dough, sauce, cheese, and olive oil.

MAKES 2 PIZZAS

1 batch pizza dough (see preceding recipe)

½ to ¾ cup marinara sauce (see page 108)

4 ounces fresh mozzarella, thinly sliced

1 tablespoon extra-virgin olive oil

A pizza stone, as it is called, is usually a rectangular tablet made of stone or terra-cotta that you place in your oven. It helps make good crusty pizza and focaccia because it heats to high temperature and disperses the heat evenly over the bottom of the pizza, cooking evenly and crisp. A pizza stone should not be washed, since it is porous; you just scrape and brush off any remaining debris. If you do not have a stone, baking the pizza on a baking sheet or in a cast-iron skillet will work, too.

Pizza Margherita

Chicago Deep-Dish Pizza

# Chicago Deep-Dish Pizza

*Pizza Alta di Chicago*

One could call this dish pizza bread, and it is a cross between a focaccia and a pizza. In Sicily, they make a high pizza called *sfincione,* topped with tomatoes, oregano, and a few anchovies. It is sold in warm squares as street food from a cart. The idea for deep-dish pizza came from the early Sicilian immigrants who settled in Chicago, although the excessive toppings are not something one would find in Sicily.

Pour 1 cup plus 3 tablespoons warm (90 to 110 degrees F) water into a bowl, then stir in the sugar and yeast. Let sit until the yeast begins to bubble, about 5 minutes.

In an electric mixer fitted with the paddle attachment, mix the flour, cornmeal, and salt on low to combine. Pour in the yeast mixture and the olive oil to combine while still mixing. Once the dough comes together, switch to the dough hook, and knead on medium-high speed to make a smooth dough, about 2 to 3 minutes. Add a little more water or flour as needed to make a soft dough. Put the dough in an oiled bowl, cover, and let rise until doubled in size, from 1¼ to 1½ hours.

Preheat oven to 400 degrees F. Punch down the dough, and press it into a 14-by-10-inch oiled baking pan or an oiled 12-inch cast-iron skillet, gently pressing the dough up the sides to make a shell. Fill the shell with an even layer of the provolone and mozzarella, then spread the sauce to cover the cheese completely. Top with the pepperoni, and sprinkle with the grated cheese and oregano. Cover with foil, and bake 45 minutes. Then uncover, and bake until the crust is deep golden brown and the pizza is bubbly, about 20 minutes more. Let sit about 5 to 10 minutes before cutting into wedges and serving.

MAKES I PIZZA

FOR THE DOUGH

½ teaspoon sugar

1 packet instant dry yeast (2¼ teaspoons)

3½ cups all-purpose flour, plus more for kneading the dough

½ cup fine cornmeal

½ teaspoon kosher salt

¼ cup extra-virgin olive oil, plus more for bowl and pan

FOR THE TOPPING

4 ounces provolone, sliced

4 ounces mozzarella, sliced

1 to 1½ cups marinara sauce (see page 108)

2 ounces pepperoni, sliced

½ cup grated Grana Padano or Parmigiano-Reggiano

½ teaspoon dried oregano

# Stuffed Pizza Dough

*Calzone*

3 tablespoons extra-virgin olive
oil, plus more for brushing

4 garlic cloves, crushed and
peeled

12 ounces sweet Italian sausage
without fennel seeds, removed
from casing

1 bunch spinach or escarole,
washed, dried, and chopped
(about 12 ounces)

1 pound fresh ricotta, drained

1 batch pizza dough (see page
82)

All-purpose flour, for rolling

Preheat oven to 400 degrees F. Line two baking sheets with parchment.

Heat the olive oil in a large skillet. When the oil is hot, add the garlic and the sausage. Cook over medium heat, breaking up the sausage with a wooden spoon, until browned, about 4 minutes. Toss in the chopped spinach or escarole, and cook, stirring, until tender and wilted, about 7 minutes. Remove from heat, and scrape into a bowl to cool. When the sausage mixture is cooled, stir in the ricotta.

Roll out the dough on a floured work surface to a rectangle about ¼ inch thick. Using a 4½-inch round, cut out as many circles as you can, rerolling the dough to get more circles. You should have about eighteen.

Fill each circle with about 2 tablespoons of the filling. Brush the edges of the dough with water, then fold over and crimp edges together with a fork. Poke holes in the top of each calzone. Place on the baking sheets, and brush the tops of the calzones lightly with olive oil. Set the baking sheets with the calzones in the oven, rotating the pans front to back halfway through baking, until calzones are golden brown, about 25 minutes.

# St. Louis Pizza

*Pizza alla St. Louis*

I found the St. Louis pizza to be different from any other pizza I have had before. The crust has a texture between a cracker and shortbread, and the cheese mixture recalls the milky-velvety mozzarella cheese found in Italy. The pizza is cut into squares, which makes it easy to eat. Here is a recipe I developed after several visits to Imo's in St. Louis, and I think it is quite close to the St. Louis original.

In the bowl of an electric mixer fitted with the dough hook, combine the flour, baking powder, and salt. Mix ½ cup plus 2 tablespoons water and the olive oil in a cup, and, with the mixer on medium speed, pour the wet ingredients into the dry. Knead the dough in the mixer until soft and smooth, about 2 minutes. Remove the dough, and knead on a well-floured counter a few times, then wrap in plastic and let rest at room temperature while you make the topping.

Preheat oven to 450 degrees F with a pizza stone on the bottom rack (see page 83). Drain and crush the canned tomatoes, squeezing out as much juice as possible (save the juices for a future sauce or soup). Coarsely chop the tomatoes, and put in a medium bowl; add the crushed garlic, olive oil, and salt. Let steep 10 to 15 minutes. After the garlic has steeped, discard it and stir in the basil.

Combine the three cheeses in a food processor, pulsing until cheese is mixed to a crumbly paste.

Divide the dough in half. On a floured work surface, roll the dough into an 11-to-12-inch round. Put the dough on a floured pizza peel, or on the back of a baking sheet lined with parchment paper. Spread with half of the sauce, all the way to the edges of the dough. Top with half of the cheese. Slide the pizza off the pizza peel or baking sheet with parchment onto the pizza stone. Bake until very crispy, about 13 to 15 minutes. Repeat with remaining sauce and dough.

## MAKES 2 PIZZAS

### FOR THE DOUGH

2 cups plus 2 tablespoons all-purpose flour, plus more for working the dough

1 teaspoon baking powder

½ teaspoon kosher salt

2 tablespoons extra-virgin olive oil

### FOR THE TOPPING

28-ounce can whole Italian plum tomatoes, preferably San Marzano

3 garlic cloves, crushed and peeled

1 tablespoon extra-virgin olive oil

¼ teaspoon kosher salt

6 tablespoons shredded fresh basil

5 ounces sharp white cheddar, cut in chunks

5 ounces Swiss cheese, cut in chunks

5 ounces smoked provolone, cut in chunks

Grilled Caesar Salad

# Salads

# Grilled Caesar Salad

## Insalata alla Cesare Grigliata

Caesar salad (see following recipe) is not a traditional Italian recipe, and the grilled Caesar salad seems to be a recent phenomenon. Nino Germano, the presiding chef-owner at La Scala in Baltimore, told us how, purely by accident, he invented the grilled Caesar salad. During a busy evening in the kitchen, a cut head of young romaine lettuce fell on the grill. Nino, a frugal *padrone,* set it aside, and when the evening was over and it was time to have his dinner, he decided to dress that grilled romaine as he would a regular Caesar salad. And so the recipe was born.

SERVES 6

3 cups ½-inch cubes of country bread

½ cup extra-virgin olive oil

Yolk of 1 large hard-boiled egg

4 garlic cloves

4 anchovy fillets

2 tablespoons red-wine vinegar

2 tablespoons lemon juice

1 tablespoon Dijon mustard

Kosher salt and freshly ground black pepper, for seasoning

3 heads (1 package) romaine hearts, trimmed and halved lengthwise

¼ cup grated Grana Padano or Parmigiano-Reggiano, plus a 2-ounce piece for shaving

Preheat oven to 350 degrees F.

Preheat a stovetop griddle that fits over two burners over medium-high heat. Scatter the bread cubes on a baking sheet, toss with 2 tablespoons of the olive oil, and toast in the oven, or scatter and toast on the griddle, until crisp throughout, about 6 to 8 minutes. Set aside to cool.

Combine the egg yolk, garlic, anchovies, vinegar, lemon juice, and mustard in a mini–food processor. Process until smooth, scraping down the sides of the work bowl as needed. With the processor running, pour 4 tablespoons olive oil through the feed tube to make a smooth dressing. Season with the salt and pepper.

Drizzle the romaine hearts with remaining 2 tablespoons olive oil, brushing all over to coat evenly. Lay the romaine on the grill pan, cut side down. Grill just until marked and slightly wilted, about 2 minutes.

Arrange the grilled romaine on a platter. Drizzle most of the dressing over them, sprinkle on the grated cheese and croutons, and then drizzle the remaining dressing on top. Use a vegetable peeler to shave slivers of Grana Padano or Parmigiano-Reggiano all over the top of the salad.

Chef Nino of La Scala Ristorante Italiano in Baltimore

# Caesar Salad

*Insalata alla Cesare*

This is not an Italian salad at all, and you would not find it in Italy. Nevertheless, it was very popular in Italian American restaurants in the 1960s and '70s, and has made a strong comeback today. You can find it in any deli or fast-food locale, often topped with grilled chicken, shrimp, or turkey. With all its different renditions and toppings, it is a great salad if made well. This recipe will produce a delicious, tangy Caesar salad.

SERVES 6

2 cups ½-inch cubes of country bread

½ cup red-wine vinegar

Yolks from 2 large hard-boiled eggs

3 garlic cloves

4 anchovy fillets

1 tablespoon Dijon mustard

⅓ cup extra-virgin olive oil

½ teaspoon kosher salt

Freshly ground black pepper

3 heads (1 package) romaine hearts, cut into 1-inch pieces crosswise

½ cup grated Grana Padano or Parmigiano-Reggiano

Preheat oven to 350 degrees F. Scatter the bread cubes on a baking sheet, and toast until crisp throughout, about 8 to 10 minutes. Set aside to cool.

Blend the vinegar, egg yolks, garlic, anchovies, and mustard in a mini–food processor. Process until the dressing is smooth, scraping down the sides of the bowl as needed. With the processor running, slowly pour in the oil to make a smooth dressing. Season with the salt and pepper.

Put the romaine and croutons in a large serving bowl. Drizzle with the dressing, toss well, sprinkle with the grated cheese, and toss again. Serve immediately.

# Spinach Salad

*Insalata di Spinaci*

As a child, I had salads in the winter that Nonna Rosa would dress with the flavorful fat rendered from pancetta or prosciutto scraps and a splash of homemade vinegar. The greens were always the tougher winter kinds, like chicory or escarole, and sometimes she even added slices of boiled potatoes, still warm. So, when I had my first spinach salad in America dressed with warm bacon pieces, I assumed my grandma's salad made with spinach was the American/Italian way.

Heat 2 tablespoons of the oil in a large skillet over medium heat. Add the bacon, cook until crisp, then drain on paper towels. Pour all but 2 tablespoons of the fat out of the pan. Toss in the mushrooms, and cook just until wilted, about 2 to 3 minutes. Combine the mushrooms and bacon in a large serving bowl, and scatter the baby spinach on top.

Set the skillet over high heat. Pour the vinegar into the pan and bring just to a boil, then remove from heat and pour over the salad. Drizzle with the remaining 2 tablespoons olive oil, and sprinkle with the grated cheese. Toss, and serve immediately.

**SERVES 4**

¼ cup extra-virgin olive oil

4 ounces bacon, cut into 1-inch pieces

2 cups sliced button mushrooms

9-ounce bag fresh baby spinach

¼ cup white-wine vinegar

¼ cup grated Grana Padano or Parmigiano-Reggiano

# Tomato and Bread Salad
## *Panzanella*

You might be familiar with this salad made with stale bread, but for some more texture and taste, try making it with *taralli,* often sold as pepper or fennel round bread biscuits at Italian specialty stores in the United States. Actually, *taralli* are small bread rounds, much in the style of bagels, which are baked and toasted to a crisp. It is a traditional food from Puglia, Calabria, and Basilicata. The story goes that the *taralli* were made specifically for the shepherds and workers to take to their fields. The *taralli* lasted and traveled well, and, once tossed with some condiments, they would revive and be delicious.

SERVES 4 TO 6

1 pint grape tomatoes, halved

1 small red onion, thinly sliced

½ teaspoon dried oregano

8 ounces *taralli*

¼ cup red-wine vinegar

¼ cup extra-virgin olive oil

½ teaspoon kosher salt

¼ packed cup fresh basil leaves, shredded

Toss together the tomatoes, red onion, and oregano in a large serving bowl. Break the *taralli* into 1-inch pieces, and add to the bowl. Drizzle with the vinegar and oil, and season with the salt.

Let the salad sit at room temperature for about 15 minutes, to moisten the *taralli* with the dressing and tomato juices. Toss with the shredded basil just before serving.

# Artichoke and Chickpea Salad

*Insalata di Carciofi e Ceci*

When you think you have nothing to eat or serve, look in your cupboard. Providing that you have shopped for these Italian ingredients (most of them in a can or jar), you can make this delicious and nutritious salad in no time. I like it best at room temperature. It is a great appetizer, but it becomes a meal when topped with some grilled chicken or a can of tuna.

Preheat the oven to 350 degrees F. Put the bread cubes on a baking sheet, and toast in oven until crisp throughout, about 8 to 10 minutes. Let cool.

Combine the bread cubes, artichokes, chickpeas, sun-dried tomatoes, and almonds in a large serving bowl. Drizzle with the vinegar and oil, season with the salt, and toss well. Add the parsley and mint, and toss again to distribute. Serve at room temperature.

SERVES 4 TO 6

3 cups day-old ½-inch bread cubes

Two 10-ounce jars artichoke halves or quarters in brine, drained

16-ounce can chickpeas, rinsed and drained

½ cup sun-dried tomatoes in oil, drained and halved

½ cup sliced almonds, toasted

5 tablespoons red-wine vinegar

3 tablespoons extra-virgin olive oil

½ teaspoon kosher salt

2 tablespoons chopped fresh Italian parsley

1 tablespoon chopped fresh mint

# The Outer Boroughs:
# From Astoria to Brooklyn

Nine months after our arrival in the United States, we moved from our first home, in North Bergen, New Jersey, to Astoria, Queens, to be close to our distant cousin Louis Matticchio and his family. Louis had heard we'd made it to America, and it felt good finally to have someone from the family near. Living in Astoria was almost like being in Italy: Broadway and Grand Avenue were lined with Italian bakeries, such as Parisi Brothers, and we went to specialty-food stores that carried Italian products. For fish we always went to Marino's, on 30th Avenue, where they even carried the dry baccalà, *stoccafisso,* from which we make *mantecato* for the holidays. For meats we went to K&T Meat Market on Broadway, where they had the whole baby lamb for Easter, the tripe that my father loved, and chicken necks for soup (the boiled necks were delicious to nibble on with some salt). And the Greek and Korean vegetable markets had the Italian produce list for every season.

Life was beautiful in Astoria, which was our epicenter for a while, but Brooklyn became our Sunday excursion. We discovered other *paesani* who'd settled there, and my mother and father would go and visit, and of course we went along to meet the kids. Brooklyn was Astoria but magnified; if Astoria seemed like an Italian town to me, then Brooklyn was an Italian city, and a big one at that. Our trips on the subway back and forth from Canarsie to Bensonhurst to Bay Ridge seemed endless, but a stop at Coney Island made it all worthwhile.

I never did get to know Brooklyn well, although I made and still make many trips to enjoy good restaurants, pizza, and Italian products. But Brooklyn has many Italian stories to tell, and nobody knows the Brooklyn Italian community better than my friend Angelo Vivolo, so I sought him out and begged him to tell the story of his family in Brooklyn. Angelo heads, with his son Frank, three establishments in Manhattan: Vivolo, Bar Vetro, and Cucina Vivolo. But Angelo started out in Brooklyn, and so he shares the story:

> Brooklyn had several Italian communities. There was Bensonhurst Brooklyn and 18th Avenue; all the Sicilians lived there. Then there is Dyker Heights, where Maria Bartiromo and Rosanna Scotto came from. Thirteenth Avenue was

another big Italian neighborhood. These Italian areas in Brooklyn all had the Italian shops—a salumeria, a *latticini* shop, and always a few bakeries. Our family made a stop every week at these shops. There were always two or three local butcher shops with special cuts of meat, such as tripe, *capuzella* (lamb's head), and hanging whole chickens and lambs. All the grocery stores in the neighborhood carried Italian specialty items: imported pasta, anchovies, marinated olives, dry fava beans, lentils, baccalà during the holidays. We kids went to the ones that sold *torrone* around Christmas and chocolate eggs at Easter. No truffles or radicchio, but Italian staples were always available, and mostly from mom-and-pop operations. There was Avenue U, with its many bakeries (most owned by Sicilians) and typical Italian pastry shops. They competed as to who had the best and most authentic pastries, but especially who had the best bread. And *everyone* spoke Italian.

My family has been in the restaurant business since 1931, and as far back as I can recall, we lived above the store. My mom, Angelina, would cook every day, but Sundays we all sat down in the restaurant for a big family meal before the rush came. The restaurant was on 26th Avenue between Bath and Harway; it was called Villa Vivolo and lasted for seventy years. It was a big place; we always knew we wouldn't be hungry and would have work. We all worked in the restaurant at some point or another. The restaurant was reminiscent of Italy: there was the typical grapevine arbor with a table underneath, and a garden with fruit trees. My dad, Francesco, was born in Italy—in Brusciano, outside of Naples. Mom was born here, but her parents and siblings were born in Corleone, Sicily. The family controversy was that my father married a Sicilian and he was Neapolitan. My father would tease my mother that her parents didn't speak Italian—they spoke Sicilian.

Church was very important to my family. I recall we would all pile into the Ford and go to church every Sunday; eventually, my father bought a Packard. I remember that most of the priests were Italian, and that there was always an Italian mass on Sunday, usually early in the morning. We went to the local public school—our local parish didn't have a Catholic school.

It was great growing up Italian. There wasn't a holiday when we weren't together. Walking through town on a Sunday, you knew what everyone was cooking. The old Italian men from the neighborhood would stand outside on Sunday and smoke Di Nobili cigars, those short, smelly cigars, and talk for hours. Music was very important to us as well, and my grandmother had all of the records of the Italian singers of the time: Carlo Buti, Claudio Villa, Ezio Pinza. Everyone thought they could sing; my grandfather did sing, and my uncle

In 2008, the esteemed pleasure of being the Grand Marshal of New York City's Columbus Day Parade was bestowed upon me, and here I am with Angelo to celebrate the occasion (above); that same year, I had the great honor of cooking for Pope Benedict XVI (bottom left). Here I am at the Vatican Apostolate in New York with Angelo, my son Joe, and his Holiness—a pinnacle of my career; together with my mother Erminia, my father Vittorio, and my brother Franco in Astoria, Queens, in 1962 (top left).

played the accordion. At special dinners people would always sing, mostly typical Neapolitan songs. And there was always wine, a gallon of wine at the table. As kids, we drank red wine with cream soda, and that became my brother's favorite drink. I met my American wife, Denise, in Manhattan and I was the only one who didn't marry an Italian. I always tell my kids, they missed out on growing up Italian in Brooklyn.

# Radicchio and Beet Salad

*Insalata di Radicchio e Barbabietole*

Radicchio belongs to the chicory family. Sweet and bitter at the same time, it is delicious in salads, braised alone, in risotto, and for making pasta sauces. On my recent trip to the Salinas Valley in California, I was astounded to see how radicchio prospered, and how much of it was being produced.

Trim the beet stems, leaving about 1 inch of the stems on the beets. Reserve the greens. Put the beets in a pot, and fill with water to cover them by 2 inches. Bring to a boil, and cook until the beets are almost tender, about 30 minutes. Add the trimmed beet greens, and cook until the beets and greens are tender, about 15 minutes more. Drain and let cool.

Peel the cooled beets, and slice them into ¼-inch half-moons, then put them in a serving bowl. Squeeze out the excess liquid from the beet greens, and chop coarsely. Combine with the shredded radicchio and provolone or cheddar, and toss them into the serving bowl. Drizzle with the vinegar and olive oil, and season with salt. Toss well again, and serve.

SERVES 4 TO 6

1 bunch beets, with greens (about 4 medium beets)

1 head radicchio, cut into ½-inch shreds (about 8 ounces)

6 ounces mild provolone or white cheddar, cut into ¼-inch cubes

2 tablespoons balsamic vinegar

3 tablespoons extra-virgin olive oil

½ teaspoon kosher salt

The vibrantly colored radicchio at Royal Rose Radicchio in Salinas, California

# Radicchio, Goat Cheese, and Raisin Salad

*Insalata di Caprino e Radicchio*

This quick salad delivers a lot of flavor. The radicchio has a touch of bitterness, but the raisins bring in the sweet element, and the goat cheese the creamy complexity. It is a great appetizer, or can be a main course.

SERVES 6

¾ cup golden raisins

3 tablespoons balsamic vinegar

2 pounds radicchio, cut into 1-inch shreds

3 tablespoons extra-virgin olive oil

1 teaspoon kosher salt

1 pound fresh goat cheese (or Gorgonzola—*dolce,* or sweet, is best)

Put the raisins in a small bowl, and pour the vinegar over them. Let soak for 15 minutes.

Pour the raisins and vinegar over the shredded radicchio in a large serving bowl. Drizzle with the olive oil, and season with the salt. Toss well to coat the salad with the dressing. Crumble the goat cheese into chunks over the salad, and gently toss again to distribute the cheese, taking care to keep it in chunks.

Radicchio, Goat Cheese, and Raisin Salad

# Radicchio, Endive, and Walnut Salad

*Insalata di Radicchio, Indivia Belga, e Noci*

The harmony of this salad is that both the radicchio and the endive are from the chicory family, sweet and slightly bitter at the same time.

SERVES 6 TO 8

12 ounces walnut pieces

1 cup grated Grana Padano or Parmigiano-Reggiano

4 heads radicchio di Treviso (about 1¼ pounds), cut into 1-inch pieces

3 heads Belgian endive (about 12 ounces), cut into 1-inch pieces

3 tablespoons extra-virgin olive oil

3 tablespoons balsamic vinegar

1 teaspoon kosher salt

Toast walnuts in a large nonstick skillet over medium heat, about 3 to 4 minutes. Reduce heat to low, and sprinkle with ½ cup of the grated cheese; cook, stirring constantly, until cheese just melts and coats the nuts, about 1 minute. Remove the pan from heat, but leave the nuts in the skillet so they stay warm (but not hot).

Combine radicchio and endive in a large serving bowl. Drizzle with the oil and vinegar, and season with the salt. Toss to coat the leaves with the dressing. Sprinkle with remaining ½ cup grated cheese, and add the warm walnuts. Toss well again, and serve.

# Red Cabbage and Bacon Salad

*Insalata di Verza e Pancetta*

In America, commonplace coleslaw is made from green cabbage, but I do see shreds of red cabbage tossed into a mixed salad every now and then. When I was a child in northern Italy, we ate a lot of the cabbage family, from regular cabbage to Savoy cabbage to black kale. We ate red cabbage braised next to a roast, but we also made a lot of differently dressed salads with it. The secret—and the work—was in slicing the cabbage thin. But given today's food processors and all their different attachments, and the reasonable prices of mandoline slicers, this salad is a cinch to make. You can even slice the cabbage a few hours in advance; just remember to toss it with some vinegar as soon as you slice it to keep its color bright.

SERVES 4 TO 6

Put the shredded red cabbage in a large serving bowl. Heat 1 tablespoon olive oil in a large skillet over medium heat. Cook the bacon until crisp, about 5 to 6 minutes. Pour off most of the fat, and return the pan to the heat.

Add the remaining olive oil and the vinegar to the skillet. Bring to a full boil, and pour over the cabbage in the bowl. Mop out the skillet with a handful of the cabbage to get the crusty bits from the bottom of the pan, and add to the bowl. Season with salt, and toss well so the cabbage doesn't stick together. Serve warm or at room temperature.

1 small head red cabbage, very finely shredded, by hand or on a mandoline

¼ cup extra-virgin olive oil

1 pound bacon, cut into 1-inch pieces

5 tablespoons balsamic vinegar

Kosher salt

Capellini with Vegetables

# Pasta

# Spaghetti with Garlic and Oil
## *Spaghetti Aglio e Olio*

Spaghetti *aglio e olio* is one of those basic recipes that just about every household in Italy, and every Italian American household, has made at one time or another. Searching for flavors of home, Italian immigrants could create a tasty dish with just pasta, olive oil, and flavorful garlic. The simplicity of these three ingredients and the technique used here is what makes it so good. Do not burn the garlic, and add pasta water to make it into a sauce—the secret is as simple as that.

In my recipe, I have added some shredded basil, since I've found in my travels that the addition of basil to a garlic-and-oil sauce is quite common. I often add basil to recipes: when in season, it brings freshness and that pleasant garden bouquet to many dishes.

SERVES 6

Kosher salt to taste

10 garlic cloves, sliced

⅓ cup olive oil, plus more as needed

1 pound spaghetti

½ teaspoon peperoncino flakes

½ cup chopped fresh Italian parsley

1 packed cup fresh basil leaves, shredded

½ cup grated Grana Padano or Parmigiano-Reggiano

Bring a large pot of salted water to boil for the pasta.

Heat the olive oil in a large skillet over medium heat. Add the garlic, and let sizzle until it begins to turn golden, about 2 minutes. Once you begin to cook the garlic, drop the spaghetti into the boiling water and give it a stir.

Once the garlic is golden, toss in the peperoncino and let toast for a minute, then ladle in 2 cups pasta water and stir. Bring the sauce to a rapid boil, and season with salt to taste (depending in part on how salty your pasta water is). Once the sauce has reduced by about half and the spaghetti is al dente, ladle the pasta from the water and into the sauce. Sprinkle in the parsley. Cook and toss to coat the pasta with the sauce. Remove from heat, and add the basil and grated cheese. Toss once more, adding a final drizzle of olive oil, and serve immediately.

NOTE This recipe can be transformed into a different sauce without major effort or investment. You can add four anchovy fillets when you cook the sliced garlic, or add ½ cup drained capers when you add the pasta water, or you can add both.

Emilio Mignucci standing amid the array of cheeses at Di Bruno Brothers in Philadelphia

# Basic Marinara

*Sugo alla Marinara*

MAKES 4 CUPS OF SAUCE,
ENOUGH TO DRESS AT LEAST
1 POUND OF PASTA

4 cups canned San Marzano or other Italian plum tomatoes, with juices (one 35-ounce can)

⅓ cup extra-virgin olive oil

½ cup sliced garlic

¼ teaspoon peperoncino flakes, or more to taste

1 cup hot water

1 teaspoon salt or more to taste

1 stalk or big sprigs fresh basil (with 20 or so whole leaves)

FOR DRESSING THE PASTA

⅓ cup shredded fresh basil leaves, packed (about 12 whole leaves)

¾ cup freshly grated Grana Padano or Parmigiano-Reggiano

Pour the tomatoes and their juice into a big mixing bowl. Using both hands, crush the tomatoes and break them up into small pieces. (You don't have to mash them to bits; I like chunkiness in my marinara, with the tomatoes in 1-inch pieces.)

Pour the oil into a big skillet, scatter in the garlic slices, and set over medium-high heat. Cook for 1½ minutes or so, until the slices are sizzling, then push the garlic aside to clear a dry spot to toast the peperoncino for another ½ minute. Shake and stir the pan until the garlic slices are light gold and starting to darken. Immediately pour in the crushed tomatoes, and stir in with the garlic. Rinse out the tomato can and bowl with 1 cup of hot water, and dump this into the skillet as well.

Raise the heat; sprinkle in the salt and stir. Push the stalk or sprigs of basil into the sauce until completely covered. When the sauce is boiling, cover the pan, reduce the heat slightly, and cook for 10 minutes at an actively bubbling simmer. Uncover the pan, and cook another 5 minutes or so. The sauce should be only slightly reduced from the original volume—still loose and juicy. Before adding pasta, remove the poached basil stalk or sprigs from the skillet and discard (shaking off the sauce that's clinging to it). Keep sauce at a low simmer until the pasta is ready.

To dress the pasta with the marinara sauce, toss and cook them together, incorporating the shredded basil. Remove the skillet from the heat, and toss in the cheese just before serving.

# Spaghetti with Tomatoes and Capers

*Spaghetti con Pomodori e Capperi*

This is one of those "I have nothing in the refrigerator" dishes. Well, look in the cupboard. Capers, the small unopened buds of the caper bush, have been used for thousands of years. They are mentioned as an ingredient in *Gilgamesh,* possibly the oldest written story known, which describes events dating back to about 2000 B.C., found on ancient Sumerian clay tablets.

Bring a large pot of salted water to boil for pasta.

Heat ½ cup of the olive oil in a large skillet. Toss in the bread crumbs, and toast until they are crisp, about 3 to 4 minutes. Scoop out the bread crumbs with a slotted spoon and drain on paper towels.

Now add the sliced garlic to the skillet, and cook over medium heat. Once the garlic is sizzling, add the chopped tomatoes, capers, salt, and peperoncino. Adjust heat, and cook until the tomatoes break down and give off their juices, and the sauce reduces, about 8 to 10 minutes.

Slip the spaghetti into the boiling water. When the spaghetti is al dente and the sauce is ready, remove the spaghetti with tongs from the pot and add directly to the sauce. Sprinkle on the shredded basil, and drizzle in remaining 2 tablespoons olive oil. Toss to coat the pasta with the sauce. Remove from heat, and sprinkle with the grated cheese. Toss, and transfer to serving bowls or plates. Sprinkle with the reserved bread crumbs, and serve.

**SERVES 6**

1 teaspoon kosher salt, plus more for pasta pot

½ cup plus 2 tablespoons extra-virgin olive oil

1 cup coarse bread crumbs (see note)

6 garlic cloves, sliced

2 pounds ripe fresh tomatoes, cored, and chopped into ½-inch pieces

3.5-ounce jar capers, drained

¼ teaspoon peperoncino flakes

1 pound spaghetti

10 large fresh basil leaves, shredded

½ cup grated Grana Padano or Parmigiano-Reggiano

NOTE To make the coarse bread crumbs, grate a piece of stale country bread on the large holes of a box grater.

# Spaghetti with Basil Pistachio Pesto

*Spaghetti al Pesto di Basilico e Pistacchi*

Everybody loves a quick and tasty pasta dressing, and there is nothing better than a pesto. All you need is a blender. Combine all the ingredients, and—*voilà*—you have a sauce. Everybody by now is familiar with pesto made with basil and pinoli nuts, but during one of my visits to Sicily, I enjoyed a pleasant pesto surprise: the pinoli were replaced with pistachios. Although Sicily is known for its delicious pistachios, 98 percent of the pistachios eaten in the United States come from California. So do try this pesto rendition.

MAKES 3 CUPS PESTO, ENOUGH FOR 1 POUND PASTA, SERVING 6 PEOPLE, AND 1½ CUPS EXTRA *(see note)*

½ teaspoon salt, plus more for pasta pot

3 packed cups fresh basil leaves

2 packed cups fresh parsley leaves

1 cup unsalted pistachios, toasted

8 garlic cloves, peeled

1 pound spaghetti

1½ cups plus 2 tablespoons extra-virgin olive oil

½ cup grated Grana Padano or Parmigiano-Reggiano

Bring a large pot of salted water to boil for pasta.

Pulse the basil, parsley, pistachios, garlic, and salt in a food processor. Pour in 1½ cups of the olive oil in a slow, steady stream. Process to make a smooth paste, stopping to scrape down the sides of the bowl occasionally.

Slip the spaghetti into the boiling water, and cook until al dente. Scrape half of the pesto into a large skillet, and add 1 cup pasta water (no need to heat the sauce). Use a spider to drain pasta and transfer to the skillet. Drizzle with remaining 2 tablespoons olive oil, and toss to coat the pasta with the pesto. Toss with the grated cheese and serve.

NOTE You can freeze the remaining half of the pesto for future use. Just pack it into a plastic container and pour a thin film of olive oil over the top. Thaw in refrigerator before using. Or you can cut the recipe in half, if you just want enough for 1 pound of pasta.

Toasting any nuts brings out their oils and flavors, so always toast them just before using. Here are two quick options: You can set the nuts in a baking pan and toast in a 350-degree preheated oven, shaking them periodically, until golden on all sides. Or you can toast them in a sauté pan on top of the stove, shaking them often to make sure they do not burn.

# Fusilli with Spinach Walnut Pesto
*Fusilli al Pesto di Noci*

Spinach and walnuts go well together and make a great pesto to dress pasta. This recipe is ideal for a quick meal; sometimes I like to add a few tablespoons of fresh ricotta to the pasta.

Bring a large pot of salted water to boil for pasta.

Pulse the spinach, basil, walnuts, garlic, and salt in a food processor. Pour in 1½ cups of the olive oil in a slow, steady stream. Process to make a smooth paste, stopping occasionally to scrape down the sides of the bowl.

Pour the fusilli into the boiling water, and cook until al dente. Scrape half of the pesto into a large skillet, and add 1 cup pasta water (no need to heat the sauce). Use a spider to drain the pasta and transfer to the skillet. Toss to coat the pasta with the pesto. Drizzle with the remaining 2 tablespoons of olive oil. Toss with the grated cheese and serve.

MAKES 3 CUPS PESTO, ENOUGH FOR I POUND PASTA, SERVING 6 PEOPLE, AND I½ CUPS EXTRA *(see note)*

1 teaspoon kosher salt, plus more for pasta pot

9-ounce bag fresh spinach, stems trimmed

2 packed cups fresh basil leaves

2 cups walnut halves, toasted

4 garlic cloves, peeled

1½ cups plus 2 tablespoons extra-virgin olive oil

1 pound fusilli

½ cup grated Grana Padano or Parmigiano-Reggiano

NOTE You can freeze the remaining half of the pesto for future use. Just pack it into a plastic container and pour a thin film of olive oil over the top. Thaw in refrigerator before using. Or you can cut the recipe in half, if you just want enough for 1 pound of pasta.

Walnuts abound at the Arthur Avenue Retail Market in the Bronx.

While roaming through the aisles at Venda Ravioli in Providence, Rhode Island, I discovered Chef Salvatore Cefaliello and owner Chris Costantino.

# Fusilli As Made by Ladies of the Evening

*Fusilli alla Puttanesca*

Puttanesca sauce originated in Naples and derives its name from "ladies of the evening." The story goes that, between clients, the women of the evening in Naples would make this quick and delicious pasta dish. The easy procedure and simple ingredients—found in the cupboard, most likely—created a quick dish they could make without any major interruption of business.

This dish was big on the Italian American restaurant scene in the seventies, I guess because it called for authentic Italian ingredients that were newly available then. Cured olives and cured capers are used a lot in southern Italy, to deliver a wallop of flavor with a small investment, and so this traditional dish continues today in Italian homes and restaurants across America.

SERVES 6

Bring a large pot of salted water to boil for pasta. When the sauce is about halfway done, stir the pasta into the boiling water.

Heat ¼ cup of the olive oil in a large skillet over medium heat. Toss in the garlic, and cook until it sizzles and is just golden around the edges, about 2 minutes. Add peperoncino, let toast a minute, then add the tomatoes. Slosh out the tomato can with 1 cup pasta water, add it to the skillet, and stir. Season with the ½ teaspoon salt. Stir in the tuna and olives, bring the sauce to a simmer, and cook until thickened, about 10 minutes. Add the capers and parsley, and simmer a few minutes more.

When pasta is al dente, transfer the pasta to the sauce with tongs. Cook and toss the pasta in the sauce until all of the pasta is coated. Drizzle with the remaining 2 tablespoons olive oil, and toss again. Remove from heat, and toss with the grated cheese. Serve immediately.

½ teaspoon kosher salt, plus more for pasta pot

1 pound fusilli

6 tablespoons extra-virgin olive oil

6 garlic cloves, sliced

¼ teaspoon peperoncino flakes

28-ounce can Italian plum tomatoes, preferably San Marzano, crushed by hand

5-ounce can Italian tuna in olive oil, drained

1 cup pitted olives, a mix of black oil-cured and green, halved

⅓ cup drained tiny capers in brine

¼ cup chopped fresh Italian parsley

½ cup grated Grana Padano or Parmigiano-Reggiano

# Spaghetti with Sun-Dried Tomato Pesto

*Spaghetti con Pesto di Pomodori Secchi*

The important thing is that pesto is a raw sauce and should not be cooked when dressing the pasta. Just toss the hot pasta with a little of its cooking water and the pesto. Stir well, add some cheese, and dinner is ready.

MAKES 3½ CUPS PESTO, ENOUGH FOR I POUND PASTA, SERVING 6 PEOPLE, AND I¾ CUPS EXTRA *(see note)*

Kosher salt

2 cups oil-packed sun-dried tomatoes, drained

2 packed cups fresh basil leaves

2 packed cups fresh parsley leaves, plus 2 tablespoons chopped

1 cup pine nuts, toasted

4 garlic cloves, peeled

1¾ cups extra-virgin olive oil

1 pound spaghetti

½ cup grated Grana Padano or Parmigiano-Reggiano

Bring a large pot of salted water to boil for pasta.

Pulse sun-dried tomatoes, basil leaves, 2 cups parsley leaves, pine nuts, and garlic in a food processor. Pour in 1½ cups of the olive oil in a slow, steady stream. Process to make an almost smooth paste, stopping occasionally to scrape down the sides of the bowl.

Slip the spaghetti into the boiling water, and cook until al dente. Scrape half of the pesto into a large skillet over low heat, and add 1 cup pasta water. Use tongs to drain the pasta and transfer to the skillet. Drizzle with the remaining ¼ cup olive oil, and toss to coat the pasta with the pesto. Remove from heat, and toss with the grated cheese and the chopped parsley.

NOTE You can freeze the remaining half of the pesto for future use. Just pack it in a plastic container with a thin film of olive oil on top. Thaw in refrigerator before using. Or you can cut the recipe in half, if you just want enough for 1 pound of pasta.

# Bucatini with Pancetta, Tomato, and Onion
## *Bucatini all'Amatriciana*

As the impoverished residents of Amatrice moved to Rome in the eighteenth and nineteenth centuries, this recipe came along with them; today it is as Roman as the Colosseum, but you would never know it. Throughout America, 99 percent of Italian restaurants have this tubular-spaghetti dish on their menus, so it might as well be American now.

You can use garlic here instead of onions, as the original recipe calls for. But unless your *amatriciana* contains *guanciale* (cured pig jowl), you are not even close to the original. Since pig jowl is not found in every corner store, making the dish with bacon or pancetta will yield delicious results as well. In this recipe I used onions, as in most of the American *amatriciana* recipes, but the bay leaves are my addition.

The precursor to *amatriciana* sauce is *sugo alla gricia,* which does not contain tomatoes. The dish seems to have roots before the discovery of the New World; tomatoes came back from there to Italy. The *gricia* sauce contains *guanciale,* coarsely ground black pepper, and grated pecorino cheese to dress the pasta. This dish is still made today and is very popular in and around Rome, where it is called *pasta alla gricia.*

Bring a large pot of salted water to boil for pasta. Slip the bucatini into the water, and cook until it is al dente.

Heat olive oil in a large skillet over medium heat. Add the bacon or pancetta, and let the meat render its fat until the edges begin to crisp, about 3 to 4 minutes. Add the sliced onion and the bay leaves, cover, and cook until the onion begins to soften, about 3 to 4 minutes.

Uncover, and sprinkle in the peperoncino and tomatoes. Slosh out the can with 1 cup pasta cooking water, add it to the sauce, and stir. Season with salt, bring the sauce to a simmer, and cook until thickened, about 10 to 12 minutes.

When pasta is ready, transfer to the sauce with tongs. Cook and toss the pasta in the sauce until all of the pasta is coated. Remove from heat, and toss with the grated cheese. Serve immediately.

SERVES 6

1 teaspoon kosher salt, plus more for pasta pot

1 pound bucatini

1 tablespoon extra-virgin olive oil

4 ounces slab bacon or pancetta, cut into ½-inch pieces

1 large onion, sliced ¼ inch thick

2 fresh bay leaves

¼ teaspoon peperoncino flakes

28-ounce can Italian plum tomatoes, preferably San Marzano, crushed by hand

½ cup grated Grana Padano or Parmigiano-Reggiano

½ cup grated Pecorino Romano

# Spaghetti with Egg, Onion, and Bacon
## *Spaghetti alla Carbonara*

Spaghetti carbonara has humble roots in the Apennine hills of central Italy, not far from Rome, and was the shepherds' favorite as they roamed the hilly pastures following the movement of flocks, a practice known as the *transumanza*. They carried with them some bacon, and made the cheese as they went along. Eggs were used only if available; of course they render the dish richer and creamier, but it is delicious with or without them.

Of all of the pasta recipes that I have served in my restaurants throughout the years (starting with Buonavia in 1971, to today's Felidia, Becco, Lidia's KC, and Lidia's Pittsburgh), spaghetti carbonara is definitely the crowd pleaser. It has some of the flavors loved most by Americans: bacon, eggs, cheese, and of course pasta. I've added some chopped scallions for freshness; I hope you like it.

SERVES 6

Kosher salt

1 pound spaghetti

6 ounces bacon, chopped

Extra-virgin olive oil, if needed

1 small onion, chopped (about 1 cup)

2 large egg yolks

1 bunch scallions, trimmed and chopped (about 1 cup)

1 teaspoon freshly ground black pepper

1 cup grated Grana Padano or Parmigiano-Reggiano

Bring a large pot of salted water to boil. Slip the spaghetti into the boiling pasta water, and stir.

Cook the bacon in a skillet over medium heat until the fat has mostly rendered, about 4 to 5 minutes. (If your bacon is very lean, you can add a drizzle of olive oil to help start the rendering of the fat.) Push the bacon to one side of the pan, and add the onion. Let both cook separately until the onion is tender, about 5 minutes, then mix the two back together. (If you like, you can drain off the excess bacon fat here and replace it with olive oil.)

Ladle 4 cups pasta water into the skillet with the bacon and onion, bring to a rapid boil, and quickly reduce the sauce. Meanwhile, whisk the egg yolks with ¼ cup hot pasta water in a small bowl.

When the sauce has reduced by about half and the spaghetti is al dente, scoop the pasta into the sauce with tongs or a spider. Add the scallions, pepper, and salt to taste. Toss the pasta until it is coated in the sauce and the scallions are wilted. Remove the pan from the fire, and quickly mix in the egg yolks, stirring until creamy. Toss the pasta with the grated cheese, and serve immediately.

# "Straw and Hay"

## *Paglia e Fieno*

"Straw and hay," as the name of this pasta recipe translates, is a common dish in Italy, especially in northern Italy, Emilia-Romagna, the heart of fresh pasta making. It always includes a little prosciutto, the sauce is cream-based, and it needs lots of grated cheese. Here I added some chopped scallions for freshness, although the dish always has peas. It is best if made with fresh pasta, but dry fettuccine will still yield a perfectly delicious dish.

Bring a large pot of salted water to boil for pasta.

Melt the butter in the olive oil in a large skillet over medium heat. Stir in the onion, and cook until softened but not browned, about 5 minutes. Add prosciutto, peas, and scallions. Cook until scallions are wilted, about 2 to 3 minutes. Season with the salt, then add the stock and cream. Adjust heat so the sauce is cooking rapidly, then simmer until thickened, about 5 minutes.

Slip the fettuccine into the boiling water, and cook until al dente. When the pasta and sauce are ready, remove the pasta with tongs and add directly to the sauce, along with ½ cup pasta cooking water. Increase the heat so the sauce is boiling, and toss to coat the pasta with the sauce. When the sauce is thickened and coats the pasta, remove the skillet from the heat and sprinkle with the grated cheese. Toss well, and serve immediately.

SERVES 6

½ teaspoon kosher salt, plus more for pasta pot

3 tablespoons unsalted butter

2 tablespoons extra-virgin olive oil

1 small onion, thinly sliced

6 ounces prosciutto, sliced, cut into 1-inch strips

2 cups frozen peas, thawed

1 bunch scallions, trimmed and finely chopped

1 cup chicken stock (see page 40)

1 cup heavy cream

1 pound "straw and hay" (green and yellow) or plain fettuccine

1 cup grated Grana Padano or Parmigiano-Reggiano

# Fettuccine Alfredo

*Fettuccine alla Alfredo*

Fettuccine Alfredo began as regular *fettuccine al burro* until the Roman restaurateur Alfredo di Lelio enriched it with a double and a triple dose of butter for his pregnant wife, who could not keep anything down. The dish was so delicious he kept it on the menu of his restaurant, Alfredo alla Scrofa, in Rome. Mary Pickford and Douglas Fairbanks had it during their 1920 honeymoon trip to Rome, loved it, brought the recipe back, and served it to their friends when they returned to Hollywood. And so another Italian came to America.

Fettuccine Alfredo has most certainly been eaten more in the States than in Italy since then. The dish is used as the base for many different versions, topped with shrimp, broccoli, asparagus, and more. Since butter separates readily when heated, cream is added to make the sauce creamier. In this version, I also add a few leaves of sage, since sage and butter are a marriage made in heaven.

SERVES 6

1 teaspoon kosher salt, plus more for pasta pot

1 pound dried fettuccine

2 cups heavy cream or half-and-half

4 tablespoons unsalted butter

10 fresh sage leaves

½ cup grated Grana Padano or Parmigiano-Reggiano

Bring a large pot of salted water to boil for pasta. When you are ready to begin the sauce, slip the fettuccine into the water.

Combine the cream, 1 cup pasta cooking water, the butter, sage, and half of the grated cheese in a large skillet over medium heat. Stir to melt the butter and bring just to a simmer. Let simmer lightly for a minute or two, so the cream infuses the sage leaves.

When the fettuccine is al dente, transfer it directly to the skillet with the simmering sauce. Season with the salt, and return to a simmer. Simmer, tossing with the tongs, just until the sauce begins to coat the pasta, another minute or two. Remove from heat, sprinkle with the remaining grated cheese, and toss. Serve immediately.

Romana Raffetto in Raffetto's on West Houston Street in New York City

# Rigatoni Woodsman Style

## *Rigatoni alla Boscaiola*

This is a recipe that everybody loves, easy to make and exemplary of Italian home cooking. Its roots are most likely somewhere with the shepherd community of the Apennines. Traditionally, it includes pasta, ricotta, and some meat in a casing, like sausage or salami. The other ingredients are delicious contemporary additions.

### SERVES 6

1 teaspoon kosher salt, plus more for pasta pot

1 pound rigatoni

3 tablespoons extra-virgin olive oil

1 medium onion, chopped

1 pound sweet Italian sausage without fennel seeds, removed from casing

1 pound mixed fresh mushrooms (button, cremini, shiitake, oyster), thickly sliced

6 fresh sage leaves

28-ounce can Italian plum tomatoes, preferably San Marzano, crushed by hand

1 cup frozen peas

1 bunch scallions, chopped

½ cup heavy cream

1 cup grated Grana Padano or Parmigiano-Reggiano

Bring a large pot of salted water to boil for pasta. Slip the rigatoni into the pasta water, and cook until al dente.

Heat the olive oil in a large skillet over medium heat. Add the onion, and cook until softened, about 4 minutes. Add the sausage, and cook, crumbling with a wooden spoon, until the sausage is no longer pink, about 4 minutes.

Add the mushrooms, then cover, and cook until the mushrooms release their juices, about 2 minutes. Uncover, and add the sage and tomatoes. Bring to a simmer, slosh out the tomato can with 1 cup pasta cooking water, and add it to the sauce, along with the salt. Bring the sauce to a simmer, and cook, uncovered, until thickened, about 10 minutes.

Once the sauce is thickened, toss in the peas and scallions. Cook until the scallions wilt, about 2 minutes. Pour 1 cup pasta water and the heavy cream into the sauce. Bring to a boil, and cook until thickened, about 2 minutes.

When it is cooked, remove the pasta with a spider and add directly to the sauce, tossing until the pasta is coated. Remove from heat, and sprinkle with the grated cheese. Toss again, and serve immediately.

# Pittsburgh

I have gotten to know Pittsburgh pretty well during the past ten years, doing research and then ultimately, in 2001, opening Lidia's Pittsburgh, our restaurant on Smallman, in the Strip District. Pittsburgh is a beautiful city laid between two rivers, the Allegheny and the Monongahela. It was the city of steel, and of course now it is the city of the Steelers. With its coal mines, steel foundries, and the building of the Reading Railroad, western Pennsylvania had many jobs to offer immigrants. A group of northern-Italian Waldensians arrived in New Castle, Delaware, in 1665, and Filippo Mazzei, a leading scientific and literary figure and friend of Benjamin Franklin and Thomas Jefferson, visited Philadelphia in 1779. But it was toward the end of the nineteenth century that Italian immigrants looking for work began settling in Pennsylvania en masse.

When we opened our restaurant, we chose to open it near Penn Avenue, where there was already a welcoming Italian community. The Pennsylvania Macaroni Co., run by the Sunseri brothers, is a prime retail store offering Italian specialties, and on Saturdays the line snakes around its shelves, stocked with tomatoes, pasta, and all kinds of Italian products. Three generations ago, the Sunseri brothers came from Sicily; with hard work and determination, they started to manufacture pasta. Several years into their success, a fire destroyed their business, yet this only made the brothers more resilient. In reopening, they blossomed into a retailer of spices, olive oils, specialty products, prosciutto, salamis, mortadella, and a wide selection of Italian cheeses and condiments.

The Strip District, which has been the home for vegetable wholesalers, is just two streets from Penn Avenue, and the market is still operating to this day. In the 1930s, Joe Primanti set up a cart in the Strip District and started selling sandwiches from 3 a.m. to 3 p.m. to the vegetable truckers. The demand for his sandwiches prompted him to open a little restaurant on 18th Street, and now the Primanti name graces five restaurants around Pittsburgh. There is a whole list of sandwiches on Primanti's blackboard, but all the sandwiches have one thing in common: with whatever meat you choose, a pile of vinegary coleslaw is served, topped by French fries. You need the jaws of an alligator to bite into the sandwich, but somehow everybody manages to come back for more. Amy Stevenson, my culinary director and recipe tester, hails from Pittsburgh, and one of her childhood food memories is a Primanti Brothers sandwich. She recalls that the only way she could take a first bite out of the Primanti sandwich was by squishing it down with her two hands.

But the official title of Pittsburgh's Little Italy belongs to the Bloomfield area, and there Amy also had a favorite place where, growing up, she would go for special-occasion meals with her family: Del's Bar & Ristorante DelPizzo. It is a transgenerational Italian restaurant: the DelPizzo family came from Italy in 1908, and started with a small grocery store. Eighty-year-old Grandma Josephine still greets customers at the door; John, her son, is in the kitchen; and Marianne, her daughter, manages the dining room. I ate some good stuffed shells when I visited, but what intrigued me most was the Mafalda sauce, which one could choose to dress one of four different pastas offered. We opted for rigatoni, and the sauce was a good marinara with some cream added to it, which made it pink and rich.

We were told not to miss Merante Gifts, a shop on Liberty Avenue, not too far from Del's Bar & Ristorante DelPizzo. Maria Merante Palmieri is the queen of Liberty

Maria Merante Palmieri, the "queen of Liberty Avenue" in Pittsburgh,
making some of her freshly brewed espresso with a hint of orange peels

Avenue, where her family has run a grocery store for twenty-seven years. On one of her visits to New York's Little Italy, Maria was inspired to begin selling memorabilia along with the groceries. Her father objected at first, but the ceramic plates, tapes of Italian songs, and religious relics sold, and sold well. Now they even sell Italian seeds for radicchio, tomatoes, kale, and cabbage.

As we walked in, a heated Italian-style discussion was taking place between two women and a man: Maria; her husband, Mario; and her sister Gina. Hearing the man speaking Italian, I could not keep myself from chiming in, and we became friends in no time. I wanted to know about them and their family. Maria and Gina were born here, but were from Calabrese parents. The husband came as a young emigrant from Abruzzo. Maria is involved not only in the store, but in the whole neighborhood. She runs a modest cooking school in the apartment where her parents lived above the store. Up the steps we went, to the school in the apartment with a mural of sunny Italy. There were some cream-puff shells cooling on the counter, and some recipes piled on the table awaiting the next class. (The cooking lesson she was about to give that day was certainly Italian—Italian greens and beans with sausage, *pasta in brodo alla Zia Lina,* and cream puffs.)

But before we knew it, Maria had pulled out the Napoletana, the hourglass-shaped coffeepot, and made some coffee. She did something I have never seen before: she peeled the skin from half an orange and put it in the top receptacle of the coffeepot. As the coffee slowly oozed up the spout into the top, it brought out the orange flavor of the peels. The orange flavor in the coffee was unique and delicious. All of this was happening as the two sisters bubbled with information and history: how they grew up, how they went back to Italy to find their relatives, and how they felt ever more Italian.

# Fettuccine with Mafalda Sauce

*Fettuccine al Sugo di Mafalda*

I had this dish at Del's Bar & Ristorante DelPizzo, on Liberty Avenue in Pittsburgh, the local restaurant that caters to the neighborhood crowd, not too far from our restaurant Lidia's on Smallman Street. This velvety combination of tomato and cream sauce is good on any pasta. The day we were there, it was offered with shells. But I think it is even better served with fettuccine.

**SERVES 6**

Kosher salt

3 cups marinara sauce (see page 108)

1 cup heavy cream

1 pound fettuccine

10 large fresh basil leaves, shredded

½ cup grated Grana Padano or Parmigiano-Reggiano

Bring a large pot of salted water to boil for pasta. Bring the marinara sauce to a simmer in a large skillet. Stir in the heavy cream, bring to a simmer, and cook until thickened, about 5 to 6 minutes.

Slip the fettuccine into the boiling water. When the pasta is al dente and the sauce is ready, drop the pasta directly into the sauce. Add the shredded basil, then toss to coat the pasta with the sauce. Remove from heat, stir in the grated cheese, and serve immediately.

# Penne Rigate in a Vodka Sauce

*Penne Rigate alla Vodka*

If there is one dish that I can affirm is Italian American, this is it. It has all the pedigree of being Italian, though it was definitely born in America. This is one of those few recipes that crossed the Atlantic in the other direction, and the Italians in Italy have been enjoying it as well. The first references we find to vodka sauce are from the early 1980s.

SERVES 6

Bring a large pot of salted water to boil for the pasta. When the sauce is almost done, slip the pasta into the pasta pot, stir around, and cook until al dente.

Melt the butter in the olive oil in a large skillet over medium heat. Toss in the diced onion and crushed garlic, and let them sweat a few minutes, without coloring. Clear a "hot spot" and toast the peperoncino for a minute. Then ladle in about ½ cup pasta water, stir, and let simmer to break down the onion, about 2 to 3 minutes.

Once the onion has softened, pour in the crushed tomatoes. Slosh out the can with about a cup of pasta water, and add it to the sauce. Season with salt, bring to a simmer, and cook until thickened, about 10 to 12 minutes.

When the sauce has thickened, remove the garlic cloves, then add the half-and-half and vodka. Bring to a boil, and cook until the sauce comes together and thickens again. When the pasta is al dente, scoop out of the pot with a strainer or spider, and drop it directly into the sauce. Cook and toss the pasta in the sauce until coated all over. Remove from heat, and toss with the grated cheese and basil. Serve immediately.

1 teaspoon kosher salt or to taste, plus more for pasta pot

1 pound penne rigate

2 tablespoons unsalted butter

1 tablespoon extra-virgin olive oil

½ cup finely diced onion

2 garlic cloves, crushed and peeled

¼ teaspoon peperoncino flakes

28-ounce can Italian plum tomatoes, preferably San Marzano, crushed by hand

½ cup half-and-half

⅓ cup vodka

1 cup grated Parmigiano-Reggiano or Grana Padano

¼ cup shredded fresh basil leaves

# Capellini with Vegetables
## *Capellini alla Primavera*

Pasta with spring vegetables—or, for that matter, any vegetables—has always been a staple of Italian cuisine. But Sirio Maccioni, the renowned Italian restaurateur who has owned Le Cirque for decades, claims to be the one to baptize it *primavera* in 1974. Along with Romeo Salta, and the Giambelli brothers, Sirio was at the lead in bringing the fine Italian dining experience to New York. Sirio runs a restaurant that is French by name but serves *pasta primavera*.

**SERVES 6**

1 teaspoon salt, plus more for pasta pot

1 pound capellini

½ cup extra-virgin olive oil

4 garlic cloves, crushed and peeled

8 ounces green beans, cut into 1-to-2-inch lengths

8 ounces asparagus, peeled, cut into 1-to-2-inch lengths

1 pint grape tomatoes

1 bunch scallions, chopped

1 cup frozen peas, thawed

½ cup heavy cream

½ cup fresh basil leaves, loosely packed, shredded

½ cup grated Grana Padano or Parmigiano-Reggiano

Bring a large pot of salted water to boil for pasta. Once it is boiling, slide in the capellini, and cook until al dente.

Pour ¼ cup of the olive oil into a large skillet over medium-high heat, then toss in the garlic cloves. Once the garlic begins to sizzle, slip in the green beans, asparagus, and salt. Pour in ½ cup pasta water, then cover and let steam until crisp-tender, about 4 minutes.

Once the asparagus and green beans are crisp-tender, add the grape tomatoes, and cook until they begin to wrinkle, about 2 to 3 minutes. Pour the scallions and peas into the skillet. Drizzle with 2 tablespoons olive oil, and ladle in about 2 cups pasta water. Bring to a rapid boil, and cook until reduced by about half.

When the capellini is al dente, transfer it to the sauce. Pour in the cream, the remaining 2 tablespoons oil, and up to ½ cup more pasta water if the sauce is too dense. Bring to a boil, and cook until sauce coats the pasta; toss with the shredded basil. Remove from heat, and toss with the grated cheese.

# Orecchiette with Broccoli Rabe

*Orecchiette con Broccoli Rapini*

Broccoli rabe, the leafy bitter almond-flavored vegetable consumed by the Italians for centuries, has found its way into American hearts. It is great just braised with olive oil and garlic; it makes an excellent soup; it is also delicious stuffed and as a flavoring in some crunchy Italian bread. But I love it with pasta, and not with just any pasta—I love it with orecchiette (little earlobes).

Rapini, as it is called in Italy, is a plant in the mustard family that grew wild, especially in southern Italy. In America, the largest producer is Andy Boy, a company founded by Stephen and Andrew D'Arrigo, emigrants from Sicily, who officially named the rapini "broccoli rabe." They knew that the vegetable that was part of their family table in Italy would make it to the American table.

Bring a large pot of salted water to boil for pasta. Plop the orecchiette into the boiling water, and cook until al dente.

Cook the garlic in 3 tablespoons olive oil in a large skillet over medium heat. Once the garlic is sizzling, crumble in the sausage, and cook, breaking up the clumps with the back of a wooden spoon, until browned, about 3 minutes. Season with the peperoncino. Add the broccoli rabe, and season with the salt and the remaining 2 tablespoons olive oil. Toss to coat the broccoli with the oil. Pour in 1 cup pasta water, then cover and cook until broccoli rabe is tender, about 15 minutes.

When the broccoli rabe is tender, uncover, add 1 more cup pasta water, and bring to a boil. When the orecchiette is al dente, scoop the pasta from the water and add to the sauce. Toss to coat the pasta with the sauce. Remove from heat, sprinkle with the Pecorino Romano, and toss. Serve immediately.

SERVES 6

¼ teaspoon kosher salt, plus more for pasta pot

1 pound orecchiette

6 garlic cloves, sliced

5 tablespoons extra-virgin olive oil

1 pound sweet Italian sausage, removed from casing

¼ teaspoon peperoncino flakes

2 bunches broccoli rabe, trimmed, chopped into 1-inch pieces

1 cup grated Pecorino Romano

# Orecchiette with Artichokes and Bacon

*Orecchiette con Carciofi e Pancetta*

The artichoke is in the thistle family. One medium to large artichoke will yield approximately 2 ounces of delicious edible flesh. An artichoke is fresh when it squeaks as you squeeze it, and feels heavy in your hand for its size. Look for a deep olive green on the outside, and pale tender green on the inside of the petals. Artichokes will last fresh about a week. To store them, sprinkle them with cold water, and refrigerate in an airtight bag. Wash only before using.

Italians have endless ways to enjoy artichokes, but I love them in this pasta dish with a little bacon added, a perfect harmony.

SERVES 6

¼ teaspoon kosher salt, plus more for pasta pot

1 pound orecchiette

6 medium artichokes

2 lemons

8 ounces bacon, cut into 1-inch pieces

3 tablespoons extra-virgin olive oil

6 garlic cloves, crushed and peeled

¼ teaspoon peperoncino flakes

⅓ cup chopped fresh Italian parsley

1 cup grated Pecorino Romano

Bring a large pot of salted water to boil. Once it is boiling, plop in the orecchiette and cook until al dente.

Clean and prepare the artichokes as detailed on page 18. Then cut all of the artichokes into ½-inch-thick slices, and leave in the water while you start the sauce.

Put the bacon, 1 tablespoon of the olive oil, and the crushed garlic in a large straight-sided skillet over medium heat. Cook the bacon until most of the fat has rendered, about 5 minutes. Drain the artichokes, pat dry, and add to the skillet along with the juice of the remaining lemon. Season with the salt and peperoncino. Cover, and let the artichokes cook gently until they begin to soften and caramelize, about 10 minutes. Uncover, and add about 1 cup pasta water, then bring to a simmer and cook, uncovered, until the artichokes are tender, about 10 minutes more.

When the pasta is al dente, scoop it out of the water and add to the sauce. Drizzle with the remaining 2 tablespoons olive oil, and add the chopped parsley. Cook, tossing to coat the pasta with the sauce. Remove from heat, sprinkle with the grated Pecorino Romano, and toss. Serve.

# Linguine with Red Clam Sauce

*Linguine alle Vongole in Salsa Rossa*

SERVES 6

Bring a large pot of salted water to boil. Once it is boiling, slip the linguine into the pot and cook until al dente. Drain the pasta, reserving the cooking water.

Heat 4 tablespoons of the olive oil in a large, deep straight-sided skillet or Dutch oven over medium heat. Toss in the sliced garlic, and cook until garlic is sizzling, about 1 to 2 minutes. Season with the peperoncino, let toast for a minute, then pour in the tomatoes. Rinse out the tomato can with a cup of the reserved pasta cooking water, pour it into the sauce, and stir. Season with the salt, and bring to a simmer. Cook, uncovered, to thicken the sauce and develop the flavors, about 8 to 10 minutes.

Add the clams to the sauce, and cover the pan. The clams will take about 7 to 8 minutes to open. Check them occasionally, removing to a bowl any that have opened fully. Carefully remove hot clam meat from the shells, using a towel if the clams are too hot to handle comfortably.

Once all of the clams have opened and been removed, add the shredded basil to the sauce. Add the cooked linguine to the sauce. Drizzle with remaining 2 tablespoons olive oil, and put the shucked clams back in. Toss for a minute to coat the pasta with the sauce, and serve.

½ teaspoon kosher salt, plus more for pasta pot

1 pound linguine

6 tablespoons olive oil

6 garlic cloves, sliced

¼ teaspoon peperoncino flakes

28-ounce can plum tomatoes, preferably San Marzano, crushed by hand

36 littleneck clams, scrubbed

10 large fresh basil leaves, shredded

# Linguine with White Clam Sauce

*Linguine alle Vongole*

This is the quintessential Italian pasta dish, especially in Naples and Rome. The ingredients are three; the clams are the smaller ones—*vongole veraci*—and they are always cooked in their shells. Once they open, the sauce is done. Here in the States, linguine with clam sauce is made with chopped clams, and I guess this adjustment makes sense, especially since the clams here can be quite large, from littlenecks (small to medium) to topnecks (large) to quahogs or chowder clams (very large). Today, though, one is ever more likely to find smaller cockles on the market; if you find them, by all means use them.

SERVES 6

6 tablespoons extra-virgin olive oil

6 garlic cloves, sliced

4 anchovy fillets, sliced

36 littleneck clams, scrubbed

¼ teaspoon peperoncino flakes

¼ teaspoon dried oregano

1 pound linguine

¾ cup chopped fresh Italian parsley

Bring a large pot of water to boil for pasta. In a large straight-sided skillet, heat 4 tablespoons of the olive oil over medium heat. Add sliced garlic, and cook until sizzling, about 1 to 2 minutes. Add anchovies, and stir until the anchovies break up and dissolve into the oil, about 2 minutes.

Add the clams to the skillet, along with the peperoncino and oregano. Ladle in about 2 cups pasta water. Bring to a simmer, cover, and cook until clams open, about 5 to 7 minutes. As the clams open, remove to a bowl. Meanwhile, add linguine to boiling pasta water.

When all the clams are out, increase heat to high and add ½ cup of the parsley. Cook until liquid is reduced by half. Meanwhile, shuck the clams.

When the linguine is al dente and the sauce is reduced, add the pasta directly to the sauce, and drizzle with remaining 2 tablespoons olive oil. Cook and toss until the pasta is coated with the sauce. Add shucked clams and remaining ¼ cup chopped parsley. Cook a minute more, to blend the flavors, and serve.

Linguine with red clam sauce is almost never found in Italy, but a big seller in Italian American restaurants here in the United States. So, when you go to Italy, eat it as they do, with white clam sauce, and never, ever ask for cheese to put on your linguine with clam sauce.

# Spaghetti with Crab Sauce
## *Spaghetti al Sugo di Granchio*

This dish is especially good when made with live blue-claw crabs, but sometimes they are difficult to find. The snow crab—or its more expensive cousin, the Alaskan king crab—will yield a most delicious sauce as well. In immigrant Italian American fishing communities, such as those in Delaware and Rhode Island, this dish was made by the fishermen's wives from the unsellable catch.

**SERVES 6**

2 teaspoons kosher salt, plus more for pasta pot

1 pound spaghetti

½ cup extra-virgin olive oil

8 garlic cloves, sliced

Two 28-ounce cans Italian plum tomatoes, preferably San Marzano, crushed by hand

1 teaspoon dried oregano

3 pounds snow-crab legs, broken into pieces, ends snipped off the legs to let in flavor

3 tablespoons chopped fresh Italian parsley

Bring a large pot of salted water to boil for pasta. Slip the spaghetti into the boiling water, and cook until al dente.

Heat 4 tablespoons of the oil in a large Dutch oven over medium heat. When the oil is hot, add half of the sliced garlic. Once the garlic sizzles, add the tomatoes. Slosh out the can with 1 cup pasta water, and add that as well. Bring to a simmer, add the salt and oregano, and simmer until slightly thickened, about 10 minutes.

Meanwhile, heat the remaining 4 tablespoons olive oil in a large skillet over medium-high heat. When the oil is hot, add the remaining sliced garlic. Once the garlic sizzles, add as many crab-leg pieces as will fit in the pan in one layer (you will need to do this in batches). Sauté crab legs, turning, until they turn from blue to bright red, about 3 minutes per batch. Remove to a plate, and repeat with remaining crab legs. Once all of the crab is sautéed, and after the sauce has cooked 10 minutes, add the crab legs to the sauce. Simmer until the crab is cooked through and the sauce is flavorful, another 10 minutes or so.

When the pasta is ready, pour about 3 cups of the sauce into a large skillet, and bring to a simmer. Transfer the drained pasta directly into the sauce in the skillet. Sprinkle with the chopped parsley, and toss to coat the pasta with the sauce. Serve the pasta in shallow bowls, with the extra sauce and crab legs piled over the top.

Spaghetti with Breaded Shrimp

# Spaghetti with Breaded Shrimp
*Spaghetti con Gamberi Impanati*

I first encountered this dish in Chicago. While the sauce for the pasta has all the makings of a *primavera,* the fried shrimp on top is very much Sicilian.

Bring a large pot of salted water to boil for pasta. Once it is boiling, slip the spaghetti into the pot, and cook until al dente.

Meanwhile, pour the flour into one shallow bowl, beat the eggs with a pinch of salt in another, and spread the bread crumbs in a third. Season the shrimp with salt, then dredge them in the flour, tapping off the excess. Dip the shrimp in the eggs, letting excess drip back into the bowl, then dredge them in the bread crumbs. Set the breaded shrimp aside while you start the pasta sauce.

Melt 2 tablespoons of the butter in the olive oil in a large skillet over medium heat. Once the butter has melted, add the garlic and let sizzle for a minute, until fragrant. Add the broccoli, mushrooms, and asparagus, and season with the salt and peperoncino. Sauté the vegetables, tossing occasionally, until they begin to wilt, about 3 minutes. Ladle in ½ cup pasta water, cover the skillet, and let cook until the vegetables are almost tender, about 5 minutes.

Meanwhile, heat ½ inch vegetable oil in another skillet over medium heat. When ready (the tip of a shrimp will sizzle on contact), fry the shrimp in two batches until crispy and golden, about 3 minutes per side. Drain on paper towels, season with salt, and keep warm.

Once the vegetables in the sauce are almost tender, uncover, and add the scallions and 1 cup pasta water. Bring the sauce to a simmer, and cook until it is reduced and the vegetables are tender, about 8 to 10 minutes.

When the pasta is al dente, plop it directly into the sauce. Add the remaining 2 tablespoons butter, and toss to melt. Remove from heat, and toss with the grated cheese. Serve the pasta in bowls, topping each serving with three breaded shrimp. Serve with lemon wedges to squeeze over the shrimp.

SERVES 6

FOR THE SHRIMP

1 cup all-purpose flour

2 large eggs

Kosher salt

2 cups fine dry bread crumbs

18 jumbo shrimp (about 1 pound), peeled and deveined, tails on

Vegetable oil, for frying

1 lemon, cut into 6 wedges

FOR THE SPAGHETTI

1 teaspoon kosher salt, plus more for pasta pot

1 pound spaghetti

4 tablespoons unsalted butter

3 tablespoons olive oil

2 garlic cloves, sliced

2 cups small broccoli florets

2 cups sliced cremini mushrooms

1 cup 1-inch pieces asparagus

Pinch peperoncino flakes

1 bunch scallions, finely chopped

1 cup grated Grana Padano or Parmigiano-Reggiano

# Orecchiette with Mussels and Broccoli Rabe

*Orecchiette con Cozze e Rapini*

Broccoli rabe grew wild in Italy, especially in southern Italy; in places like Puglia, Calabria, Basilicata, and Sicily it was abundant and free for the picking, and thus used especially to dress pasta dishes. Orecchiette, a pasta that has an indentation from being dragged with the finger on a board, was the pasta of choice. All of these regions are on the sea, and mussels were cheap and abundant as well. So it would seem natural that the three ingredients come together to make this wonderful dish. Now broccoli rabe is abundant in the United States, thanks to Andy Boy vegetable growers in California. This recipe is a delightful combination.

SERVES 6

Kosher salt

1 pound orecchiette

½ cup extra-virgin olive oil

11 garlic cloves, 6 crushed, 5 sliced

2 pounds mussels, cleaned

1 bunch broccoli rabe, trimmed, chopped into 2-inch pieces

Pinch peperoncino flakes

½ cup grated Grana Padano or Parmigiano-Reggiano

Bring a large pot of salted water to boil for pasta. Once it is boiling, plop the orecchiette into the pasta water, and cook until al dente.

Meanwhile, heat 3 tablespoons of the oil over medium-high heat in a large skillet. When the oil is hot, add the crushed garlic. Let the garlic sizzle a minute, then add the mussels. Cover, and cook until the mussels open, about 5 minutes, then scoop the mussels up with a spider and put them in a bowl to cool slightly. Reserve any leftover liquid.

Heat 3 tablespoons olive oil over medium-high heat in another large skillet. Add the sliced garlic, and cook until sizzling and fragrant, about 1 to 2 minutes. Toss in the broccoli rabe and peperoncino, and strain the reserved mussel cooking liquid into the skillet. Cover, and cook until the broccoli rabe is tender, about 10 minutes. If there is too much liquid left in the skillet and it looks soupy, uncover and bring to a rapid boil to reduce and thicken the sauce.

Pluck the mussels from their shells, and put the meat in a small bowl. (No need to save the shells.) When the pasta is ready, use a spider to transfer it directly into the skillet with the broccoli rabe. Return the mussels to the skillet, drizzle with the remaining 2 tablespoons olive oil, and toss to coat the pasta with the sauce. Remove from heat, toss with the grated cheese, and serve.

# Calamari Fra Diavolo over Linguine

*Linguine con Calamari Piccanti*

There was a time when calamari was not much consumed in America and it was considered a cheap fish. But Italians love calamari, and it became the fish of choice of the Italian immigrants. You can find calamari today as a delicacy in contemporary restaurants of every ethnicity. Spicy calamari with linguine is a trademark of Italian American restaurants all over America.

Bring a large pot of salted water to boil for pasta. Stir the linguine into the boiling water.

Pour 4 tablespoons of the olive oil into a large skillet over medium-high heat. When the oil is hot, toss in the sliced garlic, and cook until it sizzles, about 1 to 2 minutes. Season with the peperoncino, let it toast for a minute, then pour in the tomatoes. Slosh out the tomato can with a cup of pasta water, add that to the sauce, and stir. Season with the oregano and salt. Bring to a simmer, and cook, uncovered, to thicken the sauce and develop the flavors, about 8 to 10 minutes.

When the sauce is ready, stir in the calamari and simmer until just cooked through, about 2 to 3 minutes. When the pasta is al dente, drain and toss it directly into the sauce. Drizzle with the remaining 2 tablespoons olive oil, toss well to combine, and serve immediately.

SERVES 6

½ teaspoon kosher salt, plus more for pasta pot

1 pound linguine

6 tablespoons extra-virgin olive oil

8 garlic cloves, sliced

½ teaspoon peperoncino flakes

28-ounce can plum tomatoes, preferably San Marzano, crushed by hand

1 teaspoon dried oregano

1 pound cleaned calamari, bodies cut into 1-inch rings, tentacles roughly chopped

# Spaghetti and Meatballs
## Spaghetti con Polpette di Carne

Everybody loves meatballs. I think meatballs are an example of Americana and they belong on the American table. This is a great and simple recipe. It calls for three types of meat, but a combination of any two—or even a single meat—will work as well.

The recipe makes four dozen meatballs, but you can cut it in half and it will work just as well. The sauce and meatballs freeze well, but are best frozen in smaller quantities (½ pint, or six to eight meatballs and sauce) so that they reconstitute quickly.

Spaghetti and Meatballs

Preheat oven to 425 degrees F.

Combine the carrot, celery, and onion in a food processor, pulsing to make a fine-textured paste or *pestata*. Scrape the *pestata* into a large bowl, and add the three meats, eggs, oregano, parsley, bread crumbs, and salt, mixing with your hands to combine well.

Roll the meat into golf-ball-sized balls, and place on baking sheets lined with parchment paper. (You should get about forty-eight meatballs.) Bake the meatballs until browned all over, about 18 to 20 minutes. (They do not need to be entirely cooked through, because they will cook more in the sauce.)

While the meatballs are baking, bring a large pot of salted water to boil for pasta. Slip the spaghetti into the boiling water and cook until al dente. Drain the pasta, reserving ½ cup of pasta water.

Begin the sauce: heat the olive oil in a large pot over medium heat. Toss in the onion, and sauté until it turns transparent, about 2 to 3 minutes. Ladle in the reserved pasta water, and simmer the onion to break it down, about 2 to 3 minutes.

Once the water has cooked away, sprinkle in 1 teaspoon of the salt, the bay leaves, and peperoncino. Let the peperoncino toast for a minute, then pour in the tomatoes. Slosh out the tomato cans and bowl with 4 cups hot water, add to the pot, and stir. Stir in the remaining teaspoon of salt, and bring the sauce to a simmer while the meatballs finish baking; simmer sauce about 10 minutes more.

When the meatballs have finished baking, gently add them to the sauce and return to a simmer. Simmer, shaking the pan periodically to move (but not break) the meatballs, until the sauce is thick and flavorful, about ½ hour.

Plop the spaghetti back into the empty pasta cooking pot. Add half of the sauce (with no meatballs) and toss. Set in a hot bowl, and top with meatballs and additional sauce if necessary. Serve immediately, offering the remaining sauce and meatballs at the table with the grated cheese.

MAKES ENOUGH FOR I POUND PASTA, SERVING 6 PEOPLE, PLUS ABOUT 3 QUARTS EXTRA *(total of about 4 dozen meatballs and 3 quarts sauce)*

FOR THE MEATBALLS

1 medium carrot, coarsely chopped

2 stalks celery, coarsely chopped

1 medium onion, coarsely chopped

1 pound ground beef

1 pound ground pork

1 pound ground veal

2 large eggs, beaten

1 teaspoon dried oregano

½ cup chopped fresh parsley

2 cups bread crumbs

1 tablespoon kosher salt

FOR THE SAUCE

¼ cup extra-virgin olive oil

1 medium onion, chopped (about 1½ cups)

2 teaspoons kosher salt, plus more as needed

2 fresh bay leaves, or 3 dried bay leaves

½ teaspoon peperoncino flakes

Three 28-ounce cans Italian plum tomatoes, preferably San Marzano, crushed by hand

1 pound spaghetti

1 cup grated Grana Padano or Parmigiano-Reggiano

# North Bergen, New Jersey

There are more than two million descendants of Italian immigrants in New Jersey. Totowa, Hackensack, and Nutley all have strong Italian American communities. One of the first Italian immigrants to live in New Jersey, Giovanni Battista Sartori, settled in Trenton and founded both the first spaghetti factory in America and the first Catholic Church in New Jersey. Most immigrants came and worked at manual-labor jobs or as longshoremen. Some worked in factories; many were artisans. Weavers and cloth dyers from Lombardy found jobs in Paterson's silk industry, and craftsmen and sculptors from Tuscany were employed at the Perth Amboy Terra Cotta Company. For over a century in Hoboken, the Feast of Saint Ann has been celebrated and men have been convening at the Monte San Giacomo Club. However, Italians in New Jersey are not restricted to the places across from La Grande Mela (the Big Apple); they are spread over all of New Jersey.

Ralph's Famous Italian Ices resides in Hoboken (as did Frank Sinatra), and some of the first ravioli made in America came from Bruno Ravioli in Hackensack. In 1888, Bruno Cavalli left his home in Piedmont and came to America. He started work as a waiter and noticed that many customers were asking for fresh ravioli. So, in 1905, Bruno opened his first shop, making fresh ravioli for people to take home, stuffing them with meat and cheese and delivering them in shoe boxes by bicycle. Four generations later, the business is going strong, with several stores in Manhattan.

One Saturday morning, I decided to revisit North Bergen, where my family first lived as new immigrants. This is where my American story began in 1958. Our first home here was a small ranch perched on the Jersey cliffs, overlooking the Manhattan skyline. I still recall that my brother and I would sit on those rocks under the star-studded sky for hours into the night, looking at the twinkling magic of the big city, a far cry from the lights of the thirty houses that lined Busoler, the little town where Grandma Rosa lived. The house on those Jersey cliffs had no paved road then, and although I went several times trying to locate that spot, somewhere behind Kennedy Boulevard East in North Bergen, I could not find it. Big buildings stand there now, and surely they engulfed our first little house in America. My mother worked as a seamstress for Evan Picone, which is no longer operating. I recall that I went to the Sacred Heart elementary school; although the church still exists, the school has closed down. Yet, even if my first home in New Jersey is gone, the state remains a beehive of Italians, busy working and living their lives.

New Jersey has many good Italian restaurants as well, and around lunchtime, on that return visit with my research assistant, we found ourselves close to the Di Palma Brothers Restaurant on Kennedy Boulevard, family-run and open since 1907. The restaurant was unusual in that it was furnished with antiques, which one could buy as

The dining room at Di Palma Brothers Restaurant in North Bergen, NJ, where you can find a good Italian meal as well as beautiful antiques

Visiting with Jerry Turci and Joe "Mozzarella" at Jerry's Gourmet in Englewood, New Jersey

well as a good meal. Fortunata and Raffaele Di Palma, a mother-and-son team, run the restaurant, and the food was good. I especially liked the eggplant meatballs and the fried zucchini stuffed with fontina cheese, and I must say the apple tart, which had just come out of the oven, was quite good as well. Raffaele was charming, so I asked him: if he was born in Italy, how could the restaurant have been operated by the same New Jersey–based family since 1907? Well, as immigrant stories go, sometimes the immigrants become homesick and do return to Italy. But in this case their children returned to America and took up the family business.

We had eaten well, and we needed to get moving. We went to Englewood, the next town over, to visit Jerry's Gourmet, acclaimed for its extraordinary collection of Italian products. Indeed, the store was buzzing with activity, everybody buying in anticipation of cooking and eating Italian. Gennaro "Jerry" Turci and his wife, Isabella, who hail from Sorrento, are first-generation immigrants. They have worked hard and have a thriving business. It felt like being a part of a New Jersey neighborhood again.

Trimming ravioli

# Ricotta and Sausage–Filled Ravioli

*Ravioli di Salsicce e Ricotta*

The first mention of ravioli seems to have been at the fourteenth-century household of Francesco di Marco Datini, merchant of Prato, who describes pasta pockets stuffed with meat and (during Lent) with herbs and cheese. One of the first ravioli shops in America, Bruno Ravioli, was started by Bruno Cavalli in 1905 in Hackensack, New Jersey. Ravioli is less popular on Italian American menus today, but in the 1950s, '60s, and '70s it was all the rage.

For Italians, ravioli is a Sunday meal, more common in the north of Italy, where fresh pasta is made, than in the south, where dry pasta is used more. Everybody loves the sense of accomplishment of making ravioli, stuffing the little pasta pockets with savory and delicious fillings. I think one of the major ingredients in filling ravioli is love. When the family gathers at the table and a steaming platter of ravioli arrives, there are always sounds of exaltation. This is an easy recipe, made with readily available sausage and ricotta, a delicious combination.

Simple marinara or butter sauce will be the perfect dressing.

**MAKES ABOUT 2 DOZEN, SERVING 4 PEOPLE**

1 small onion, quartered

1 small stalk celery, cut into chunks

1 small carrot, cut into chunks

3 tablespoons extra-virgin olive oil

¼ cup dry white wine

12 ounces sweet Italian sausage without fennel seeds, removed from casing

1 cup fresh ricotta, drained

¼ cup grated Grana Padano or Parmigiano-Reggiano, plus more for serving

¼ cup chopped fresh Italian parsley

Pulse together the onion, celery, and carrot in a food processor until finely chopped, to make a *pestata*. Heat the olive oil in a large skillet over medium-high heat. Once the oil is hot, scrape in the vegetables and cook until they begin to soften, about 3 to 4 minutes.

Pour the white wine over the sausage in a medium bowl, and crumble the sausage into small pieces with your fingers. Add the sausage and wine to the skillet with the vegetables, breaking up the sausage as finely as possible with a wooden spoon. Sauté until the sausage is completely cooked through, about 4 to 5 minutes. Scrape into a bowl to cool. When the sausage is completely cooled, stir in the ricotta, grated cheese, and parsley.

Roll the dough: Cut it into four equal pieces. (You could roll the dough out with a rolling pin, but a small Imperia pasta machine is not expensive; it rolls the dough out in even strips and makes ravioli making so much easier.) Flatten a piece of dough into a rectangle, approximately 2 inches by 2 inches, and roll through the widest setting on the pasta machine. Fold this rectangle of dough like a letter, and roll through again. Repeat the rolling and folding a few more times, to knead and smooth the dough. Repeat with the remaining pieces of dough.

Switch to the next-narrowest setting on the machine. Roll a dough strip through, short end first. Repeat with the remaining dough strips. Continue this process with narrower settings, now rolling each strip only once through each setting, until you've gotten to the next-to-last setting and the dough strips are about as wide as the machine (6 inches).

Lay one strip out on a floured counter, and place a heaping teaspoon of filling at about 4-inch intervals down the center of the strip (you will get about six or seven large ravioli per strip). Brush around the filling with water, fold the strip of dough over the fillings, the edges touching evenly, and seal the edges by pressing lightly. Using a serrated pastry cutter or pizza cutter, cut the ravioli evenly between the fillings into rectangles. Repeat with remaining dough and filling.

Keep the ravioli on a baking sheet lined with a clean kitchen towel, and covered, until you are ready to cook them; up to 2 or 3 hours is fine. To cook the ravioli, bring a large pot of salted water to a boil. Drop the ravioli into the pot one by one, stirring with a wooden spoon periodically so they do not stick to the bottom.

Have a sauté pan with the bubbling sauce ready to dress the ravioli. Once the ravioli are in the boiling water, cook for 3 minutes, then fish them out with a spider or slotted spoon. Drain them, and set them in the sauce. Stir gently to coat the ravioli with sauce. When ready to serve, toss some grated cheese over the ravioli plate, and spoon the remaining sauce on top.

1 recipe pasta dough (see page 150—same as cannelloni)

Kosher salt

---

NOTE You can serve these with a simple marinara and some grated Grana Padano or sautéed with butter and sage and some grated Grana Padano.

. . .

NOTE If you want to freeze the ravioli: Once you have set them on a lined baking sheet, cover with a film of plastic wrap and set in the freezer for 2 or 3 hours, till frozen. Gently collect the frozen ravioli, set them flat in a ziplock bag, and lay the bag flat in a sealed plastic container. They will last in the freezer for a month or more.

Macaroni and Cheese

# Macaroni and Cheese
## *Maccheroni al Formaggio*

Macaroni and cheese has to be one of the quintessential American comfort foods. To most people it brings back fuzzy memories of a childhood family table. Even Thomas Jefferson had a thing or two to say about this dish. He ordered a macaroni-making machine and instructed the cook to use cheese liberally on the pasta and bake it like a casserole. It appears that this "macaroni" was more similar to the spaghetti of today. A lot of the versions of macaroni and cheese that you may have eaten would have had some form of cream sauce or *roux,* but here I'll give you a recipe for this dish as an Italian in Italy would make it: a simply delicious rendition.

Preheat oven to 400 degrees F.

Toss the fontina and cheddar in a large bowl. Pour the milk over the cheese, and let it sit for 30 minutes to an hour, until the cheese begins to break down and dissolve into the milk.

Bring a large pot of salted water to boil for pasta. Once it is boiling, pour the pipette into the water and cook until just al dente (3 or 4 minutes shy of package cooking time). Drain, and return the pasta to the pot.

Grate the bread on the coarse holes of a box grater to get about 1½ cups coarse crumbs. Melt the butter in a small skillet over medium heat. When it is melted, stir in the bread crumbs, and toss until crisp and toasted, about 3 minutes. Scrape the crumbs into a bowl, and let cool. Butter a 15-by-10-inch baking dish, and coat the bottom and sides with a thin layer of some of the crumbs. Stir 1 cup of the grated Grana Padano or Parmigiano-Reggiano into the remaining crumbs.

Pour the cheese and milk into a pot set over medium-low heat, and whisk in the sage leaves. Cook until the cheese melts, about 7 to 8 minutes. Stir in the remaining 1 cup grated cheese.

Pour the cheese sauce into the pasta pot, and stir until all of the pasta is coated with the sauce. Scrape the pasta into the baking dish, and sprinkle the remaining bread crumbs with cheese over the top. Bake until browned and bubbly, about 20 minutes.

SERVES 6 TO 8

3 cups grated fontina

5 cups grated cheddar

4 cups milk

Kosher salt

1 pound pipette (elbow macaroni is commonly used for this dish in America, but I suggest using pipette, a pasta that looks like a bent pipe)

3-to-4-inch piece day-old Italian bread

2 tablespoons unsalted butter, plus more for the baking dish

2 cups grated Grana Padano or Parmigiano-Reggiano

4 large fresh sage leaves

# Baked Ziti

*Ziti al Forno*

Baked ziti is a real crowd pleaser. It is easy to assemble, one of those recipes that you can multiply and make double or triple the amount on those occasions when you have to feed your kids' soccer team. It is also a versatile recipe as we become more attentive to our intake of nutritious proteins and vegetables; it is delicious with additional steamed or leftover vegetables or chicken. Legend has it that, as Attila approached Rome, Pope Leo I brought baked ziti with him to meet the invader. After the meal, Attila developed serious gas, considered a bad omen by the gods, and turned around and left Rome untouched.

I don't know many who could leave a steaming plate of baked ziti untouched. Sicilian in origin, this was a favorite of many Italian immigrants, who could take the ziti into the fields or mines with them and have a tasty lunch.

SERVES 6 TO 8

Kosher salt

1 pound ziti

5 cups marinara (see page 108)

1 pound fresh ricotta, drained

9 fresh basil leaves, shredded

1 pound low-moisture mozzarella, cut into ¼-inch cubes

1 cup shredded provola

Preheat oven to 400 degrees F. Bring a large pot of salted water to boil, and add ziti. Cook the ziti until just al dente, about 10 to 12 minutes, and drain.

Meanwhile, bring the marinara sauce to a simmer in a large skillet. Stir in the ricotta and basil leaves.

Spread ½ cup of the sauce in the bottom of a 15-by-10-inch Pyrex baking dish. Layer half of the ziti on top of the sauce. Sprinkle with half the mozzarella cubes and half of the provola. Pour 2 cups of the sauce over the cheese, and spread in an even layer. Top with the rest of the pasta, and spread 2 cups sauce over that layer of pasta. Sprinkle with the remaining cheeses, and dollop with the remaining ½ cup of sauce.

Place the dish in the oven, and bake, uncovered, until browned and bubbly, about 30 minutes. Let rest 5 minutes before cutting. (If you want to assemble this ahead, bake for 15 minutes covered with foil, then, when ready to serve, uncover and bake for an additional 20 minutes.)

Freshly made provola from Casa della Mozzarella on Arthur Avenue in the Bronx

# Baked Stuffed Shells

## *Conchiglie Ripieni*

I don't encounter stuffed shells in Italy much; stuffed paccheri (big and floppy rigatoni-lookalikes) are much more common there. But I have sold a lot of stuffed shells throughout my restaurant days. This is comfort food—pasta stuffed with milky ricotta and topped with oozing melted cheese, and just about everybody loves it. It is a common dish, present in many Italian American restaurant menus and households. It is also very convenient, because the oven does the work, and you can feed a large number of guests.

SERVES 6 TO 8

FOR THE SAUCE

6 tablespoons extra-virgin olive oil

6 garlic cloves, crushed and peeled

Two 28-ounce cans Italian plum tomatoes, preferably San Marzano, crushed by hand

1 teaspoon kosher salt

½ teaspoon dried oregano

¼ teaspoon peperoncino flakes

FOR THE SHELLS AND FILLING

Kosher salt

1 pound large shells

1 pound fresh ricotta, drained

8 ounces frozen peas, thawed

1 pound low-moisture mozzarella, 12 ounces cut into ¼-inch cubes, 4 ounces shredded

2 cups grated Grana Padano or Parmigiano-Reggiano

3 tablespoons chopped fresh Italian parsley

1 large egg, beaten

Preheat oven to 400 degrees F.

Bring a large pot of salted water to boil for pasta. While the sauce cooks, add the shells to the boiling pasta water and cook two-thirds of the recommended cooking time—shells should still be firm. Drain and set all the shells on sheet trays, set apart so they won't stick to each other.

For the sauce: Heat the olive oil in a Dutch oven over medium heat. Sauté the garlic until the edges are golden, about 2 minutes, then pour in the tomatoes. Slosh out the tomato cans with 1 cup hot water each, and add that to the pot. Stir in the salt, oregano, and peperoncino, and bring to a rapid simmer. Cook, uncovered, until thickened, about 20 minutes.

For the filling: Stir together the ricotta, peas, cubed mozzarella, 1 cup of the grated Grana Padano or Parmigiano-Reggiano, the parsley, and egg in a bowl. Mix the shredded mozzarella and remaining grated Grana Padano or Parmigiano-Reggiano in a bowl, and set aside.

Spread 2 cups of the sauce in a 15-by-10-inch Pyrex or ceramic baking dish. Stuff each shell with a tablespoon of the stuffing, and arrange in the baking dish. Divide any remaining stuffing between and around the stuffed shells. Top evenly with 2 cups more sauce, and sprinkle with the reserved grated-cheese mixture. Dollop the remaining sauce evenly over the top. Make a tent with foil over the baking dish. Bake, and after 25 minutes, check: the sauce should be bubbly all over. Remove foil, and bake until golden and crusty, 5 to 10 minutes more.

# Chicken Tetrazzini

*Pollo alla Tetrazzini*

Chicken Tetrazzini is an American creation. The one thing we know about it for sure is that it was named after the famed Italian soprano Luisa Tetrazzini, also known as the Florentine Nightingale. She was a favorite with the San Francisco Opera audiences, and it is said that the dish was invented there, but there are some conflicting claims that the dish was created in New York, at the then Knickerbocker Hotel, where most of the Metropolitan Opera stars stayed in the early 1900s.

Another confusion about Tetrazzini is whether chicken, turkey, or salmon should be used in the recipe. As far as I am concerned, any or all of these options can make a good Tetrazzini.

SERVES 6 TO 8

Preheat oven to 375 degrees F. Butter a 9-by-13-inch Pyrex or ceramic baking dish. Bring a large pot of water to boil for pasta.

Heat the chicken stock in a small pot. Melt 3 tablespoons of the butter with 2 tablespoons oil in a large straight-sided skillet over medium heat. When the butter is melted, add the mushrooms and season with ½ teaspoon salt. Cook the mushrooms until their moisture has evaporated and they are browned, about 3 to 4 minutes. Add the sage, and cook until fragrant, about 2 minutes. Scrape into a bowl.

In the same skillet, melt the remaining butter and olive oil over medium-low heat, then stir in the flour to make a smooth paste. Cook and stir until the *roux*—or butter-flour mixture—is light brown in color, then season with the remaining teaspoon of the salt. Whisk in the hot stock, making sure to get out all the lumps. Increase the heat to medium, and bring to a simmer. Whisk in the milk and nutmeg, bring back to a simmer, and cook for about 5 minutes.

Slip the broccoli and linguine into the boiling water. Cook until linguine is just al dente and the broccoli is tender. Drain the broccoli and linguine well. Add the shredded chicken, linguine, and broccoli to the sauce, and stir until smooth and hot. Remove from heat, and stir in ½ cup of the grated cheese. Pour into the prepared baking dish. Mix together the remaining grated cheese and the bread crumbs, and sprinkle over the baking dish. Place the dish in oven, and bake until the top is browned and bubbly, about 30 minutes.

5 tablespoons butter, plus more for the baking dish

1½ teaspoons kosher salt, plus more for pasta pot

2½ cups chicken stock (see page 40)

4 tablespoons extra-virgin olive oil

1 pound white mushrooms, sliced

6 fresh sage leaves, chopped

¼ cup all-purpose flour

3 cups milk

Pinch freshly grated nutmeg

½ head broccoli, in small florets

1 pound linguine, broken in half

4 cups shredded or chopped leftover cooked chicken, without skin and bones

1 cup grated Grana Padano or Parmigiano-Reggiano

¼ cup dry bread crumbs

# Cannelloni

Cannelloni—that delicious stuffed pasta, literally translated as "big reeds"—is always a sign of a festive occasion in Italy. This baked dish can be made in advance and serve a large group of people, and it is loved by most. What you stuff it with almost does not matter, although a meat-and-vegetable combination is the most common choice. Cannelloni was a big-hit item on menus of Italian American restaurants in the sixties and seventies.

If you have a gathering of family and friends, as Italians often do, this is a good dish to make.

SERVES 8 OR MORE

FOR THE PASTA

2 cups all-purpose flour, plus more for working the dough

2 large eggs

¼ cup extra-virgin olive oil

Kosher salt

FOR THE FILLING

¼ cup extra-virgin olive oil

1 large onion, finely chopped

1½ pounds ground pork

1 cup dry white wine

2 medium carrots, finely chopped

2 stalks celery, finely chopped

2 teaspoons kosher salt

1 teaspoon chopped fresh rosemary

2 tablespoons tomato paste

1 quart hot chicken stock (see page 40)

10-ounce bag fresh spinach, roughly chopped

8 ounces mortadella, finely chopped

Make the pasta: Put the flour in the bowl of a food processor, and pulse to aerate. Mix together the eggs, oil, and 3 tablespoons water in a separate bowl, and pour through the feed tube into the food processor while running. Process until the dough forms a ball and sticks to the blade, about 30 seconds. Add more water or flour as necessary to achieve the right consistency—a smooth, homogenized, compact dough. Transfer the dough to a floured work surface and knead a few times, just to bring it together. Wrap the dough in plastic, and let rest at room temperature for an hour. In the meantime, make the filling and the besciamella sauce.

*Make the filling:* Heat the olive oil in a large skillet over medium heat. Toss in the onion, and cook until it starts to soften, about 5 minutes. Add the ground pork, and cook, crumbling with a wooden spoon, until no longer pink, about 5 minutes. Pour in the white wine, and cook until the wine and meat juices have cooked away and the meat is sizzling, about 10 minutes.

Add the carrots, celery, salt, and rosemary. Push the vegetables and meat to the side to clear a "hot spot" in the pan to plop in the tomato paste. Let the tomato paste toast a minute or two, then stir it into the meat and vegetables. Pour in the hot chicken stock, and simmer until it is thickened and the flavors come together, about 10 minutes. Add the spinach, and cook until tender, about 5 minutes. Scrape filling into a bowl to cool. When it is cooled, stir in the mortadella, grated cheese, parsley, and lemon zest.

*Make the sauce:* Warm the milk with the bay leaves in a small saucepan. Melt the butter in a medium saucepan over medium heat. When melted, stir in the flour to make a smooth paste. Cook, stirring with a wooden spoon, until the *roux* smells toasty but has not darkened in color, about 4 minutes. Pour in the hot milk, whisking to avoid lumps. Bring to a simmer, whisking until thickened, about 5 minutes. Season with the salt, nutmeg, and pepper. Remove from heat, and whisk in the grated cheese, then strain.

When an hour has passed, roll out the dough: Cut it into four equal pieces. Flatten a piece of dough into a rectangle, 2 by 2 inches, and roll through the widest setting on a pasta machine. Fold this rectangle of dough like a letter, and roll through again. Repeat the rolling and folding a few more times, to knead and smooth the dough. Repeat with the remaining pieces of dough.

Switch to the next-narrowest setting on the machine. Roll a dough strip through, short end first. Repeat with the remaining dough strips. Continue this process with narrower settings, now rolling only once through each setting, until you've gotten to the next-to-last setting and the dough strips are about as wide as the machine (6 inches).

Cut dough strips into 4-by-6-inch rectangles. Bring a large pot of salted water to boil for pasta. Place a large bowl or pot of ice water next to the boiling pasta water. Boil the dough rectangles, just about a minute, then remove with a spider and place in the ice bath to cool. Drain, and spread out on baking sheets lined with damp kitchen towels.

Preheat oven to 400 degrees F. To assemble the cannelloni: Spread 1 cup besciamella in the bottom of a 3-quart 9-by-13 Pyrex or ceramic baking dish. Top with ½ cup of the marinara sauce and spread. Fill the dough rectangles with about ½ cup of the filling, then roll up the long way like a cigar and fit them snugly together in the baking dish. Spread the remaining besciamella on top, then drizzle the remaining 1 cup marinara sauce over the besciamella. Sprinkle with the grated cheese. Tent the baking dish with aluminum foil, and bake until heated through, about 10 to 15 minutes, then uncover and bake until browned and bubbly, about 10 to 15 minutes more.

2 cups grated Grana Padano or Parmigiano-Reggiano

¼ cup chopped fresh Italian parsley

Zest of 1 lemon

FOR THE BESCIAMELLA
(BÉCHAMEL SAUCE)

1 quart low-fat or whole milk

2 fresh bay leaves, or 3 dried bay leaves

4 tablespoons unsalted butter

¼ cup all-purpose flour

¾ teaspoon kosher salt

Pinch freshly grated nutmeg

Pinch white pepper

3 tablespoons grated Grana Padano or Parmigiano-Reggiano

FOR ASSEMBLY OF THE
CANNELLONI

1½ cups marinara sauce (page 108)

½ cup grated Grana Padano or Parmigiano-Reggiano

# Lasagna

*Lasagne*

There are endless renditions of lasagna: with just cheese, with vegetables, with mushrooms, with meat. Once you have mastered the art of cooking and layering the pasta, the filling can be your choice. But here I give you the Italian American rendition, one that you make with store-bought dry pasta. The major effort here is in making the Bolognese sauce, and in the Bolognese recipe I give you on page 158, you can make the sauce in advance and freeze it, all ready for when you decide to make a lasagna.

## SERVES 10 OR MORE

Kosher salt

7 to 8 cups Bolognese sauce (see page 158)

28-ounce can Italian plum tomatoes, preferably San Marzano, crushed by hand

1¾ cups fresh ricotta, drained

½ cup heavy cream

½ cup loosely packed fresh basil leaves, roughly chopped

2 boxes lasagna

1½ pounds fresh mozzarella, thinly sliced

1½ cups grated Grana Padano or Parmigiano-Reggiano

Bring a large pot of salted water to boil for the pasta. Preheat the oven to 400 degrees F. Warm the Bolognese in a pot, pour in the crushed tomatoes, and simmer together while the pasta cooks. Stir together the ricotta, cream, and basil in a bowl.

When the water is boiling, slip in the lasagna and cook until just al dente, several minutes less than the cooking time on the package. (Don't crowd the noodles in the pot or they'll stick; boil in batches, if necessary.) Remove the lasagna to a large bowl or roasting pan filled with ice water to stop the cooking process. Drain the lasagna, and lay the strips on damp kitchen towels, in layers, on a baking sheet.

Spread ½ cup of the Bolognese in a thin layer in the bottom of a 13-by-9-by-3-inch baking dish. Make one layer of the lasagna noodles so they extend over the long edges of the pan and meet in the middle, covering the sauce completely. Spread half of the ricotta mixture on top, and top that with a layer of 2 cups Bolognese.

Add another layer of noodles, perpendicular to the first layer. You no longer need to overlap the sides, so trim the noodles to fit just the bottom of the pan. Spread 1½ cups Bolognese, half the sliced mozzarella, and the remaining ricotta mixture on top.

Make another layer of lasagna noodles, parallel to the last layer, then cover with 1½ cups Bolognese and the remaining mozzarella, and sprinkle with ½ cup of the grated cheese.

Add a final layer of lasagna noodles. Cover with 1 cup sauce, and sprinkle with ½ cup of the grated cheese. Flip over the noodles from the edges of the pan to encase the last layer, and spread with the remaining sauce, which should be about 1 cup. Sprinkle with the remaining grated cheese.

Tent the lasagna dish with foil, and bake until bubbly, about 40 to 45 minutes. Uncover, and bake until the top is browned and crusty, about 15 to 20 minutes more. Let the lasagna rest at least 20 minutes before cutting and serving.

Michael James shops with his mother for tomatoes at Trinacria in Baltimore.

Gnocchi with Gorgonzola and Peas

# Gnocchi with Gorgonzola and Peas

*Gnocchi con Gorgonzola e Piselli*

At our home, when we were newly arrived immigrants, for Sunday dinner it was either gnocchi or garganelli with *sugo.* The *sugo,* a rich sauce, was made of either chicken or cubed veal or pork—all second cuts of meat—which created a first-class sauce. The *sugo* does take two to three hours to make, so, if you have no time for the *sugo* and have a good piece of Gorgonzola, try this sauce. It will take no more than ten minutes once you have the gnocchi done.

Boil the unpeeled potatoes in water to cover until tender. When the potatoes are cool enough to handle, peel them and put them through a potato ricer or food mill. Spread the mashed potato out on a baking sheet, season with the salt, and let cool.

When the potatoes are cooled, pour the beaten eggs over them and sprinkle with half of the flour. Gather the dough together and knead, adding more of the flour as needed, until the dough comes together and is not sticky. Don't knead too much or add too much flour, or the gnocchi will be heavy.

Bring a large pot of salted water to boil for the gnocchi. To make the gnocchi, cut the dough into three pieces. Keeping your hands and the work surface floured, roll one piece into a long snake, about ½ inch thick, then cut into ½-inch pieces.

Roll each piece lightly in the palms of your hands. Take each rolled piece of dough and, holding a fork with one hand at a 45-degree angle, using your thumb, press lightly on the piece of dough starting high on the inside tines of the fork. Roll the dough down the whole length of the tines to create a ridged gnocco with an indentation where your thumb was. Repeat with the remaining pieces of dough. Dust the gnocchi with flour, and place them on floured baking sheets.

For the sauce: Melt the butter in a large skillet over medium-high heat. Pour in the cream and stock, and once the mixture simmers, scatter in the peas. Bring the sauce to a rapid simmer, and cook until reduced to a creamy consistency, about 5 minutes. Stir in the Gor-

*(continued)*

SERVES 6

1½ pounds russet potatoes

¾ teaspoon kosher salt, plus more for pasta pot

2 large eggs, beaten

1½ to 2 cups all-purpose flour, plus more for work surface

2 tablespoons unsalted butter

½ cup heavy cream

1 cup chicken stock (see page 40), vegetable stock, or pasta water

10-ounce box frozen peas, thawed

6 ounces Gorgonzola, crumbled

¼ cup grated Grana Padano or Parmigiano-Reggiano

*(Gnocchi with Gorgonzola and Peas, continued)*
gonzola until it dissolves in the sauce. Keep the sauce warm while you cook the gnocchi.

Shake the excess flour from the gnocchi, and drop them into the boiling water (don't crowd them: depending on the size of the pot, you may want to cook in two batches). Once the gnocchi rise to the surface, simmer until cooked through, about 2 minutes. Using a spider, move the gnocchi directly to the sauce. Toss the gnocchi in the sauce for a minute; add a little pasta water if needed to loosen the sauce (there should be just enough sauce to coat the gnocchi). Remove from the heat. Sprinkle with the grated cheese, toss, and serve.

# Tagliatelle with Bolognese Sauce
## *Tagliatelle alla Bolognese*

This sauce seems like a chore, but once you get everything in the pot, it simmers and cooks on its own and yields enough sauce for several luscious meals. (It also freezes well.) When unexpected guests arrive, just cook some pasta and you have dinner ready. What makes this meat sauce unique is the cinnamon, which adds an unexpected, unidentifiably delicious flavor. The kids absolutely love it with gnocchi.

**SERVES 6, PLUS A QUART OF SAUCE FOR THE FREEZER**

¼ cup extra-virgin olive oil, plus more for drizzling

1 large yellow onion, finely diced

1 large carrot, peeled and grated

2 stalks celery, finely diced

1 tablespoon kosher salt, plus more for pasta pot

1 pound ground beef

1 pound ground pork

1 pound ground veal

1 cup dry white wine

Two 28-ounce cans Italian plum tomatoes, preferably San Marzano, crushed by hand

4 fresh bay leaves, or 6 dried bay leaves

½ teaspoon peperoncino flakes

Scant ¼ teaspoon ground cinnamon

1 pound dried egg tagliatelle

½ cup grated Grana Padano or Parmigiano-Reggiano, plus more for passing

Heat the olive oil in a large Dutch oven set over medium heat. Add the onion, and let cook until slightly softened, about 2 to 3 minutes. Add the carrot and celery, and season with 1 teaspoon salt. Cook and stir until the onion is translucent, about 3 to 4 minutes more. Meanwhile, put the ground meats in a large bowl, and pour the wine over the meat into the bowl. Use a fork to stir and crumble the meat to mix with the wine and break the meat into small clumps. Add the meat to the pot, season with 1 teaspoon salt, and cook, stirring with a wooden spoon to break down the clumps, until the meat has given up all of its liquid. Increase heat to medium-high, and reduce away the liquid until you hear a crackling sound coming from the bottom of the pan, about 15 minutes in all.

When the bottom of the pan is dry and the meat is lightly browned, pour in the tomatoes and slosh out the cans with 2 cups hot water. Pour that into the pot along with the bay leaves, and season with the peperoncino, cinnamon, and remaining salt.

Bring the sauce to a boil, then lower the heat to a rapid simmer. Set the cover slightly ajar, and cook until the sauce is thick and flavorful, about 1½ hours, adding up to 4 cups more hot water during the cooking time to keep the meat covered in liquid.

Bring a large pot of salted water to boil for pasta. Heat half of the sauce in a large skillet (refrigerate or freeze the remaining sauce for another day!). Plop the tagliatelle into the boiling water. When the pasta is al dente, drain and transfer it directly into the simmering sauce. Drizzle with olive oil, and toss to coat the pasta with the sauce. Remove from heat, and toss in grated cheese. Serve immediately, passing more grated cheese.

# California:
# The North and San Francisco

California Italians contributed a great deal to the new state. In 1883, Anthony Caminetti was the first American-born Italian American to be elected to the State Assembly, and in 1913 he would be appointed by President Wilson to serve as the commissioner of immigration. California Wine Country was developed by Italian immigrants in the 1880s. In 1904, the Bank of Italy was founded by Amadeo Giannini; it was later to become the Bank of America.

Many early Italian immigrants settled at the foot of the Sierra Nevada, lured by the promise of work in the gold mines and on the land. The immigrants came mostly from northern Italy, primarily from Genoa. The climate in California is quite similar to that of Italy, and Italian immigrants remained in San Francisco and the surrounding areas to take on work in agriculture and wine production, and to dig for gold. Sicilians and Ligurians mainly settled in San Francisco, though many of them moved to San Diego after the San Francisco Fire of 1906.

Ligurian Italians, many of whom hailed from small fishing villages, found that San Francisco Bay gave them an opportunity to do what they did best—fish—and as early as 1870, Italian fishermen were providing 90 percent of all fish consumed in San Francisco. Italian immigrants became known as some of the most skilled workers in the city. They also farmed their new land as they had farmed their own land back in Italy. A vibrant agricultural industry developed around fruit, vegetables, and olive-oil production, and was a direct result of the skills and drive of these immigrants. Italians began food distribution by opening general stores to accommodate the needs of the large influx of immigrants. By the 1880s, Italians dominated the California mining, fishing, and agricultural industries.

I had a lot of places to go visit in California, but I first had to stop to see Giovanni Giotta in San Francisco, and have one of his espressos. Tanya and I headed for North Beach, where there are Italian cafés, restaurants, and shops. But we went directly to Caffe Trieste on Vallejo Street, presided over by Giovanni Giotta. Giovanni and his family came to San Francisco as my family had, as immigrants from Trieste. Trieste is a city of great coffeehouses and long-standing coffee tradition, and it was in the same spirit that Giovanni opened his café in North Beach, a place where the walls are covered with pictures of famous personalities who have had his coffee, and where creative minds gather and talk over a stimulating cup of Italian coffee. Giovanni is an artist himself, and you can still catch him at times strumming his guitar and projecting nostalgic songs with his *dolce* tenor voice. His family now carries on the coffee business— *torrefazione,* the art of roasting coffee, as it is called in Italy—and the tradition of the café.

A short walk from Caffe Trieste brought us in front of Saints Peter and Paul Church, which sits in the shadow of the famous Coit Tower and was the Italian religious center of San Francisco, mostly known as the church that Joe DiMaggio and Marilyn Monroe took wedding pictures in front of after their wedding in City Hall. By then it was time for lunch, and I felt like pizza, so I paid a visit to Shelley Lindgren at A16. Shelley is not Italian, but she took a school trip to Italy, fell in love with the culture, and then dedicated her whole professional career to Italian food and wine. Even the name of her restaurant is Italian, A16 being the *autostrada* that connects Naples in Campania to Bari in Puglia; the Italian food she fell in love with abounds on the menu.

(Above) At A16 in San Francisco with chef/owner Liza Shaw and Shelley Lindgren; (left) Nic Romano at Villa Romano Green Farms in San Clemente, California; (below) my friend Papa Gianni, otherwise known as Giovanni Giotta, from Caffe Trieste in the heart of San Francisco

Artichokes growing under the California sun

# Vegetables and Sides

# Stuffed Artichokes

## *Carciofi Ripieni*

Italians love their artichokes in a thousand ways, and stuffed with seasoned bread crumbs is a favorite. This recipe is an Italian American rendition, much richer and with more stuffing and ingredients than the one found in Italy. It was often an appetizer on the menu of Italian American restaurants in the 1950s, '60s, and '70s, and most likely the first way that many Americans tasted artichokes Italian-style. And I am sure the charm of it was the discovery of how to eat this curious thistle with not much pulp but lots of flavor.

SERVES 6

Juice from 2 lemons

Zest of 1 lemon

6 large artichokes

1½ cups fine dry bread crumbs

½ cup grated Grana Padano or Parmigiano-Reggiano

½ cup toasted pine nuts, coarsely chopped

½ cup plus 2 tablespoons chopped fresh Italian parsley

½ cup plus 3 tablespoons extra-virgin olive oil

2 large hard-boiled eggs, finely chopped

¾ teaspoon kosher salt

1 cup dry white wine

⅛ teaspoon peperoncino

Preheat oven to 400 degrees F. Zest one of the lemons, and set aside.

Clean and prepare the artichokes for stuffing as detailed on page 18.

For the stuffing: Mix together the bread crumbs, grated cheese, and pine nuts in a bowl. Stir in ½ cup of the parsley, ½ cup of the olive oil, the eggs, ¼ teaspoon salt, and the reserved lemon zest. Toss with a fork until all the crumbs are moistened with the olive oil.

Remove the cleaned artichokes from the water, and drain them upside down on a kitchen towel. Spread the leaves of an artichoke open, and fill the center with stuffing. Continue to work outward, sprinkling and packing stuffing into the rows of leaves as you separate them. Put the artichoke in a baking dish that will hold all six snugly. Repeat with the remaining artichokes.

Pour the wine and 1 cup water around the artichokes in the baking dish, and add the lemon juice and artichoke stems. Season the liquid with the remaining salt and the peperoncino. Drizzle the remaining 3 tablespoons of olive oil over the artichokes. Tent the dish with foil and bake for about 30 minutes. Uncover, and bake until the artichokes are tender all the way through and the crumbs are browned and crusty, about 20 to 30 minutes more (depending on the size and toughness of your artichokes). If the cooking juices are too thin, pour them into a small pot and boil for a few minutes to reduce. Stir in the remaining 2 tablespoons of chopped parsley. Serve the artichokes in shallow soup plates, topped with the cooking juices.

Stuffed Artichokes

# Fried Zucchini

*Zucchine Fritte*

You might be used to breaded and fried zucchini cut in French-fry fashion, but when my mother fried zucchini, she would always cut them in rounds or slices. I liked them that way: they made great sandwich stuffers, especially when the flavors and moistness of the zucchini seeped into the bread. For over-the-top flavor, add a few slices of Swiss cheese and melt under the broiler or in a sandwich press. The perfect Italian lunch.

SERVES 6 TO 8

Vegetable oil, for frying

4 large eggs

Kosher salt

2 tablespoons chopped fresh mint

2 cups all-purpose flour

3 cups fine dry bread crumbs

1 cup grated Grana Padano or Parmigiano-Reggiano

2 pounds medium zucchini, sliced into ¼-to-½-inch-thick rounds on the bias (see note)

Heat 1 inch of the vegetable oil in a large skillet over medium heat. Beat the eggs in a bowl with a pinch of salt, and stir in the mint. Put the flour in one shallow bowl, and mix the bread crumbs and grated cheese in another.

Dredge the zucchini, in batches, in the flour, then the egg, then the bread crumbs, shaking off the excess. Let the rounds rest on sheet trays while you finish all of the zucchini. When the oil reaches about 365 degrees (or when a piece of zucchini sizzles on contact), slip a batch of zucchini into the oil. Fry, turning occasionally, until crisp and golden all over, about 2 minutes. Drain the zucchini on paper towels, and season with salt. Let the oil return to temperature between batches, and repeat with the remaining zucchini, seasoning with salt as soon as they come out of the oil.

NOTE Cut slices ¼ inch thick if you like crispier slices, or ½ inch thick if you like meatier slices.

# Stuffed Tomatoes

*Pomodori Farciti al Forno*

Italians will stuff anything, but when it comes to a nice summer tomato, this is *the* recipe. It is good just out of the oven, and delicious at room temperature. Wonderful as an appetizer, a vegetable, and also a main course, this dish is popular at Italian family gatherings and festivities, and it looks great on the buffet table.

Preheat oven to 400 degrees F.

Bring 2 cups water with ½ teaspoon of the salt and the bay leaves to a boil in a small pot. Stir in the rice and 1 tablespoon of the olive oil. Bring to a simmer, and cook, uncovered, until rice is al dente and liquid is almost all gone, about 10 minutes. Scrape into a bowl to cool.

Remove any stems and leaves from the tomatoes, then slice off the tops and set them aside. Scoop out only the inner center flesh and seeds of the tomatoes with a spoon, leaving an outer flesh shell intact. As you work, put the scooped-out flesh in a strainer set over a bowl, to collect the juices. Once all of the tomatoes are scooped out, season the insides of the tomatoes with ½ teaspoon of the salt.

Chop the strained tomato flesh, and put in the bowl with the rice. Add the mozzarella, ham, ½ cup of the grated cheese, the basil, the oregano, and the remaining ¼ teaspoon salt to the bowl. Toss to combine.

Pour the reserved tomato juices into the bottom of a 9-by-13-inch baking dish. Spoon the stuffing evenly into the tomatoes. Arrange the reserved tomato tops, cut side down, in the baking dish, and place a stuffed tomato on each top, so it is being held up as if on a pedestal. Depending on the size of your tomatoes, you may have a little leftover stuffing; if so, roll it into "meatballs" and place in the open spaces of the baking dish. Drizzle the tomatoes with the remaining tablespoon of olive oil, and sprinkle the tops with the remaining grated cheese. Bake until tomatoes are soft and juicy and stuffing is browned on top, about 20 to 25 minutes.

SERVES 8

1¼ teaspoons kosher salt

2 fresh bay leaves, or 3 dried bay leaves

¾ cup Arborio rice

2 tablespoons extra-virgin olive oil

8 firm-ripe medium tomatoes

¾ cup fresh mozzarella cut into small cubes

2 ounces ham, cut into small cubes

½ cup plus 2 tablespoons grated Grana Padano or Parmigiano-Reggiano

10 large fresh basil leaves, chopped

½ teaspoon dried oregano

Stuffed Tomatoes, Fried Zucchini, Stuffed Artichokes, and Meat-Stuffed Eggplant

# Stuffed Vegetables

*Verdure Farcite*

What makes this dish truly good is the old bread soaked in milk. Not only is it flavorful and mellow, but the traditions are steeped in preserving and respecting food: waste not, want not. It makes for a great vegetarian main course. With some old bread and whatever was growing in the garden, the Italian immigrants could make a delicious meal.

Preheat the oven to 400 degrees F. Pour the milk over the bread in a bowl, and let sit for 20 minutes, pressing the bread into the milk.

Prepare the vegetables for stuffing: Halve the zucchini crosswise, then lengthwise, to make twelve pieces. Scoop out the centers to make "boats." Finely chop the scooped-out centers, and put them in a large bowl. Cut the celery stalks into 4-inch lengths. Cut each bell pepper into four segments, at the natural breaks in the ribs, and remove stems and seeds. Peel onions, halve them crosswise, then cut each in half crosswise again, to get eight rings in all. Remove the inner pieces of onion, to make onion boats. Set the boats aside, and chop and reserve the smaller inner parts of the onions.

Squeeze the excess milk from the bread. Combine the bread with the chopped zucchini. Add the scallions, 1 cup of the grated cheese, the provola, the parsley, and 1 teaspoon of the salt. Mix well.

Season the vegetables to be stuffed with ¼ cup olive oil and the remaining 2 teaspoons salt. Brush two large baking dishes with 3 tablespoons olive oil each. Scatter the chopped onion in the bottom of the baking dishes. Fill the vegetables with the stuffing, and put the stuffed zucchini and peppers in one dish, the onions and celery in another. Sprinkle the tops of the vegetables with the remaining 1 cup grated cheese. Cover the baking dishes with foil, and bake until the vegetables release their juices and are almost tender, about 30 minutes. Uncover, and bake until vegetables are tender and the stuffing is browned and crispy, about 30 minutes more. (The peppers and zucchini may be done before the onions and celery; check them after 20 minutes.) Serve warm or at room temperature.

SERVES 8 OR MORE AS AN APPETIZER, OR 6 AS A MAIN COURSE

4 cups 1-inch cubes of day-old country bread

1½ cups milk

3 medium zucchini

3 large stalks celery, peeled

2 red bell peppers

2 sweet onions, such as Vidalia or Walla Walla

1 cup finely chopped scallions (about 1 small bunch)

2 cups grated Grana Padano or Parmigiano-Reggiano

4 ounces provola, cut into small cubes

½ cup chopped fresh Italian parsley

1 tablespoon kosher salt

10 tablespoons extra-virgin olive oil

# Stuffed Escarole

## *Scarola Farcita*

Italians love the chicory family of vegetables, of which escarole is a member. Escarole was one of the abundant leafy green vegetables that they could readily find in the States. Today it has fallen out of favor, but when I opened Buonavia, my first restaurant, in 1971, we were cooking escarole by the bushel. We served it in soups, braised with garlic and oil as a side dish, in salads, and for an appetizer; or we would stuff it, as in the recipe below. In Italy, stuffed greens served with beans would often have been the whole meal, not just a side.

SERVES 4 TO 6

1 large head escarole

3 cups cubes of day-old country bread

2 garlic cloves, crushed and peeled

7 tablespoons extra-virgin olive oil

¼ cup chopped oil-cured black olives

½ cup finely shredded provola

3 tablespoons drained tiny capers in brine

3 tablespoons toasted pine nuts

½ teaspoon dried oregano

¼ teaspoon kosher salt

½ cup grated Grana Padano or Parmigiano-Reggiano

Preheat the oven to 375 degrees F.

Bring a large pot of water to boil for blanching the escarole. Separate the escarole into leaves, and blanch in the boiling water until the leaves are limp, about 2 minutes. Remove the leaves with tongs, reserving the cooking water. Cool the leaves in ice water, and pat dry. Set aside the twelve largest leaves (or combine two smaller leaves to make one large one if necessary) for stuffing, and chop the rest of the escarole. Squeeze any excess water from the chopped escarole and set aside.

Pour about 2 cups of the hot escarole cooking water over the bread cubes in a bowl. Let soak for a few minutes, then strain the bread. (Weight the top of the strainer with a bowl and some heavy cans, and let the bread drain and cool.)

Cook the garlic with 2 tablespoons of the olive oil in a small skillet over medium-high heat. Once the garlic is sizzling, add the chopped escarole, and sauté for a few minutes to cook off any residual moisture, then add the olives. Cook and toss a few minutes, then transfer to a large bowl to cool slightly.

When the escarole has cooled, add the soaked, drained bread, the provola, capers, pine nuts, and oregano, and stir to combine. Spread the twelve escarole leaves flat on your work surface. Place the stem part of one flattened leaf closest to you, and evenly distribute the filling among the leaves, spreading the filling out on the leaf but leaving an inch or so of border all around. Fold the sides in over the bowl, then begin rolling from the side closer to you till you have rolled it up completely. Flip the tip of the leaf up snugly around to make a tightly stuffed escarole roll. Repeat with the remaining leaves. Brush a 9-by-13-inch baking dish with 3 tablespoons olive oil, and arrange the rolls, seam side down, in the dish. Sprinkle the tops of the rolls with the salt and grated cheese. Drizzle the remaining 2 tablespoons olive oil over all. Cover the baking dish with foil, and bake 20 minutes. Uncover, and bake until the tops of the rolls are browned and crusty, about 15 minutes.

To salt or not salt the water, that is the question. I used to boil vegetables in salted water, but I found that if I boiled them in unsalted water they would retain more of their natural flavors. After draining them, but while they are still steaming hot, I toss them with some coarse salt, to enhance their natural goodness. Does it really make a difference? Indeed it does.

Instead of making a saline solution out of the boiling water, which permeates the vegetable throughout, salting later allows the vegetable to retain its pure flavor. In addition, the sprinkled salt adds another dimension by seeping into the vegetable while it is still hot.

# Eggplant Parmigiana
## *Melanzane alla Parmigiana*

While the word *parmigiana* literally means "from Parma," a town in northern Italy, this dish is clearly Sicilian in origin. Here you have the traditional eggplant-parmigiana recipe that everyone loves. This versatile dish can be made in advance and baked when your guests arrive. It reheats well as a leftover and makes a great sandwich as well. In Italy, sometimes it is not even baked, but assembled with sauce and a generous sprinkling of grated Grana Padano, eliminating the mozzarella, and eaten straightaway. And at Roberto's, on Arthur Avenue in the Bronx, I found alternating layers of eggplant and zucchini—delicious.

SERVES 8

2½ pounds medium-size, firm eggplant, sliced lengthwise ½ inch thick

1 tablespoon plus 2 teaspoons kosher salt

3 cups dry bread crumbs

4 cups grated Grana Padano or Parmigiano-Reggiano

1 cup plus 2 tablespoons extra-virgin olive oil

4 large eggs

½ cup milk

1½ cups all-purpose flour, for dredging

3 garlic cloves, crushed and peeled

14 ounces fresh spinach, washed and trimmed

5 cups marinara sauce (see page 108)

1 pound low-moisture mozzarella, shredded

Salt the eggplant slices all over with 1 tablespoon kosher salt. Layer them in a large colander set in the sink. Lay a plate over the eggplant and weight it down with cans to help press out excess liquid. Let drain about ½ hour, then rinse and pat dry.

Preheat the oven to 375 degrees F. Toss together the bread crumbs, 2 cups of the grated cheese, and 1 cup of the olive oil in a large shallow bowl. Season with ½ teaspoon salt. Beat the eggs and milk with a pinch of salt in another shallow bowl. Spread the flour on a plate.

Dredge the eggplant slices in flour, then the eggs, then the bread crumbs, pressing the crumbs in to make sure they adhere. Lay the eggplant slices on parchment-lined baking sheets, making sure they are not touching. Place in the oven, and bake the eggplant, rotating the sheets halfway through baking, until it is cooked through and the crumbs are crisp and golden, about 25 minutes. Remove, and let cool slightly.

Heat the remaining 2 tablespoons olive oil in a large skillet over medium-high heat. Add the crushed garlic, and sauté until just golden, about 1 to 2 minutes. Toss in the spinach with any water clinging to the leaves, season with remaining salt, then cover and cook until wilted, about 3 to 4 minutes. Check occasionally to make sure the bottom of the pan is not dry, adding water a tablespoon at a time if necessary. Once the spinach is wilted, uncover, and cook until spinach is tender and excess water is gone, about 4 minutes.

To assemble the eggplant: Spread ¾ cup of the marinara sauce in the bottom of a 10-by-15-inch baking dish. Make a layer of half of the baked eggplant in the dish. Spread 1 cup of the marinara sauce over it, and sprinkle on ½ cup of the grated Grana Padano and half the shredded mozzarella; spread all of the spinach in one layer on top. Cover with 2 more cups marinara, and sprinkle on the remaining shredded mozzarella and ½ cup grated Grana Padano. Top with an even layer of the remaining eggplant. Spread the remaining sauce on top, and sprinkle with the remaining grated Grana Padano. Tent the baking dish with foil so it is not touching the cheese, and bake until bubbly, about 30 minutes. Uncover, and bake until the cheese is browned and crusty and sauce is bubbling all over, another 15 minutes. Let cool and set 5 to 10 minutes before cutting and serving.

Ripe and ready for picking—deep purple eggplants at the Maugeri farm in Swedesboro, New Jersey

# Potato Croquettes

*Crocchette di Patate*

Potato croquettes are not served much in Italy, except around Rome. When I first began working in Italian American restaurants, potato croquettes were always paired with a vegetable as a side dish. I grew fond of the dish, I guess, because it combines two things Americans love: mashed potatoes and fried things.

MAKES ABOUT 24 CROQUETTES

2 pounds Yukon Gold potatoes

1 tablespoon extra-virgin olive oil

½ cup finely diced prosciutto

4 large eggs

1 cup grated Grana Padano or Parmigiano-Reggiano

2 tablespoons chopped fresh parsley

1½ teaspoons kosher salt, plus more as needed

¼ cup whole milk

1 cup all-purpose flour, for dredging

1 cup fine dry bread crumbs

¼ cup sesame seeds

Vegetable oil, for frying

Put the unpeeled potatoes in a saucepan with water to cover by an inch. Bring to a simmer, and cook until tender, about 20 to 35 minutes, depending on the size of the potatoes. Drain, and when cool enough to handle, peel, and pass the potatoes through a ricer into a large bowl.

Heat the olive oil in a small skillet over medium heat, and toss in the diced prosciutto. Sauté the prosciutto until the fat is rendered and the prosciutto is slightly crisp, about 3 to 4 minutes. Remove from heat, and let the prosciutto cool, then add to the bowl with the potatoes. Beat one egg and add, plus the grated cheese, parsley, and 1½ teaspoons salt.

Using about 3 tablespoons per croquette, form the potato mixture into twenty-four 2-inch cylinders, and place on a baking sheet lined with parchment. Refrigerate the potato mixture until firm, about ½ hour.

Whisk together the remaining eggs and the milk in a wide, shallow bowl. Spread the flour on a plate, and mix the bread crumbs and sesame seeds on another plate. Season each dish with salt. Working in batches, dredge the croquettes in flour to coat them lightly, and tap off the excess. Dip the croquettes into the eggs, turning well to coat evenly. Let the excess egg drip back into the bowl, then dredge the croquettes in bread crumbs. Turn to coat all sides well, pressing gently with your hands until the bread crumbs adhere. For easier frying, refrigerate ½ hour after breading.

When you are ready to fry, heat ½ inch vegetable oil in a large skillet over medium heat; it is ready for frying when the end of a croquette sizzles. Fry the croquettes in batches, turning on all sides, until golden, about 2 to 3 minutes per batch. Drain on paper towels, seasoning with salt while still hot. Serve warm or at room temperature.

# Braised Fennel with Sausage

*Finocchio Brasato con Salsicce*

Italians love fennel, *finocchio,* but Americans are just getting familiar with it. It is terrific raw, and in Piedmont is dipped raw into hot oil with anchovies. It is also great served solo as a braised vegetable. I love the hint of anise flavor in it, as well as the crunchy crack under my teeth when I eat it raw as a snack. The crumbled sausages make this a very flavorful vegetable dish that can also be used to dress pasta. It can be made in advance, keeps well, and reheats well. What more could you ask of a vegetable?

Heat the olive oil in a large skillet over medium-high heat. When the oil is hot, sauté the onion and sausage, crumbling the sausage with the back of a wooden spoon, until the meat is no longer pink, about 3 to 4 minutes.

Push the sausage and onion to the sides of the pan to create a clear spot in the center, and plop in the tomato paste. Let the tomato paste toast for a minute or two, then stir it into the vegetables. Toss in the fennel, and season with the salt and peperoncino. Lower the heat, cover the skillet, and cook, stirring occasionally, until the fennel is tender and caramelized, about 15 to 20 minutes. Uncover, and increase the heat to cook away any excess liquid in the pan, if necessary.

SERVES 4 TO 6

3 tablespoons extra-virgin olive oil

1 medium onion, sliced ¼ inch thick

8 ounces sweet Italian sausage without fennel seeds, removed from casing

1 tablespoon tomato paste

2 medium fennel bulbs, trimmed, cored, cut into 1-inch chunks

1 teaspoon kosher salt

Pinch peperoncino flakes

Meat-Stuffed Eggplant

# Meat-Stuffed Eggplant
## *Melanzane Ripiene*

I recall having a version of this dish in Greece, and I am sure the Greeks brought it to Sicily, and I am sure the Sicilians brought it to America. I have found it at weddings and on the menus of Italian restaurants across America. It is a great dish for a large party and for a buffet table. I like it best hot out of the oven, but it is also good at room temperature. "Eggplant" is a misnomer: the vegetable is neither white nor shaped like an egg. However, the first eggplants to arrive in Europe were a rare oval-shaped white variety, and the name stuck. When buying eggplants, look for even color and firm feel. The eggplant should be heavy relative to its size; when you pick it up at the market, it should be firm and crisp, not spongy, to the touch.

SERVES 6

6 small eggplants (about 2 pounds total)

½ cup extra-virgin olive oil

1 small onion, finely chopped

1 pound ground beef

⅓ cup dry white wine

1 red bell pepper, finely chopped

2 teaspoons kosher salt

2 cups cubes of day-old country bread

1 cup milk

1 cup grated Grana Padano or Parmigiano-Reggiano

½ cup chopped fresh Italian parsley

1 hard-boiled egg, chopped

2 plum tomatoes, seeded and chopped

Preheat oven to 400 degrees F.

Cut the eggplants in half lengthwise. Scoop out the flesh to make a shell about ½ to 1 inch thick. Finely chop the flesh and set aside.

Heat 4 tablespoons of the olive oil in a large skillet over medium-high heat. Toss in the onion, and cook until it begins to soften, about 3 to 4 minutes. Crumble in the ground beef, and pour the wine over the meat. Cook, breaking up the beef with the back of a wooden spoon, until the meat releases its juices and they then cook away, about 6 or 7 minutes. Add the bell pepper and chopped eggplant, and season with 1 teaspoon of the salt. Cover, and cook until the vegetables are tender, about 10 minutes. Scrape into a bowl to cool.

Pour the milk over the bread cubes in a small bowl. Once the bread has softened, squeeze out the excess milk and put the bread in the bowl with the cooled meat filling. Add the grated cheese, parsley, egg, and tomatoes, and mix well.

Put the eggplant halves in a large baking dish, and drizzle with the remaining 4 tablespoons oil. Sprinkle with the remaining teaspoon salt, and toss well to coat all of the eggplant with the oil. Fill the eggplant halves with the filling, and arrange snugly in the baking dish. Cover the dish with foil, and bake until the eggplant is tender all the way through, about 40 to 45 minutes. Uncover, and bake until the top of the filling is browned and crispy, about 10 minutes more.

# Broccoli with Garlic and Anchovies

*Broccoli con Aglio e Acciughe*

SERVES 4

3 tablespoons extra-virgin olive oil

6 garlic cloves, sliced

2 anchovies, chopped

1 large head broccoli, cut into 1½-inch florets

¼ teaspoon peperoncino flakes

¼ teaspoon kosher salt

Heat the olive oil in a large straight-sided skillet over medium-high heat. Toss in the garlic; once the garlic is sizzling, add the anchovies. Cook and stir until the anchovies dissolve and sizzle in the oil, about 1 to 2 minutes.

Add the broccoli to the skillet, and season with the peperoncino and salt. Pour ½ cup of water into the skillet, bring to a simmer, cover, and cook until the broccoli is tender, about 4 to 5 minutes. Remove the lid, and increase heat to high to boil away any excess liquid. Serve.

Fresh garlic just harvested at LJB Farms in San Martin, California

# Peas with Bacon

*Piselli e Pancetta*

I found versions of this dish on menus across America, Italian and non-Italian. I guess everybody loves its appealing flavors. It is delicious made with frozen peas, but when I was a child, my grandma made it only with the sweetest first pods of peas. I also remember that it was my job to shell them, and I ate quite a few of those raw peas.

Pancetta is pork belly cured with salt, pepper, and other seasonings, then made into a roll, but not smoked like bacon. You can substitute bacon or Canadian bacon for the pancetta, and substitute fresh peas for frozen.

SERVES 4

Combine the olive oil, pancetta, and onion in a large skillet over medium heat. Cook until the pancetta fat is rendered, about 5 to 7 minutes.

Pour in the peas. Cook, stirring occasionally, until the onion and peas are tender and flavored with the pancetta. Stir in the pine nuts. Cook and toss for a minute, then serve.

3 tablespoons extra-virgin olive oil

3 ounces pancetta, finely chopped

1 small onion, finely chopped

1 pound frozen peas, thawed, or 1 pound fresh peas blanched for 5 minutes

¼ cup pine nuts, toasted

# Sautéed Escarole

*Scarola Strascinata*

Escarole is a big ingredient in the Italian American pantry, so one will see it frequently on an Italian American table. Escarole has always been abundant in American markets, whereas the dark-green vegetables such as chicory and broccoli rabe made their appearance much later. The usual recipe for sautéed escarole is *scarola strascinata,* "dragged" in the pan with garlic and oil. In this rendition, the addition of anchovies and black olives makes it more festive and gives the dish more complexity.

SERVES 4

3 tablespoons extra-virgin olive oil

4 garlic cloves, crushed and peeled

3 anchovy fillets

1 large bunch escarole, about 1 pound, leaves trimmed, separated, and washed

¼ teaspoon kosher salt, plus more as needed

¼ cup pitted oil-cured black olives

Heat the olive oil in a large skillet over medium heat. Add the garlic and anchovies, and cook, stirring, until the anchovies dissolve, about 2 minutes.

Add the whole escarole leaves to the skillet, with a little water from washing still clinging to them, and season with the salt. Stir in the olives. Once the escarole begins to wilt, cover the skillet and cook until the leaves are tender, about 8 to 10 minutes. Check occasionally to make sure the pan is not dry; if it is, add a few tablespoons of water and re-cover.

Once the escarole is wilted and tender, uncover and cook for another minute or two to evaporate any excess liquid. Season with salt (keeping in mind that the anchovies and olives contain salt), and serve warm.

Sautéed Escarole

# Spinach with Bacon

*Spinaci con Pancetta*

Everything tastes better with bacon, and so does spinach. The Italians often use rendered pieces of pancetta or prosciutto to flavor their vegetables, especially the winter vegetables such as chicory, kale, Savoy cabbage, cauliflower, and the like.

**SERVES 4**

2 tablespoons extra-virgin olive oil

6 garlic cloves, crushed and peeled

6 ounces pancetta or regular bacon, cut into ¼-inch pieces

Two 10-ounce bags fresh spinach, washed and trimmed

¼ teaspoon kosher salt

Heat the olive oil in a large skillet over medium heat. When the oil is hot, toss in the garlic. Let the garlic sizzle for a minute or two, then add the pancetta. Sauté until the pancetta fat is rendered and the pancetta is crisp, about 4 to 5 minutes.

Add the spinach, ½ cup water, and the salt. Cover, and cook until the spinach is tender, about 4 to 5 minutes. Uncover, and increase heat to high to cook away excess liquid, about 1 minute. Serve immediately.

# Swiss Chard and Potatoes

*Bietole con Patate*

I grew up on Swiss chard, but in the United States it has only become a popular part of the leafy-vegetables section in markets during the last ten years. I love the vegetable: I love cooking with it and using it in soups, as well as in pastas, risottos, and fish dishes. To me, everything is good when served with Swiss chard. This simple dish is a family recipe my grandmother made for us, and it is still a favorite at our table. The children love it as well.

Fill a large pot with cold salted water, and add the whole peeled potatoes. Bring to a simmer, and cook the potatoes about halfway, about 15 minutes. Add the shredded chard, and cook until the leaves are very tender, 15 minutes or more, depending on the size. Drain well in a colander.

Wipe out the pot, and return it to the stovetop. Pour ⅓ cup of the olive oil and the crushed garlic into the pot set over medium heat. Cook until the garlic is light golden, about 3 to 4 minutes. Slice in the butter; once it has melted, add the drained potatoes and chard. Drizzle with the remaining 3 tablespoons olive oil, and season with 1 tablespoon salt. Mash coarsely with a potato masher. Let cook a few minutes to remove any excess liquid, stir in the almonds, and serve hot.

SERVES 6

1 tablespoon kosher salt, plus more for the pot

2 pounds large russet potatoes, peeled

2 bunches Swiss chard (about 2 pounds), trimmed (see note) and coarsely shredded

⅓ cup plus 3 tablespoons extra-virgin olive oil

6 garlic cloves, crushed and peeled

2 tablespoons unsalted butter

½ cup sliced almonds, toasted

NOTE If you buy young Swiss chard, cook the stems and leaves all at the same time. If you buy Swiss chard with larger leaves and stalks, trim the stems from the leaves and cook them for 10 minutes before adding the leaves.

# Braised Artichokes

*Carciofi Brasati*

The love Italians have for the artichoke is evident at the table. It is also evident as you visit markets in Italy, when you search through the pickled and canned vegetables in the Italian section of specialty stores in America, and when you consider the endless number of recipes dedicated to this thistle.

SERVES 4

2 pounds baby artichokes
(about 16)

8 garlic cloves, crushed and
peeled

Zest and juice of 1 lemon

2 tablespoons chopped fresh
mint

2 tablespoons chopped fresh
Italian parsley

¾ teaspoon kosher salt

¼ teaspoon peperoncino flakes

3 tablespoons extra-virgin
olive oil

3 tablespoons unsalted butter,
cut into small pieces

1½ cups dry white wine

1 tablespoon dry bread crumbs

Clean and prepare the artichokes as detailed on page 18.

Combine the artichokes, garlic, lemon zest and juice, mint, parsley, salt, and peperoncino in a saucepan of the size in which the artichokes will snugly fit in one layer. Nestle the artichokes in the pan with the ingredients, drizzle with the olive oil, and dot with the butter. Pour 3 cups water and the wine into the saucepan. Bring to a simmer, cover, and cook until the artichokes are tender all the way through, about 40 minutes.

Uncover the pan, sprinkle with the bread crumbs, and simmer until the bread crumbs dissolve and thicken the sauce, just a minute or two.

Holding a flowering artichoke at Pezzini Farms in Castroville, California

# Southern California and the Italian Vegetable Trail

After investigating the canning industry in San Diego, Tanya and I took a ride north to San Clemente, and along the highway, I could not help noticing field upon field of artichokes. I wanted to stop, but we were heading to meet Nic Roma, an advertising executive who gave it all up to become a farmer and return to his earthy Italian roots. His family came from Tricarico, Basilicata, in 1909. "My people didn't bring valuables with them, they brought values." His passion and quest is to work the land as his ancestors did, while making use of all the technical innovations today. He is not an immigrant, but, rather, an American with Italian roots. He wants to spread an appreciation for the Italian varietals of vegetables, and with them his ancestors' respect for the land.

A delicious *merenda* (snack) awaited us when we greeted Nic at VR Green Farms in San Clemente. Under the pergola (entryway), we were surrounded by exemplary Mediterranean species of vegetables, from artichokes to fava beans. We walked through orchards of olive trees, and munched on fresh pecorino cheese drizzled with mango honey. We dunked our crunchy multigrain bread into olive oil made in the nearby hills, and popped local almonds into our mouths.

Nic is committed to bringing Italian varietals of vegetables and fruits to California. I promised him that I would send him some seeds and together we would start a radicchio-zuccherino salad revolution in America.

We were well fed on our way north to Salinas Valley, and arrived bright and early one morning at the immense fields of the D'Arrigo Brothers' farm. The broccoli rabe was still moist from the morning dew—I had never seen so much broccoli rabe in one place, or, for that matter, such a quantity of any vegetable in one place.

Stephen and Andrew D'Arrigo, two brothers originally from Messina, Sicily, had moved to California in the early 1900s from Boston, and invested in a small farm growing fennel and broccoli in 1925. They had the vision that their compatriots would appreciate their native broccoli rabe, and brought some broccolini rapini (as the broccoli rabe is called in Italy) seeds from Sicily in the 1950s. They began growing it and renamed it broccoli rabe.

The vegetable's popularity spread like wildfire. Andy Boy (the D'Arrigos' company) is now the largest producer of broccoli rabe in the United States, but they also cultivate

With Margaret D'Arrigo in the abundant fields of broccoli rabe at Andy Boy Farms

broccoli, cauliflower, and romaine lettuce. Now another generation of D'Arrigos run the farm—Andrew, and his son and daughter John and Margaret. As I walked the fields with Margaret, I noticed that besides the broccoli rabe there were endless fields of prickly pears, their Sicilian heritage prevailing again. Margaret's twin sons were not too far behind us, playing hide-and-seek. Even while playing, the fourth generation of D'Arrigo farmers are being groomed.

Our next stop was the Royal Rose Radicchio growing company, and here the Italian story is quite different. Lucio Gomiero and Carlo Boscolo are Italian businessmen, both from the Veneto region of Italy. Lucio has a successful construction business in Italy and produces wine; the Boscolos are Italy's largest growers of radicchio. Fate brought them together on a construction project, and they became friends; in 1988, Lucio took a gamble and proposed to Carlo that they had a real opportunity to grow radicchio in California. After extensive research on the Salinas Valley, they bought twenty acres and began farming. They now sell more than ten million pounds of radicchio a year and even export it to Italy. Clearly, this was a story of Italians with ambitions looking for their own opportunities, rather than looking for work under someone else.

The Salinas Valley in California, one would say, is a second Italy, it is so similar in climate. Missing the products from their home, immigrants transported seeds and knowledge, and developed one of the largest agricultural communities growing Italian produce: garlic, artichokes, purple asparagus, and red radicchio, just to name a few.

There is almost no professional chef who does not use some of this Italian American–grown produce. When we came to the farm, a sea of radicchio heads lay before us. Most of them were of the round, cabbagelike Chioggia varietal, although farmers here also grow the Treviso varietal and are beginning to grow the Rosa di Castelfranco—a radicchio that looks like a rose—a radicchio of red and yellow. The bittersweet quality of these salads of the chicory family is much loved and enjoyed in Italy, and it seems that the American palate is following closely behind.

The next morning, we were at the Pezzini Farms in Castroville bright and early, where there were silvery-green artichoke plants as far as the eye could see. Artichokes are one of the oldest foods known to humans: the Greek philosopher and naturalist Theophrastus wrote of them being grown in Sicily in 300 B.C. However, the Italians were not the first to bring the artichoke to the American shores. It was the French, who brought it into New Orleans in 1806, and from there the Spaniards took it to California. Andrew Molera, a landowner in the Salinas Valley, decided to lease his land (previously dedicated to growing sugar beets) to Italian farmers who were growing the new vegetable. In the 1920s, it was the Italians who turned most of the cornfields of California's Central Coast into a garden of artichokes. As a result, today we have Castroville, the Artichoke Capital of the World. Every May, the Artichoke Festival takes over the town, and visitors are offered field tours and are able to taste artichokes cooked in every method imag-

Guido and Tony Pezzini and me in the fields at Pezzini Farms—home of nine different sizes of artichokes

inable. There is an antique-car show, a show of agro art (three-dimensional artworks made of produce), and also a run and walk through the artichoke fields.

California accounts for 99.9 percent of the artichokes grown in the United States, and the cooler coastal climate allows them to thrive, growing like little palm trees planted in rows. The Pezzini Farms are known for Green Globe artichokes, a varietal much sought after by chefs and home cooks alike across America, and they offer these artichokes in nine different sizes. Tony Pezzini claims that each artichoke is picked and packed by hand, and that each is unique in flavor and texture.

We were met by three generations upon our arrival at the farm: the grandfather Guido, his son Tony, Tony's wife, Jo Lynn, their son Sean, and a beautiful all-black shepherd guard dog. Guido explained that it was his father, an emigrant from Lombardy, who started the farm, and then Guido began to specialize in the artichoke. There is nothing mechanical about farming artichokes: everyone in the Pezzini family has to work hands-on, and they even have a well-supplied stand where they sell fried artichokes.

To cook all of these great Italian vegetables, you need garlic, lots of garlic, and at the LJB Farms in San Martin we found just that. Mounds upon mounds, braid after hanging braid of garlic. The LJB Farms are run by a fourth generation of garlic farmers: Louie and Judy Bonino and their sons, Brent and Russ, work very hard at growing garlic. But with the competition from China, they had to diversify. So they have set up a bountiful farm stand where they sell deliciously succulent tree- and vine-ripened fruits and vegetables. The fifth generation, Jeremy and Anthony, were at the farm as well. When they talked about their plans, the future did not include garlic growing, but becoming a pilot and a fireman. Still, I have the feeling that the business of their grandfather and father will beckon them at some time. We left with handfuls of garlic braids, and the aroma of garlic wafted as a delicious reminder of the salad of tomato, cucumber, onion, basil, and garlic that was prepared for us by Judy.

As we made our way northward, we took a detour to Modesto, where Dino and Tom Cortopassi, a delightful Italian American family I have known for years, make olive oil and grow and can some of the best Italian plum tomatoes in this country. Used mainly in the food-service industry, their tomatoes are of the highest quality. They believe that if you use the highest-quality ingredients your dish is bound to be good. The Cortopassi packing facility is fast-moving, with tomatoes whizzing by twenty-four/seven, and they pack everything fresh. They must complete their entire yearly production and get it packed within the three-month growing season. In their freshness of taste, the Cortopassis' tomatoes reflect the commitment to quality in the three generations of passionate farming.

It was time to head for the airport and fly to Seattle, where I was to meet my son-in-law Corrado Manuali. Seattle does not have a big Italian American population, but Italian food and wine are doing well there. One of the men to be credited with spreading the

With the Bonino family at LJB Farms (left to right): Brent, Luci, Louie, Tanya, Judy, Jeremy, Lidia, Russ, Raquel, and Anthony

flavors of the Italian table in Seattle is Armandino Batali, with his famous Armandino's Salumi, at 309 Third Avenue South. His daughter Gina now runs this popular eatery, where at lunchtime the line wraps around the block. But I have an in with the family, and get privileged access—for, after all, his son Mario Batali is a dear friend and partner with my son Joseph and with me in several restaurants.

In the tradition of the farmers and entrepreneurs we have met through our travels, in October 2010 we opened Eataly, a new retail-restaurant complex, bringing the Italian food experience in America ever closer to Italy. It is so much like the Italian shopping experience that people leave the 50,000-square-foot complex saying, "It feels and tastes like Italy in there." Americans are ever more knowledgeable and appreciative of traditional Italian food and products, and at Eataly we deliver just that: the authenticity of Italian products, Italian cooked meals, and the Italian lifestyle. Most of the products are Italian and are chosen under the guidance of the Slow Food philosophy, designed to enhance the rich experience of beautifully made food. Other goods such as our breads, desserts, and mozzarella are made on the premises by Italian masters collaborating with American talent. We have also incorporated local American artisanal meats, vegetables, fruits, dairy and egg products, all selected here in America with the same criteria as the Italian products are selected in Italy. At Eataly, the best of two great cultures come together at the table, just as they have in restaurants and homes across America.

Sam Maugeri holding lusciously ripe Roma tomatoes at the family farm in New Jersey

# Braised Cauliflower with Tomatoes

*Cavolfiore Brassato al Pomodoro*

Cauliflower braised in tomato sauce is not a new recipe, but I had this delicious rendition, which I share with you here, at Torrisi.

Heat 3 tablespoons of the olive oil in a large skillet over medium-high heat. When the oil is hot, add the garlic, and let it sizzle for a minute. Toss the cauliflower florets and leaves, and stir to coat with the oil.

Sprinkle in the olives, oregano, salt, and peperoncino, and stir. Pour in the tomatoes and capers, and bring the sauce to a rapid simmer. Cover, and cook 10 minutes. Uncover, and simmer until the cauliflower is tender and the sauce has thickened, about 10 to 12 minutes. Drizzle with the remaining 2 tablespoons olive oil, and tear the basil leaves into the skillet. Stir to combine, and serve hot.

SERVES 4 TO 6

5 tablespoons extra-virgin olive oil

6 garlic cloves, crushed and peeled

1 large head cauliflower, cut into 2-inch florets, and any tender leaves coarsely chopped

¼ cup pitted oil-cured black olives, halved

½ teaspoon dried oregano

½ teaspoon kosher salt

¼ teaspoon peperoncino flakes

28-ounce can Italian plum tomatoes, preferably San Marzano, crushed by hand

¼ cup drained tiny capers in brine

8 large fresh basil leaves

# Stewed Eggplant, Peppers, Olives, and Celery
## *Caponata*

This dish exemplifies Sicilian cooking, especially in the late-summer months, when eggplant, tomatoes, and peppers are at their best. The same kind of summer-vegetable preparation also appears in French ratatouille. But the difference is that the Sicilians make it *agrodolce,* sweet and sour: cooking some vinegar and sugar, then tossing with the vegetables. The acidity in the vinegar hinders spoilage, and in hot New Orleans summers, this dish keeps well without refrigeration.

Caponata requires a lot of preparation, but once done it keeps well in the refrigerator for up to ten days, and freezes well, so it makes sense to make a big batch. It is a very versatile dish—as an appetizer with some cheese, as a side dish, or as a delicious sandwich stuffer. Actually, it improves if left to steep for a while. I love it at room temperature with a piece of grilled meat or fish.

SERVES 8 TO 12

¼ cup extra-virgin olive oil

1 large red onion, cut into ¾-inch chunks

1 fennel bulb, trimmed, cored, cut into ¾-inch chunks

4 stalks celery, peeled if necessary, cut into ¾-inch chunks

2 red, yellow, or orange bell peppers, seeded, cut into ¾-inch chunks

2 teaspoons kosher salt, plus more as needed

2 fresh bay leaves, or 3 dried bay leaves

1 cup vegetable oil

2 small, firm eggplants, cut into ¾-inch chunks

2 medium zucchini, cut into ¾-inch chunks

Heat the olive oil in a large skillet over medium heat. Add the onion, fennel, celery, and peppers, season with 1 teaspoon salt, and drop in the bay leaves. Toss a few times to coat the vegetables in the oil, then cover and let sweat over low heat until tender, about 10 minutes.

Heat ½ cup of the vegetable oil in another skillet over medium-high heat. Slide in the eggplants and cook, turning to brown all sides, about 6 to 7 minutes. Drain the eggplants on a paper-towel-lined baking sheet. Add the remaining ½ cup of oil to the skillet, and repeat with the zucchini, browning on all sides, about 6 to 7 minutes. Remove the browned zucchini, and let it drain along with the eggplant.

Meanwhile, bring the vinegar and honey to a boil in a small saucepan, and cook until syrupy and reduced by about half, 2 to 3 minutes.

When the onion, fennel, celery, and peppers are tender, uncover and add the sun-dried tomatoes. Cook, uncovered, to evaporate excess liquid, about 2 to 3 minutes more. Sprinkle in the capers and oregano. Pat the eggplants and zucchini dry, and season with ½ teaspoon salt. Add the eggplants and zucchini to the skillet with the other vegetables, and toss to combine. Drizzle in the reduced vinegar mixture, season with remaining ½ teaspoon salt (or as needed), and toss for a minute or two, just until the vegetables are glazed. Serve warm or at room temperature.

Me in the eggplant fields at the Maugeri farm in southern New Jersey

⅓ cup cider vinegar

2 tablespoons honey

12 oil-packed sun-dried tomatoes, drained, cut into strips

½ cup drained tiny capers in brine

1 teaspoon dried oregano

# Skillet Cauliflower Torrisi

*Cavolfiore Affogato alla Torrisi*

Cauliflower, a good vegetable especially in the winter, can be prepared in many ways. I sometimes like just to boil it and while the cauliflower is boiling, add an egg or two to boil as well. When the cauliflower and the eggs cool, I peel the eggs, then toss the cauliflower and eggs into a great salad, dressed just with olive oil and vinegar. But the following is a recipe I got from Torrisi in New York, a deli-looking place set up with sixteen seats for dining. The cauliflower I had was delicious, and the bread crumbs used were made by Progresso, which was started by Italian immigrants in New Orleans in 1905.

SERVES 4

6 tablespoons extra-virgin olive oil

6 garlic cloves, sliced

1 large or 2 small heads cauliflower, cut into 2-inch florets

½ teaspoon kosher salt

¼ cup dry bread crumbs

¼ cup grated Pecorino Romano

Heat 4 tablespoons oil in a large skillet over medium heat. Toss in the sliced garlic, and cook until sizzling, about 1 to 2 minutes. Add the cauliflower florets, and toss to coat in the oil. Season with the salt. Cover, and cook until the cauliflower is tender, about 15 minutes. Stir occasionally, adding up to ½ cup water if the skillet starts to dry out or burn.

Mix together the bread crumbs and grated cheese in a small bowl. When the cauliflower is tender, uncover, and sprinkle with the cheese crumbs. Drizzle with the remaining 2 tablespoons olive oil and serve. For a crispy finish, bake in a preheated 375-degree oven for 15 minutes.

# Olive Oil Mashed Potatoes

*Purée di Patate all'Olio d'Oliva*

Try this recipe for a delicious Italian rendition of mashed potatoes. I recall that my grandma would fork-mash boiled potatoes, drizzle some extra-virgin olive oil, and sprinkle with coarse sea salt. Here I added some roasted garlic cloves, very much an Italian American favorite.

SERVES 4 TO 6

2 heads garlic

¼ cup extra-virgin olive oil

2 teaspoons kosher salt

2½ pounds medium russet potatoes

1 cup whole milk

Preheat oven to 375 degrees F. Cut off the tips on each garlic head, then place each garlic head on a square of foil, drizzle with olive oil, and wrap the foil to seal. Roast in the oven until the garlic is tender throughout (about 30 to 40 minutes, depending on the size of the garlic head). Let cool slightly, then squeeze the garlic cloves into a small bowl and mash with the remaining olive oil and the salt.

Meanwhile, put the potatoes in a pot with water to cover by 1 inch. Bring to a simmer, and cook until tender all the way through—about 15 to 20 minutes, depending on size. Let the potatoes cool slightly, then peel and set aside. In the pot used to cook the potatoes, warm the milk over low heat. Add the potatoes and garlic paste, and coarsely mash with a potato masher. Serve hot.

Roasted Potato Wedges

# Roasted Potato Wedges

*Fette di Patate Arroste*

Everybody loves roasted potatoes, and these have a Mediterranean twist—lots of garlic and rosemary.

The aroma of roasted rosemary in my mind conjures up images of big roasted meats and holidays, so whenever I make this dish it feels like a holiday to me.

Preheat oven to 425 degrees F.

Combine ¼ cup of the olive oil, the rosemary, garlic, and parsley in a large bowl. Let this marinade steep while the potatoes roast.

Spread the potatoes on a rimmed baking sheet, then season with the salt and toss with the remaining 3 tablespoons olive oil. Place on the lower rack of the oven, and roast until golden on one side, about 10 minutes. Flip the potatoes, and roast until golden on the other side, cooked through, and very crispy, about 10 minutes more.

Immediately dump the hot potatoes into the bowl with the garlic-rosemary mixture, and toss to coat. Season with black pepper, and use tongs to crush the potatoes lightly, so they absorb the flavored oil better. Toss again to let the exposed parts of potato get coated with oil. Serve right away. (You can pick out some or all of the rosemary and garlic before serving, if you like.)

SERVES 4 TO 6

¼ cup plus 3 tablespoons extra-virgin olive oil

3 tablespoons fresh rosemary

4 garlic cloves, sliced

1 tablespoon chopped fresh Italian parsley

2 pounds russet potatoes, cut lengthwise into 1-inch wedges

1 teaspoon kosher salt

Freshly ground black pepper

Shrimp Scampi

# Seafood

# Mussels Triestina

*Cozze alla Triestina*

This is my favorite way to eat mussels. It is how we cook them in Trieste and the surrounding area. Prepare this only when the mussels are super-fresh, and you will taste the sea in your mouth, made all velvety by the bread crumbs. I love dunking the crusty bread in the sauce. If there are any leftovers, remove the mussels from the shells and return them to the sauce; tomorrow you'll have a great pasta-with-mussels dish.

SERVES 4 TO 6

6 tablespoons extra-virgin olive oil

6 garlic cloves, crushed and peeled

1 large onion, sliced ½ inch thick

3 fresh bay leaves, or 4 dried bay leaves

½ teaspoon kosher salt

¼ teaspoon peperoncino flakes

2 cups dry white wine

3 pounds mussels, soaked and scrubbed clean

1 cup chopped scallions

½ cup chopped fresh parsley

¼ cup dry bread crumbs

Heat 4 tablespoons of the olive oil in a large Dutch oven over medium-high heat. Add the sliced garlic, and cook until garlic is sizzling and just golden around the edges, about 2 minutes. Add the onion, and cook, stirring occasionally, until softened, about 5 minutes. Sprinkle in the bay leaves and salt. Push the vegetables aside and make a dry "hot spot," then add the peperoncino and let it toast for a minute. Pour the white wine into the pot. Bring to a boil, and cook until the wine is reduced by half, about 3 to 4 minutes.

Once the wine has reduced, add the mussels and scallions. Stir, and adjust the heat so the sauce is simmering. Cover, and simmer until the mussels open, about 5 minutes.

Most of the mussels should have opened (discard any that have not). Sprinkle with the parsley and bread crumbs. Drizzle with the remaining olive oil, and toss well. Transfer the mussels to a serving bowl, and pour the juices over the top. Serve immediately.

# Mussels in Spicy Tomato Sauce

*Cozze al Pomodoro Piccante*

The Mediterranean is rich in mussels, in particular in the rocky coastal regions. They are also abundant in the coastal regions of the United States. *Cozze,* or mussels, are a very popular dish in Italy, especially around Naples. It seems that just about every Italian American restaurant has some rendition of a mussels dish: *alla Posillipo* (spicy tomato sauce), *alla marinara* (mild fresh tomato sauce), and so on. Well, here is a spicy one. Mussels are not an expensive seafood and deliver a lot of flavor if fresh and still briny from the sea. Otherwise, save your San Marzano for another dish.

SERVES 4 TO 6

Heat 5 tablespoons olive oil in a large Dutch oven over medium-high heat. Add the sliced garlic, and cook until the garlic sizzles and turns just golden around the edges, about 2 minutes. Add the tomatoes, slosh out the can with ¼ cup hot water, and add that to the pot. Season with the oregano, salt, and peperoncino. Bring to a boil, and simmer until slightly thickened, about 10 minutes.

Once the sauce has thickened, add the mussels, stir, and adjust the heat so the sauce is simmering. Cover, and simmer until the mussels open, about 5 minutes.

Once the mussels have opened (discard any that have not), stir in the basil, and drizzle with the remaining tablespoon of olive oil. Transfer the mussels to a serving bowl, and pour juices over. Serve immediately.

6 tablespoons extra-virgin olive oil

8 garlic cloves, sliced

28-ounce can Italian plum tomatoes, preferably San Marzano, crushed by hand

½ teaspoon dried oregano

½ teaspoon kosher salt

½ teaspoon peperoncino flakes

3 pounds mussels, soaked and scrubbed clean

10 large fresh basil leaves, shredded

NOTE  Instead of the canned tomatoes, you can use 2 pints of cherry or grape tomatoes, halved.

# Baltimore

Baltimore's Little Italy, between the Inner Harbor area and Fells Point, has been populated with Italians as far back as the mid-nineteenth century. The area is about twelve square blocks, and St. Leo's Church is the social center of the Italian American community. The first Italians arrived here on ships coming mostly from Genova, and most of these Italians continued west, following the lure of gold. But some of them settled and stayed close to the water. Male immigrants who came without family needed food and shelter. As a result, many Italian immigrant women began cooking and opening boarding houses to serve the growing Italian community. The second big wave of Italian immigrants, who came mostly from Naples and Sicily, opted for steady wages by working the docks and made Baltimore their home.

Baltimore is still very Italian. On one of my research trips, I went to visit our distributor of Lidia's Sauces and Lidia's Pastas in Maryland, Pastore Foods, a company that was started in 1898. Five generations have passed, and Michael Pastore and family still run the business, supplying the best Italian products to Baltimore and beyond. "Little Italy is thriving here in Baltimore," explained Michael. "We have great restaurants, bakeries, delis, St. Leo's Church, we even have an open-air Italian film festival." I recalled similar film festivals from when I was a little girl in Istria. We would climb up on the wall once the movie had started and, with our legs dangling, watch part of the movie, but mostly we ended up playing hide-and-seek. Here was Baltimore's Little Italy open-air film schedule for 2010, and I was tempted to go to Baltimore every Friday of that July and August:

*Moonstruck*
*Bread and Tulips*
*Tea with Mussolini*
*Big Night*
*It Started in Naples*
*The Italian Job*
*My House in Umbria*
*When in Rome*
*Cinema Paradiso*

Chesapeake Bay blue crabs; crabbing on the Chesapeake Bay with James "Ooker" Eskridge, the mayor of Tangier Island, Virginia

I got my Italian American experience during this trip when I went to Di Pasquale's Marketplace, which opened ninety-five years ago. What seemed a typical Italian deli unexpectedly opened up into a cozy dining room with a big kitchen in the back. Here we had a fantastic *pasta e fagioli* (it rivaled my *nonna*'s), followed by two exquisite sandwiches: the "Italian American Civic Club" (warm oven-roasted turkey, crispy pancetta, arugula, ripe tomato slices topped with pesto mayonnaise on crusty Italian bread) and the Luigi Abruzzese sandwich (juicy grilled chicken, braised rapini with significant garlic and peperoncino, melted provola on the same delicious crusty Italian bread baked in the brick oven on the premises).

I was not leaving Baltimore without some of those delicious crab cakes I had heard about at Faidley Seafood. Faidley Seafood is situated in the Lexington Market, established in 1872; it is one of America's oldest markets still running today. Unfortunately, the visit to the market was a disappointment: I anticipated stalls and counters with mounds of fresh fish, crabs, vegetables, and some good local fare like crab cakes, but most of the stalls in the market are of prepared fast food instead. However, these chunky crab cakes were the best I ever had; they looked like huge meatballs, and though it was only 10 a.m., I quickly decided to have one of those soft balls for a midmorning snack. The big lumps of crabmeat were held together by minimal amounts of condiments, and were deliciously sweet.

The urge for crab overtakes you in Baltimore, so I stopped for more at Crisfield Seafood, another Maryland institution, for a soft-shell crab sandwich that was deliciously crunchy, with specks of cornmeal on its crust, served with coleslaw on a hamburger bun. But the bun was soft and mushy. I ended up eating the soft-shell crabs and coleslaw without the bun.

# Crab Cakes
*Polpette di Granchio*

These are the crab cakes from the Faidley Seafood counter in Baltimore, the best I have ever had. Under the crisp outer layer of the crab cakes, big chunks of succulent sweet crabmeat were barely held together by condiments and what I later found out were crisp crushed saltine crackers. I managed to work out this fairly close recipe, since Faidley's would not part with the original one.

Rémoulade is a condiment that kept resurfacing on my research trip all over America. It appeared in Baltimore with the crab cakes, in New Orleans with fried artichokes, as a topping for po' boy sandwiches, and some rendition of it has even turned up as a topping for today's Big Mac. The closest Italian traditional condiment to the rémoulade is the *aglio e olio* (aioli—the emulsified rendition of olive oil and garlic which is used on the Ligurian and French coast). The French-sounding name implies some French heritage, but, then, the French played a big role in the founding of America, in particular in the Louisiana Territory.

MAKES 8 CRAB "MEATBALLS"

FOR THE RÉMOULADE

1 cup mayonnaise

½ cup chopped dill pickle

¼ cup ketchup

2 tablespoons yellow mustard

1 tablespoon red-wine vinegar

½ teaspoon Old Bay seasoning

FOR THE CRAB CAKES

1½ sleeves saltine crackers (enough to make 2 cups when crushed)

1 pound jumbo lump crabmeat

¼ cup mayonnaise

2 teaspoons yellow mustard

2 teaspoons Old Bay seasoning

Vegetable oil, for frying

For the rémoulade: whisk together all the ingredients, then cover and refrigerate until ready to serve. The recipe for rémoulade makes extra; it can be used for a variety of dishes, or you could halve that part of the recipe.

For the crab cakes: Crush the saltines with a rolling pin (while keeping them in their plastic sleeves). Empty the crumbs through a sieve into a bowl below, shaking to separate the larger crumbs from the fine crumbs. You will need about 1 to 1¼ cups fine crumbs for dredging the crab cakes.

Put the larger crumbs in a large bowl, and add the crab, mayonnaise, mustard, and Old Bay. Mix gently until you can press the mixture together to form balls. Form into eight balls, and place on a parchment-lined baking sheet. (If you have time, refrigerate for ½ hour to let them set up a bit.)

Heat ½ inch vegetable oil in a large skillet over medium heat. Dredge the crab cakes in the fine crumbs, and when oil is hot enough, drop the cakes gently into the skillet. Cook, turning on all sides without squishing or flattening, until the cakes are golden, about 6 to 8 minutes in all. Drain on paper towels, and serve hot with the rémoulade.

Scooping crab cakes at Faidley Seafood in the Lexington Market in Baltimore

Another very interesting and delicious condiment for sandwiches is the olive salad, also known as giardiniera, which I share with you in making the muffuletta sandwich (see page 64). Pickled vegetables are a big Italian tradition, the curing and preserving of vegetables when they're plentiful to be used in the less generous winter months. They were always given with a sandwich to the farmer who went out to work the land, to the factory worker, or even to office workers or kids taking their lunch with them. Giardiniera was a kind of fast food, but it was wholesome and balanced.

# Shrimp Scampi
*Scampi in Umido*

In my early restaurant days in Queens, 1971 to 1981, shrimp scampi was a major selling item on the menu, and we usually served it with some risotto, or with broccoli sautéed with garlic and oil.

"Shrimp scampi" was the name, but it is redundant, because shrimp and scampi are both species of shrimp. Shrimp scampi had significance for the early immigrants, because in Italy scampi, the spiny langouste varietal, was prepared in this fashion. In the United States, shrimp are available, not scampi, so the early immigrants prepared the shrimp they found in the scampi style they remembered.

### SERVES 4 TO 6

3 shallots, peeled and chopped (about ½ cup)

7 garlic cloves, crushed and peeled

¾ cup extra-virgin olive oil

2 pounds extra-large or jumbo shrimp, peeled and deveined

4 sprigs fresh thyme

2½ teaspoons kosher salt

2 cups dry white wine

2 tablespoons freshly squeezed lemon juice

6 tablespoons unsalted butter

½ cup chopped fresh Italian parsley

1 tablespoon dry bread crumbs, if needed

Combine the shallots, five garlic cloves, and 2 tablespoons of the oil in a mini–food processor. Process to make a smooth paste.

Pour 6 tablespoons olive oil and the remaining garlic into a large skillet over medium-high heat. Let the garlic sizzle for a minute, then add half of the shrimp and all of the thyme sprigs. Season with ½ teaspoon salt, and cook until the shrimp are seared but not fully cooked, about 1 to 2 minutes. Remove to a plate, and repeat with the remaining shrimp and another ½ teaspoon salt. Remove the shrimp and thyme from the skillet to the plate.

Add the remaining 4 tablespoons olive oil and the garlic-shallot paste to the same skillet set over medium heat. Cook, stirring constantly, until the paste has dried out and begins to stick to the bottom of the skillet, about 2 to 3 minutes. Return the thyme to the skillet, and pour in the white wine, lemon juice, the remaining 1½ teaspoons salt, 4 tablespoons of the butter, and 1 cup water. Bring the sauce to a rapid boil, and cook until reduced by half, about 4 to 5 minutes.

When the sauce has reduced, whisk in the remaining butter and return the shrimp to the pan. Cook and toss until the shrimp are coated with the sauce and just cooked through, about 2 to 3 minutes. Stir in the parsley. If the sauce still seems too thin, stir in the bread crumbs and bring to a boil just to thicken. Serve immediately.

# Shrimp Fra Diavolo

*Gamberi in Salsa di Pomodoro Piccante*

This shrimp dish is most extravagant if made with big, crunchy shrimp, but if you are price-conscious, medium-sized or even small shrimp will still be delicious. Keep in mind that the cooking time decreases as the size of the shrimp decreases. The amount of peperoncino you use to obtain the "Fra Diavolo," or "Brother Devil," is to your liking. Fra Diavolo sauce, originally made with lobster chunks still in the shell, is a creation of Italian immigrants in New York City at the turn of the twentieth century.

SERVES 6

Pour ¼ cup of the olive oil and the garlic into a large skillet over medium-high heat. Once the garlic begins to sizzle, add half of the shrimp and the thyme sprigs. Season shrimp with ½ teaspoon salt, and toss just until the shrimp are seared (but not fully cooked), a minute or two. Remove the shrimp to a plate with tongs, and repeat with the remaining shrimp and another ½ teaspoon salt.

Once all of the shrimp have been seared and removed, add the celery to skillet and cook until wilted, about 2 to 3 minutes. Add the peperoncino, letting it toast for a minute, then pour in the tomatoes. Slosh out the can with 1 cup hot water, add that to the skillet, and stir. Season with the remaining ½ teaspoon salt. Bring the sauce to a simmer, and cook until the celery is tender and the sauce has thickened, about 15 minutes. Stir in the capers, return to a boil, and return the shrimp. Simmer until the shrimp are just cooked through, about 2 to 3 minutes. Stir in the parsley, and drizzle with the remaining 2 tablespoons olive oil. Serve immediately, over rice or polenta.

6 tablespoons extra-virgin olive oil

6 garlic cloves, crushed and peeled

2 pounds extra-large or jumbo shrimp

4 sprigs fresh thyme

1½ teaspoons kosher salt

2 cups diced inner stalks and leaves of celery

¼ teaspoon peperoncino flakes, or as needed (see headnote)

28-ounce can Italian plum tomatoes, preferably San Marzano, crushed by hand

¼ cup drained tiny capers in brine

¼ cup chopped fresh Italian parsley

# Shrimp Parmigiana

*Gamberi alla Parmigiana*

Breaded shrimp is universal, but shrimp parmigiana is distinctly Italian American. I first encountered this dish when we opened Buonavia, our first restaurant, in 1971, and Chef Dino put it on the menu. Shrimp parmigiana was a regular weekly special; people loved it, and it is still a delicious dish today.

SERVES 4 TO 6

1 cup all-purpose flour

2 large eggs

2 tablespoons milk

2 cups bread crumbs

Kosher salt

1½ pounds jumbo shrimp, peeled, deveined, and butterflied

Vegetable oil, for frying

2 cups shredded low-moisture mozzarella

½ cup grated Grana Padano or Parmigiano-Reggiano

3 cups marinara sauce (see page 108)

Preheat oven to 425 degrees F. Spread the flour on a plate, beat the eggs and milk in a shallow bowl, and spread the bread crumbs on a plate. Season all three with kosher salt.

Working a few at a time, dredge the shrimp in the flour, then the egg, and then the bread crumbs. Put the breaded shrimp on a baking sheet.

Heat 1 inch of vegetable oil in a straight-sided skillet until the tip of a shrimp sizzles on contact. Fry the shrimp in batches, taking care not to crowd them, until golden on all sides, about 2 to 3 minutes per batch. Drain the shrimp on paper towels, and season with salt.

Mix together the mozzarella and grated Grana Padano in a bowl. Spread 1 cup marinara sauce in the bottom of a 10-by-15-inch Pyrex baking dish. Arrange all the shrimp in one layer, and drizzle with 1½ cups sauce. Sprinkle with the cheese mixture, and spoon dollops of the remaining ½ cup sauce on top. Place in the oven, and bake until cheese is browned and crusty and sauce is bubbly, about 15 to 20 minutes.

# Italian American Shrimp

*Gamberi all'Americana*

Vegetables are often used together with fish in traditional Italian cooking. This recipe is over the top and seems to have every available vegetable cooked with shrimp; to me it resembles jambalaya without the chicken and sausages, and it is great served over steamed rice or pasta.

SERVES 6

Pour the olive oil into a large Dutch oven over medium heat. When the oil is hot, add the garlic, let sizzle for a minute, then add the celery and carrot. Cook and stir until the vegetables are softened, about 5 minutes. Pour in the tomatoes, then slosh out the can with 1 cup hot water and add that as well. Season the sauce with the oregano and peperoncino, bring to a rapid simmer, and cook until slightly thickened, about 5 minutes.

Toss the scallions, mushrooms, zucchini, bell pepper, and salt into the pot. Bring the sauce to a simmer, and cook until the sauce is thickened and the vegetables are tender, about 10 minutes more.

Stir in the shrimp. Simmer until they are pink and just cooked through, about 3 to 4 minutes. Stir in the basil, and serve as I like to do, over rice, pasta, or even polenta.

¼ cup extra-virgin olive oil

4 garlic cloves, sliced

1 stalk celery, cut into 2-by-½-inch strips

1 large carrot, cut into 2-by-½-inch strips

28-ounce can Italian plum tomatoes, preferably San Marzano, crushed by hand

½ teaspoon dried oregano

½ teaspoon peperoncino flakes

1 bunch scallions, trimmed and chopped

8 large cremini mushrooms, sliced

1 medium zucchini, cut into 2-by-½-inch strips

1 red bell pepper, cut into 2-by-½-inch strips

½ teaspoon kosher salt

1½ pounds large shrimp, peeled and deveined

½ cup fresh basil leaves, loosely packed, shredded

Lobster Fra Diavolo

# Lobster Fra Diavolo

*Aragosta Fra Diavolo*

Although this dish has all the makings of an Italian dish, everything I have read points to its being an Italian American invention, mostly likely conceived in New York. In Italy they do make a sauce with lobsters with which they dress pasta and risotto, but it is in the form of brodetto, seafood stew—lighter than the Italian American Fra Diavolo, made with onions instead of garlic, and without oregano. Here I give you a delicious version that is a combination of both.

To prepare the lobsters: Use a large chef's knife. If you wish, stun the lobsters a bit by putting them in the freezer for 15 minutes. Put the tip of your chef's knife on the lobster's head, about 2 inches or so back from the eyes. Push the knife straight down, then through to split between the eyes. Hold the lobster with a towel where the claws meet the body, and twist to remove the claws. Twist or break the claws from the knuckles, and crack both with the back of the knife to make it easier to open when serving. Twist walking legs off the body. Split the lobster body and tail in half lengthwise, clean body cavity, leaving in the tomalley (the green digestive part of the lobster). Cut the tail from body.

Bring a large pot of salted water to boil for pasta. After you have simmered the sauce with the lobster for 10 minutes, slip the spaghetti into the boiling water, and cook until al dente.

Spread the flour on a rimmed baking sheet. Dredge the cut-side pieces of lobster body and tail (but not the claw pieces or walking legs) in the flour, tapping off the excess. Pour the vegetable oil into a large Dutch oven, and set over medium-high heat. Slip the body and tail meat into the pot, cut side down, and cook just to seal the meat, about a minute or so. Remove the pieces to a plate. Add the claw pieces, and cook just until they begin to change color, about a minute. Remove the claws to the plate.

Pour off the vegetable oil, return the pot to medium heat, and pour in 3 tablespoons of the olive oil. Add the onions and garlic. Sauté a

*(continued)*

### SERVES 4 TO 6

Two 1½-pound lobsters

1½ teaspoons kosher salt, plus more for pasta pot

1 pound spaghetti

All-purpose flour, for dredging the lobster

½ cup vegetable oil

¼ cup extra-virgin olive oil

2 medium onions, finely chopped

3 garlic cloves, crushed and peeled

2 tablespoons tomato paste

Two 28-ounce cans Italian plum tomatoes, preferably San Marzano, crushed by hand

½ to 1 teaspoon peperoncino flakes

½ cup fresh basil leaves, packed, shredded

*(Lobster Fra Diavolo, continued)*

few minutes, then add ½ cup of the pasta cooking water, and simmer to soften the onions, another 2 to 3 minutes. Increase the heat to let the water boil away, and clear a space in the pan to make a clear dry spot. Plop in the tomato paste, let sizzle a minute or two, then stir the tomato paste into the onions. Add the crushed tomatoes, and slosh out the cans with 2 cups of the pasta cooking water, adding those to the pot as well. Bring the sauce to a rapid boil, and stir in the peperoncino and salt. Add all of the lobster except for the tail pieces, and let simmer until the sauce is thickened, about 10 minutes. Add the tail pieces, and simmer until the meat is just cooked through, about 2 to 3 minutes more.

When the sauce is ready, transfer about half of the sauce (without the lobster) to a large skillet, and bring to a simmer; add the cooked and drained pasta. Drizzle with the remaining tablespoon of olive oil, and sprinkle with the shredded basil. Toss to coat the pasta with the sauce. Serve the pasta in shallow bowls, with the extra sauce and the lobster-tail pieces over top.

A Gloucester fisherman with his early morning lobster catch—getting ready to unload;
a Gloucester fishing boat coming in with its early morning catch

Seafood Soup

# Seafood Soup

*Cioppino*

Cioppino is a delicious Ligurian fish stew, and since many emigrants from Liguria settled in San Francisco, some of the best renditions of the dish on this side of the ocean are found in San Francisco. California Italians were great contributors to the American fabric, and I am sure they all enjoyed a good bowl of cioppino. It might be a bit more complicated to eat, and perhaps your guests will balk, but I like my cioppino with crab legs in their shells.

**SERVES 8**

Pour the olive oil into a large Dutch oven over medium-high heat. Spread the flour on a plate, and dredge monkfish in the flour, tapping off the excess. Slip the monkfish into oil and brown on all sides, about 3 to 4 minutes in all. Remove the monkfish to a plate.

Add the onion and celery to the pot. Cook, stirring occasionally, until onion is softened, about 5 minutes. Push aside the vegetables to make a dry "hot spot" in the pan and add the tomato paste. Let the tomato paste toast for a minute or two, then stir it into the onion and celery. Sprinkle in the peperoncino, let toast another minute, then increase heat to high, pour in the wine, and stir. Cook until the wine is reduced by half, then add the bell pepper, tomatoes, thyme, and salt. Slosh out the tomato can with 2 cups water, and add that as well. Bring to a rapid simmer, and cook until thickened, about 10 minutes.

Once the sauce has thickened, return the monkfish to the pot and let cook 2 minutes. Add the littlenecks, cover the pot, and simmer until the clams just begin to open, about 4 to 5 minutes. Add the mussels, cover, and cook until they begin to open, another 2 minutes. Finally, add the shrimp and crabmeat. Simmer, uncovered, until the shrimp are just cooked through, about 4 to 5 minutes. Stir in the parsley, and serve in warm bowls.

NOTE  Instead of the crabmeat, you can also use six king-crab legs, cracked in pieces, but if so add them just before the shrimp.

¼ cup extra-virgin olive oil

All-purpose flour, for dredging

12 ounces monkfish, trimmed and cut into 2-inch pieces

1 medium onion, chopped

1 cup chopped celery

2 tablespoons tomato paste

½ teaspoon peperoncino flakes

1 cup dry white wine

1 red bell pepper, chopped

28-ounce can Italian plum tomatoes, preferably San Marzano, crushed by hand

3 sprigs fresh thyme

½ teaspoon kosher salt

2 dozen littleneck clams, scrubbed

2 pounds mussels, scrubbed

1 pound large shrimp, peeled and deveined

8 ounces jumbo lump crabmeat, picked over

2 tablespoons chopped fresh Italian parsley

# Fried Calamari

*Calamari Fritti*

Fried calamari is one of my favorite foods. When it is lightly floured and cooked in fresh oil, rather than in a constantly reused deep-fryer, it is spectacular. But, sadly enough, I have found it to be one of the most poorly made dishes on my travels across the United States. So, if you long for good fried calamari, make yourself a batch at home. Here is my simple recipe.

SERVES 4

Vegetable oil, for frying

1½ pounds calamari (bodies and tentacles), cleaned, bodies cut into ½-inch rings

1½ cups all-purpose flour, for dredging

Kosher salt

Pour enough vegetable oil into a wide pan to come about 1 inch up the sides. Heat the oil over medium heat to about 365 degrees F, or until the edge of a piece of calamari sizzles on contact.

Pat the calamari dry with paper towels. Separate the bodies from the tentacles. Dredge the bodies in flour, and shake excess off in a strainer. Lower the bodies into the oil, and fry, turning occasionally, until golden brown and just cooked through, about 3 minutes. Lower the heat beneath the oil until you are ready to fry again. Drain the calamari on a paper-towel-lined baking sheet, and season with kosher salt.

Bring the oil back to frying temperature. Repeat the dredging process with the tentacles. Fry the tentacles until golden brown and crispy, about 4 minutes. Be careful when frying the tentacles: they tend to squirt more than the bodies, because they trap moisture. Drain the tentacles on paper towels and season with kosher salt. Serve immediately.

Fried Calamari and Shrimp Scampi

# Stuffed Calamari

## *Calamari Ripieni*

Whenever stuffing anything, one may be tempted to overstuff. Well, the elegance in this dish is to stuff the calamari lightly. When you cook fish or meat, remember that it always tightens a bit, and if there is too much stuffing, it bursts out. So keep it light—follow the recipe.

### SERVES 4 TO 6

12 medium calamari with tentacles, cleaned (about 3½ pounds)

6 tablespoons extra-virgin olive oil

1 small onion, finely chopped

1 teaspoon chopped fresh thyme

1¼ teaspoons kosher salt

⅛ teaspoon peperoncino flakes

½ cup dry white wine

1 bunch scallions, trimmed, finely chopped

¼ cup dry bread crumbs

3 tablespoons chopped fresh Italian parsley

Preheat oven to 400 degrees F. Chop the calamari tentacles and set aside.

Heat 3 tablespoons of the olive oil in a large skillet over medium-high heat. Add the chopped onion, and cook until softened, about 5 minutes. Add the chopped tentacles, chopped thyme, 1 teaspoon of the salt, and the peperoncino. Cook and stir until the tentacles are cooked through, about 2 to 3 minutes. Pour the white wine into the pan, and reduce until syrupy. Stir in the scallions, and remove from the heat. Scrape the pan's contents into a large bowl, and stir in the bread crumbs and chopped parsley. Let cool.

When the filling is cool, lay the calamari bodies out on your work surface. Fill each body with about 2 to 3 tablespoons filling, Do not overfill the calamari; it is okay if there is a little stuffing left and each raw calamari sack is half full. Pin the calamari closed by threading a toothpick up, then down again, through the wider opening of the body.

Oil a 13-by-9-inch Pyrex baking pan with 2 tablespoons olive oil. Lay the calamari in the baking pan in one layer. Sprinkle any remaining stuffing over the calamari. Pour ¼ cup water into the pan, drizzle with the remaining tablespoon olive oil, and season with remaining ¼ teaspoon salt. Cover the dish tightly with foil, and bake until the calamari are cooked through and the liquid is simmering, about 25 minutes. Uncover, and bake until the calamari are golden on top, about 10 minutes. If the calamari are done and there is still too much liquid in the pan, remove the calamari to a platter, and pour the sauce into a small skillet. Reduce on top of the stove until the sauce is slightly thickened, and serve with the calamari.

# Squid Milanese

*Calamari alla Milanese*

I have had squid prepared many ways, but never in a Milanese cutlet style until Tanya and I encountered this dish on our trip to San Diego when we went to Anthony's Fish Grotto. The calamari cutlet was a thick slab, like a veal cutlet, quite different in size from the smaller version of calamari I am accustomed to cooking on the East Coast, and yet very tender. This popular calamari may be up to 2 feet in length; the giant squid can get to approximately 43 feet; in 2003, a colossal species of squid was discovered that can be upward of 46 feet.

I'm not sure which calamari was used for my Milanese at Anthony's, but it was very good; I tested the recipe with the traditional-sized calamari, and it worked deliciously.

**SERVES 4**

Heat the oil and 2 tablespoons of the butter in a large, heavy skillet over high heat. Dredge calamari bodies in the bread crumbs and press well so that the crumbs stick. Slip the calamari into the skillet in one flat layer, and sprinkle with the oregano. Let the calamari caramelize on one side, about 1 to 2 minutes, then turn and weight the bodies down with another heavy skillet to keep them from curling. Sear until just cooked through, another 1 to 2 minutes, then remove from skillet.

Add the remaining tablespoon of butter, the capers, and lemon juice. If the pan seems dry, add a few tablespoons of water, wine, or stock to deglaze and release the browned bits from the bottom of the pan. Serve the calamari topped with the pan juices.

3 tablespoons extra-virgin olive oil

3 tablespoons unsalted butter

8 large calamari, bodies split open so they are flat (freeze the tentacles for another meal)

1 cup dry bread crumbs

½ teaspoon dried oregano

2 tablespoons drained tiny capers in brine

Juice of ½ lemon

Baked Rollatini of Sole

# Baked Rollatini of Sole

*Involtini di Sogliola al Limone*

The Sicilians have a tradition of using bread crumbs in many of their recipes, like *involtini di pesce spada,* or swordfish rollatini, which are dressed with dried-oregano-seasoned bread crumbs and olive oil. It makes sense that the large Sicilian immigrant population in the States would keep up the tradition here using fillet of sole, an easier, more economical catch than swordfish, especially for the early immigrants.

Preheat oven to 350 degrees F.

Toss together the bread crumbs, grated cheese, parsley, lemon zest, and oregano in a bowl. Drizzle with 4 tablespoons of the olive oil, and toss until the crumbs are evenly coated with the oil.

Coat the bottom of a 9-by-13-inch Pyrex baking dish with the softened butter. Arrange the lemon slices in one layer on the bottom of the baking dish. Pour in the lemon juice and white wine.

Lay the fish on your work surface, and press the crumbs into the top of the fish. Starting with the short side, roll each fillet up with crumbs on the inside, and secure closed with toothpicks. Arrange the fish in the baking dish, and scatter capers in the open spaces. Sprinkle any leftover crumbs over the fish, and drizzle with the remaining 2 tablespoons olive oil.

Place the baking dish on the bottom rack of the oven, and bake until the fish is just cooked through, about 20 minutes. Remove the toothpicks and serve.

SERVES 6

½ cup dry bread crumbs

½ cup grated Grana Padano or Parmigiano-Reggiano

¼ cup chopped fresh Italian parsley

1 large lemon, grated, then half of the lemon juiced, the other half thinly sliced

2 teaspoons dried oregano

6 tablespoons extra-virgin olive oil

2 tablespoons unsalted butter, softened

1 cup dry white wine

6 skinless fillets of sole (about 1½ pounds)

2 tablespoons drained tiny capers in brine

# Lemon Sole

*Sogliola al Limone*

I cooked this simple dish in my first restaurant, Buonavia, which I opened in 1971. I made it with fresh lemon sole and fluke, bought directly from the fishermen on Long Island when in season. But you can make it with the fillet of any white fish. It is delicious and quick.

**SERVES 4**

2 tablespoons extra-virgin olive oil

5 tablespoons unsalted butter

4 skinless fillets lemon sole, about 1½ pounds (cut fillets in half at the natural break to make easier to maneuver in the pan)

¾ teaspoon kosher salt

Flour, for dredging

5 garlic cloves, crushed and peeled

2 tablespoons pine nuts

1 cup dry white wine

2 tablespoons lemon juice

3 tablespoons drained tiny capers in brine

2 tablespoons chopped fresh Italian parsley

Put the olive oil and 3 tablespoons of the butter into a large skillet set over medium heat. Season the sole all over with ½ teaspoon salt. Lightly dredge the sole in flour, tapping off any excess, and slip the fillets into the melted butter and oil. Brown the fish on both sides, about 2 to 3 minutes per side. Once it is browned and cooked all the way through, transfer to a warmed platter while you make the sauce.

Increase the heat to medium-high. Scatter the garlic and pine nuts in the skillet. Cook and toss until the pine nuts are toasted, about 2 minutes. Add the white wine and lemon juice. Bring to a boil. Add the capers and the remaining 2 tablespoons butter. Whisk to melt the butter, and boil the sauce until reduced by about half, 2 to 3 minutes. Season with the remaining ¼ teaspoon salt. Remove the garlic cloves from the sauce, then stir in the parsley. Pour the sauce over the fish, and serve.

# Halibut with Tomato and Spinach

*Ippoglosso con Pomodori e Spinaci*

This dish is best when the tomatoes are fresh and ripe, but it will be almost as good with canned plum tomatoes. It makes a complete one-pot meal, including vegetables and protein. I used spinach, but escarole is a good Italian American substitute.

Put the tomato halves in a food processor and process to make a smooth purée. Set aside.

Season the halibut chunks with ½ teaspoon salt. Spread the flour on a plate, and lightly dredge the halibut, tapping off the excess.

Pour ¼ cup of the olive oil into a large skillet, and set over medium-high heat. When the oil is hot, add the fish and brown on all sides, until just cooked through, about 5 minutes in all. Remove the fish to a plate and keep warm.

Add the sliced garlic to the skillet. Let the garlic sizzle for a minute, then pour in the tomato purée. Slosh out the food processor's work bowl with 1 cup hot water, and add that to the skillet. Season with the peperoncino. Bring to a rapid simmer, and cook until very thick, about 10 to 12 minutes.

Season the sauce with the remaining teaspoon of salt, and stir in the remaining 2 tablespoons olive oil. Increase heat to high, add the spinach, and cook until spinach is just wilted into the sauce, about 3 or 4 minutes. Divide the spinach and sauce among plates, and serve the halibut on top.

SERVES 6

2 pounds fresh plum tomatoes, halved and cored (about 4 cups)

2 pounds skinless halibut fillet, cut into 2-inch chunks

1½ teaspoons kosher salt

All-purpose flour, for dredging

¼ plus 2 tablespoons extra-virgin olive oil

6 garlic cloves, sliced

¼ teaspoon peperoncino flakes

6 ounces fresh spinach, trimmed (about 12 packed cups leaves)

# Gloucester, Massachusetts

When we were researching the history of the Sicilian immigrants and fishing in Gloucester, Massachusetts, Nina Groppo, the wife of a Sicilian Gloucester fisherman, was our delightful companion for the day. It was a great morning for observing the fishing boats coming in with their catch, followed by the fish auction, which is one of the most advanced that I have seen in the industry. Buyers from Boston and New York communicated electronically about what was on the boats, and only a few hours after the fish was unloaded, it was the property of a bidder somewhere in the country. What is paramount in any fish preparation is the freshness of the fish, and certainly there is fresh fish to be had in Gloucester. This town is the oldest fishing port in the United States, and most of the fishermen's lineage hails from Italy—to be specific, Sicily.

With Nina Groppo from the Gloucester Fishermen's Wives Association

Even today there is still a great feeling of the Italian village and customs in the town. There are cafés and social and religious clubs where the fishermen gather to have an espresso, chat, and play cards. St. Peter's Club seemed to be the center of activities—and St. Peter is the patron saint of fishermen, after all. Late in June, the town has a feast dedicated to St. Peter, and, as is customary in Italy, the statue of St. Peter is carried in a procession around Gloucester.

As in Italy, Gloucester's fishing community is a tightly knit group of wives and families. The Gloucester Fishermen's Wives Association addresses the contemporary economic, political, and environmental problems. Fishing can be a dangerous job, and sometimes the men do not return home. In the fishing villages in Italy, the custom was that when the fleet of fishing boats returned from an extended trip at sea, all of the wives whose husbands had gone out dressed in black and waited together at the pier. Most likely one of them would find out she was a widow.

When it came time for lunch, we ate at The Gloucester House, one of the best fish houses in the area, started by the Linquata family of fishermen. The restaurant is now run by the family's fourth generation, and it is still deliciously busy. I ordered their specialty, a portion of baked halibut along with fried calamari and a steamed lobster. It did not take long for the word to spread, and we were joined by the patriarch, Michael L. Linquata, who shared the story of the four generations running this restaurant. We had a delightful lunch by the sea, watching the fishing boats glide in with their catch. The halibut was delicious, and Michael was willing to part with the recipe.

Michael Linquata of The Gloucester House

# Gloucester Baked Halibut

*Ippoglosso di Gloucester al Forno*

This delicious baked-halibut recipe came from The Gloucester House, presided over by Michael Linquata, with whom we had a lovely lunch on the porch of the restaurant. This fish is simple to make, and the recipe can easily be multiplied if you have guests coming.

SERVES 4

3 garlic cloves, sliced

¼ teaspoon kosher salt, plus more for seasoning the fish

½ cup extra-virgin olive oil

1 cup crushed saltine crackers

1 tablespoon chopped fresh thyme

1 cup grated white-cheddar cheese

Four 6-to-8-ounce skinless halibut fillets

Preheat oven to 400 degrees F. Mix garlic and ¼ teaspoon salt into the olive oil in a cup. Let steep for 30 minutes (or more, if you have the time).

Mix together the saltines and thyme in a bowl. Pour in ¼ cup of the olive oil, leaving the sliced garlic behind in the cup, to coat all of the crumbs with oil. Mix in the grated cheese.

Spread the crumbs on a plate. Brush the fish all over with the remaining oil, and season with salt. Use any oil left in the cup to grease a rimmed baking sheet. Roll the fish on all sides in the crumbs, pressing to coat well, trying to use all of the crumbs. Put the fish on the baking sheet, leaving an inch or so between pieces.

Bake the fish until the crumbs are crisp and golden and the fish is cooked through, about 20 minutes.

Louis Linquata (at left) tells me about the fish (and fishermen) on display at the fish auction in Gloucester, Massachusetts.

# Gloucester Minted Grilled Mackerel

*Sgombro di Gloucester alla Griglia con Menta e Limone*

Mackerel is not a popular fish, but I love it: it is flavorful and very nutritious. As with all fish, but especially with mackerel, the freshness of the fish is the key. This dish is very good eaten hot, but also at room temperature.

SERVES 6

Juice of 2 lemons

5 garlic cloves

1 teaspoon kosher salt

½ cup plus 2 tablespoons extra-virgin olive oil

2 pounds mackerel fillet, with skin (see note)

¼ cup fresh mint leaves, packed, shredded

Preheat a grill to medium-high heat.

Combine the lemon juice, garlic, and ½ teaspoon of the salt in a blender, and purée until smooth. With the blender running, slowly drizzle in ½ cup of the olive oil to make an emulsified dressing.

Season the mackerel with the remaining salt, and brush with the remaining 2 tablespoons olive oil. Put the fish on a rimmed baking sheet, and drizzle each fillet with 1 to 2 tablespoons of the lemon-garlic dressing. Rub or brush the dressing all over the fillets.

Grill the fish, skin side down, until the skin is marked and loosens its grip on the grill grates, about 3 minutes. Carefully flip the fillets with a large, wide metal spatula. Grill until just cooked through, about 3 to 4 minutes more. Remove the fish to a platter. (It's okay if the fish breaks up a bit; just cut the fillets into serving pieces on the platter.)

Mix the mint leaves into the remaining dressing, drizzle over the fish, and serve.

NOTE A thin row of bones runs down the dividing line of each mackerel fillet. You can have your fishmonger trim them out for you, or do it yourself with a sharp fillet knife, making sure you don't cut all the way through so the fillet stays together.

An early morning spent with the fishermen at St. Peter's Club in Gloucester: (from left to right) Mercurio Di Mercurio, Vito Ciaramitaro, Lenny Billante, and Peter Moceri

Lamb with Roasted Peppers and Broccoli with Garlic and Anchovies

# Meat

# ❧ POULTRY

# Providence, Rhode Island

Federal Hill is where things Italian happen in Providence, and Piazza De Pasquale seems to be the community's beating heart. Scattered trees and umbrellas shade the outside seating of the cafés and restaurants on the square; there is a bronze fountain gently squirting water; colorful flowers drape from the pots on the lampposts. One might as well be in a piazza in Napoli: gurgling water, people chattering, even an Italian song sung now and then. Tanya and I came early one morning to the piazza, and we had two cappuccinos, a *sfogliatella,* and a cannoli in the shade of the tree at Caffe Dolce Vita, just as we might have had in Italy.

But my plans went deeper than sweets. In the piazza next to the Dolce Vita, behind an unassuming front and a local bodegalike entrance, I could hear a flurry of activities. Antonelli Poultry is the only store in Rhode Island that still sells live chickens, rabbits, ducks, Guinea hens, partridges, and geese, and processes them to order. They also sell the eggs of many of the fowl there. As I walked in, the distinct smell of freshly processed fowl took me back to my childhood days with Nonna Rosa. When a chicken or a rabbit was sacrificed for a festive family meal, I had to assist in the process, from heating the water to plucking the chicken and collecting the innards—liver, stomach, intestines, and the unborn eggs, some of which had a soft shell, still in the making, some just yolks. These eggs ranged in size from a peppercorn to a cherry to an olive to a mature egg. After we had cleaned all the parts, a frittata made with the offal and the collected eggs was in order.

Yes, behind the plastic curtain in the back room of Antonelli Poultry, thousands of chickens are processed and sold weekly. Chris Morris is the man in charge, and he is the real deal: he loves his animals and is aware of the nutritional value and flavor in the fresh products he sells. It is an act of love: not only does he know his animals, but he could not stop talking about the different shapes, sizes, colors, and flavors of the eggs they produce for him to sell. I was happy. The tradition, though rare these days,

A day in Providence: (above) Tanya enjoying a morning cappuccino and *sfogliatella* at Caffe Dolce Vita; (right) Chris Morris at Antonelli Poultry; (below) Luigi Carchia from Frosinone serenading me at the fountain

of buying live chickens and enjoying those flavors, was alive and well, at least here in Providence.

Tanya and I were now heading toward the fountain and crossing the piazza to reach Costantino's Venda Ravioli. I had my sunglasses on, but that did not stop Luigi from recognizing me and greeting me with a spontaneous serenade. Luigi Carchia sings regularly at the festivities on the piazza, and his repertoire can range from folkloric Italian to jazz to contemporary music. It was early, but Luigi had his long handlebar mustache waxed and ready for the performance. Ah yes, this happens only in Napoli, but, no, we were in Providence, on the piazza in front of Venda Ravioli.

Venda Ravioli is like a *bomboniera,* as we say in Italian: a box of candy, full of brilliant colors and flavor and Italian products. At the small café in the front of the store, the local second-, third-, and fourth-generation Italians gather each morning, reaffirming with a cup of espresso that, indeed, they are Italian. In the back, a neat and tight kitchen produces splendid Italian fare, which is displayed and sold at the central counter, with Chef Salvatore Cefaliello at the helm. This is a family operation all the way: daughter, son, brother, cousins are all involved in running Venda Ravioli and Costantino's restaurant across the piazza.

# Roberto's Chicken Piccante

*Pollo Piccante alla Roberto*

On one of my visits to Roberto's on Arthur Avenue in the Bronx, I picked up this delightfully spicy chicken recipe. It pairs wonderfully with the tomato-and-bread salad on page 94.

Season the chicken all over with ½ teaspoon of the salt. Spread the flour on a rimmed plate, and dredge the chicken in flour, tapping off the excess. Heat the olive oil in a large cast-iron skillet over medium-high heat. When the oil is hot, add the chicken and brown on all sides, about 8 to 10 minutes in all.

Once the chicken is browned, drop the garlic into the empty spaces in the pan, and add the bell peppers and the cherry peppers. Cook until the peppers are caramelized on the edges, about 4 to 5 minutes.

Move the breast pieces on top of the rest of the chicken and vegetables (to avoid overcooking), and sprinkle everything with the oregano and the remaining 1 teaspoon salt. Cover, and cook until the chicken and vegetables are deeply caramelized, about 5 minutes.

Uncover, pour in the white wine, and simmer until the wine is almost cooked away and the chicken is cooked through, about 10 to 15 minutes more.

### SERVES 4 TO 6

3½-to-4-pound chicken, cut into 10 to 12 pieces (2 wings, 2 legs, 2 thighs, each breast halved, plus neck and back if desired)

1½ teaspoons kosher salt

All-purpose flour, for dredging

3 tablespoons extra-virgin olive oil

8 garlic cloves, crushed and peeled

2 large red bell peppers, cut into eighths

6 hot red pickled cherry peppers, drained and halved lengthwise

1 teaspoon dried oregano

1 cup dry white wine

Chatting with Chef Roberto Paciullo on a blustery winter morning outside Zero Otto Nove Restaurant

# Poached Chicken Rolls

*Petto di Pollo in Camicia*

Poached chicken served with *salsa verde* or another piquant sauce is common in Italy, and this is a perfect example of cultural blending between Italian and American styles. Today in America, Chef Fortunato Nicotra often makes this dish at our restaurant Felidia. It is light and yet very tasty, especially for lunch.

I like it over an arugula salad, but he serves it on top of a light fresh-tomato sauce as well. It is delicious both ways.

SERVES 4

2 plum tomatoes, sliced into strips

4 packed cups fresh baby spinach

6 ounces fresh mozzarella, diced

2 tablespoons extra-virgin olive oil

1 teaspoon kosher salt

4 boneless, skinless chicken breasts (about 6 to 8 ounces each)

Toss together the tomatoes, spinach, mozzarella, olive oil, and ½ teaspoon salt in a large bowl.

Slice open the chicken breasts crosswise to butterfly and use a meat mallet to pound them to an even thickness of about ½ inch. Season the chicken with the remaining ½ teaspoon of salt.

Lay each breast, cut side up, on a long piece of plastic wrap. Divide the filling over the chicken breasts, then roll them tightly in the plastic, on the diagonal, to seal the chicken completely in plastic and leave about 3 inches of plastic on either end. Twist the ends to make a tight "sausage," then tie each end with string to maintain the sausage shape.

Put the rolls in a pot with water to cover. Weight the rolls down with a plate to keep them submerged. Bring the water to a simmer, and cook until the chicken is cooked through and has an internal temperature of 165 degrees F, about 30 to 35 minutes. (The plastic wrap will not melt.) Remove the chicken, and let cool a bit. Unwrap, and slice each breast into rounds.

# Chicken Parmigiana

*Pollo alla Parmigiana*

When this dish was first made—in Emilia-Romagna, particularly in the city of Parma—it included veal and grana cheese, such as Grana Padano or Parmigiano-Reggiano. The bread crumbs, tomato, and mozzarella were all added later, and chicken has often been used as a more economical substitute for veal. This has got to be one of the most popular Italian American dishes. You can find it across America, in every Italian American restaurant, and it has now penetrated the fast-food chains, thanks to its popularity and reasonable costs. If done well with the best of products, it is a great dish.

Preheat oven to 425 degrees F. With a paring knife, make a horizontal pocket three inches deep in the chicken breasts. Season chicken with the salt. Stir together the ricotta, ¼ cup of the grated cheese, and the basil in a bowl, seasoning with black pepper to taste.

Put the cheese filling in a pastry bag with a wide tip. (If you don't have a pastry bag, you can squeeze the filling out of a regular resealable plastic bag with a corner cut off.) Pipe the filling into each pocket of the chicken breasts. Spread the flour and bread crumbs on two separate rimmed plates. Beat the eggs in a wide, shallow bowl. Dredge the chicken in the flour, tapping off the excess, then dip in the beaten egg, letting the excess drip back into the bowl. Coat the chicken on all sides in the bread crumbs.

Heat ½ inch vegetable oil in a large skillet over medium heat. When the oil is hot, add the chicken, in batches if necessary. Cook until browned and crispy, about 4 minutes per side. Drain the chicken on paper towels.

Spread 1½ cups of the marinara in a baking dish large enough to fit the chicken in one layer. Lay the chicken breasts on the sauce, and top with the remaining marinara. Layer the sliced mozzarella on the chicken, and sprinkle with the remaining ½ cup of grated cheese. Bake until the chicken is cooked through and the topping is browned and bubbly, about 20 to 25 minutes.

SERVES 6

Six 6-to-8-ounce boneless, skinless chicken breasts

½ teaspoon kosher salt

12 ounces fresh ricotta, drained

¾ cup grated Grana Padano or Parmigiano-Reggiano

8 large fresh basil leaves, shredded

Freshly ground black pepper

All-purpose flour, for dredging

2 cups dry bread crumbs

2 large eggs

Vegetable oil, for frying

4 cups marinara sauce (see page 108)

8 ounces low-moisture mozzarella, thinly sliced

# Chicken Scarpariello

*Pollo alla Scarpariello*

I would venture to say that, along with chicken parmigiana, chicken scarpariello is one of the most recognized chicken recipes in America. Chicken scarpariello is a composition of a few favorite ingredients: chicken, lots of garlic, and vinegar. In this recipe, I added some sausage, which is not unusual, especially if you have a big brood coming over. To multiply the recipe: proceed in batches; then, once you have brought the whole thing to a boil, transfer to a roasting pan and finish cooking in a 450-degree oven, stirring the chicken periodically so all the pieces get crispy.

SERVES 6 OR MORE

12 boneless, skinless chicken thighs, trimmed, each cut into 4 pieces (about 4 pounds)

2 teaspoons kosher salt

¼ cup extra-virgin olive oil

8 ounces sweet Italian sausage without fennel seeds, cut into bite-sized pieces

8 garlic cloves, sliced

½ cup white-wine vinegar

½ teaspoon dried oregano

Season the chicken all over with the salt. Pour the olive oil into a large cast-iron skillet over medium heat. Add half of the chicken and sausage (or use enough to fit in the skillet without crowding), and brown all over, about 5 minutes. Remove to a plate, and repeat with the second batch of chicken and sausage.

Return all of the chicken and sausage to the skillet. Add the garlic, and let everything brown and caramelize together for 3 or 4 minutes. Pour the vinegar into the skillet, bring to a boil, and cook until syrupy, about 2 to 3 minutes. Reduce heat to low, and sprinkle with the dried oregano. Cover the skillet, and cook until the chicken and sausage are glazed and the chicken is tender, about 20 to 25 minutes.

Chicken Scarpariello

Braised Escarole and Chicken Scarpariello

# Chicken Cacciatore

*Pollo alla Cacciatora*

This dish has roots back in the Renaissance, when people hunted for food and only the wealthy could enjoy chicken. This is good when made with a whole chicken, but I prefer it made only with drumsticks and thighs. It can be made well in advance, and will reheat and remain moist. It is great with polenta or pasta, but I love it with a chunk of crusty semolina bread.

SERVES 6

¼ cup dried porcini mushrooms, soaked in hot water, then finely chopped, liquid reserved

One 4½-to-5-pound chicken, cut into 14 pieces (see note)

2½ teaspoons kosher salt

Vegetable oil, for browning the chicken

2 tablespoons extra-virgin olive oil

2 medium onions, cut in eighths, attached at the root end

3 stalks celery, sliced into ½-inch pieces on the bias

1 cup dry white wine

1 sprig fresh rosemary

28-ounce can Italian plum tomatoes, preferably San Marzano, crushed by hand

4 cups sliced mixed mushrooms (cremini, button, shiitake)

3 red, yellow, or orange bell peppers, cut into ½-inch strips

2 teaspoons dried oregano

Season the chicken all over with ½ teaspoon salt. Pour enough vegetable oil into a large Dutch oven to cover the bottom of the pan, over medium heat. When the oil is hot, brown the chicken all over in batches, about 2 to 3 minutes per side. Remove the chicken to a plate. Discard the vegetable oil.

Add the olive oil to the pot, and bring to medium-high heat. When the oil is hot, add the vegetables. Cook, stirring occasionally, until the onions and celery are caramelized on the edges, about 5 minutes. Put the chicken back in the pot, and pour in the white wine. Drop in the rosemary. Boil until the wine is reduced by half, then add the chopped porcini and the soaking liquid, omitting any gritty residue in the soaking liquid. Once the liquid returns to a boil, add the tomatoes. Rinse out the can with 1 cup hot water and add that as well. Bring to a boil, and simmer to let the sauce come together, about 5 minutes.

Pour in the sliced mushrooms, bell peppers, oregano, and the remaining 2 teaspoons salt. Cover, bring to a simmer, and cook until the vegetables have begun to soften, about 10 minutes. Uncover, and cook until the sauce has reduced and the chicken is tender, about 15 to 20 minutes more.

NOTE The chicken gets cut up as follows: two wings, two thighs, two drumsticks, back in two pieces, breast halves in three pieces each.

# Chicken Sorrentino

## *Pollo alla Sorrentina*

*Pollo alla sorrentina* is always topped with eggplant and melted mozzarella. But what does that have to do with Sorrento? Naples and Sorrento are in the region of Campania, where the best mozzarella comes from, so it would make sense that it would be used for cooking there. In Italy, rarely do you find the name of a locale in the title of the dish. On the other hand, the names of many Italian American dishes seem to include cities in Italy. The choice seems to be driven by nostalgia, remembering and honoring one's place of birth in the recollection of how things tasted there.

Preheat oven to 400 degrees F.

Slice open the chicken breasts crosswise to butterfly and use a meat mallet to pound them to an even thickness of about ½ inch. Season the chicken with the salt. Spread the flour on a plate. Lightly dredge the chicken in flour, tapping off the excess.

Add 4 tablespoons of the butter and the olive oil to a large skillet over medium-low heat. When the butter has melted, add the chicken and lightly brown on both sides, about 2 minutes per side. Remove the chicken to a plate. Increase the heat to medium, and add the eggplant slices to skillet. Brown on both sides, about 3 minutes per side. Remove the slices to a plate lined with paper towels to drain.

Discard the oil in skillet, and set it over medium-high heat. Add the remaining 3 tablespoons butter. When the butter is melted, pour in the white wine and bring to a boil. Adjust the heat so the wine is simmering rapidly, then lay the chicken breasts back in, in one layer. Lay a slice of ham over each chicken breast. Dollop about 2 tablespoons marinara on top of each piece of ham. Drop the remaining marinara in the spaces between the chicken breasts to make the sauce. Layer the sliced cheese on top of the sauce. Sprinkle the grated cheese over top. Bake until chicken is cooked through and cheese is browned and bubbly, about 20 to 25 minutes.

SERVES 4

Four 6-ounce boneless, skinless chicken breasts, trimmed

¼ teaspoon kosher salt

All-purpose flour, for dredging

7 tablespoons unsalted butter

3 tablespoons extra-virgin olive oil

2 small eggplants (about 12 ounces total), cut lengthwise into 8 slices

1 cup dry white wine

4 slices ham (about 2 ounces total)

1 cup marinara sauce (see page 108)

6 ounces low-moisture mozzarella, thinly sliced

¼ cup grated Grana Padano or Parmigiano-Reggiano

# Braised Chicken Breast with Smoky Provola

*Pollo alla Provola Affumicata*

I had this dish at Roberto's on Arthur Avenue in the Bronx. The smokiness of the provola is the defining element that graces the dish.

SERVES 6

Six 6-to-8-ounce boneless, skinless chicken breasts

1 teaspoon kosher salt

All-purpose flour, for dredging

3 tablespoons extra-virgin olive oil

2 tablespoons unsalted butter

10 large fresh basil leaves

6 thin slices prosciutto (about 2 ounces total)

½ cup dry Marsala

½ cup dry white wine

½ cup chicken stock (see page 40)

8 ounces smoked provola, sliced

Slice open the chicken breasts crosswise to butterfly, so they open to a flattened, even thickness. Season the chicken all over with salt. Lightly dredge the chicken in flour, shaking off the excess.

Heat the olive oil and butter in a large skillet over medium heat until the butter is melted. Add the chicken to the pan, and brown each side for about 2 minutes.

Once it is browned, top each breast with a basil leaf and a slice of prosciutto. Increase the heat to medium-high. Push aside the chicken to make a dry clear spot in the center of the pan, and pour in the Marsala and white wine. Drop in the remaining basil leaves. Bring to a boil, and simmer until reduced by half, about 2 minutes. Add the chicken stock, cover, and simmer to blend the flavors, about 3 minutes.

Uncover, top the chicken evenly with the smoked provola and cover. Adjust the heat to a simmer, cooking about 5 minutes to melt the cheese, then uncover. Bring to a boil, and cook until the chicken is cooked through and the sauce is reduced to your liking, about 8 to 10 minutes more.

# Chicago

Italians have been in Chicago since the nineteenth century. The community grew slowly until the mass immigration between 1880 and 1914. In 1900, there were sixteen thousand Italians in Chicago; about five million immigrants from Italy came to the United States between 1880 and 1914. Many worked in creating the great American infrastructures such as railroads and highways and mining, but many others got involved in the food business. Italians canned tomatoes, made wine, baked their own bread, made pasta, picked wild salads and herbs, kept chickens, slaughtered pigs, and made sausage. Many women worked in the South Holland onion fields outside Chicago.

The first Italians in Chicago were from Genova and Lucca, and built the first Italian Catholic Church of the Assumption in 1881. These Italians felt a great sense of unity and sponsored many Italian events, including Chicago's first Columbus Day parade in 1868. The later mass immigration to Chicago came from the shores of southern Italy, mainly Basilicata, Campania, and Sicily. Despite being inland, Chicago was the third-largest city in the United States in 1920. Italian food was the favored ethnic food in Chicago. By 1927, Italians owned five hundred grocery stores, 257 restaurants, 240 pastry shops, and numerous other food-related businesses concentrated in the Italian neighborhoods.

Chicago's Italian heritage is evident in its deep-dish pizza (see page 85) and beef sandwich (see page 70). Locals and tourists alike enjoy sitting outside Al's for a famous beef sandwich or waiting across the street on the sidewalk for a refreshing ice at Mario's. Taylor and Polk streets, the heart of the old Italian neighborhood, have recently been enhanced by a wonderful park, Italian-piazza-style, with benches and fountains, dedicated to Joe DiMaggio, and the National Italian American Sports Hall of Fame is across the street. Whereas the original Italian neighborhood dates back to the late nineteenth century and was mainly populated by Ligurian immigrants, Chicago has a more recently populated Italian American neighborhood in the Elmwood Park section, in the area near Harlem Avenue, Grand Avenue, and West Belmont Avenue, mainly with immigrants from Puglia in the mid-twentieth century. The Italian language is still very much alive as you see familiar Italian faces trying fava beans at Caputo's grocery store or having the daily special sandwich at the Nottoli Sausage Shop.

Today Elmwood Park seems to be the last stronghold of the true Italian neighborhood, more so than Little Italy. Here you will find the flagship of Caputo's, and many small Italian-owned businesses. I have traveled often to Chicago, and love its skyline and lakeshore. I also enjoy the vibrancy of the dining-and-wine scene, and I visit periodically for the annual Housewares Show in early March. In 1995, Julia Child and I were doing a presentation together, and a book signing for the then newly released *Master Chef* series. The Windy City wreaked its vengeance that morning; as Julia and I headed for the streets, the wind felt like blades on our faces, and I recall now, with tenderness, huddling with her and forging ahead to reach our destination. I am no novice to wind, coming from Trieste, which has a regular gusty wind called La Bora, which sometimes reaches 150-plus kilometers per hour. I am not sure Chicago has a name for its wind, or at what velocity it was blowing that cold morning, but it certainly seemed to be a cousin to La Bora from Trieste.

Visiting Chicago and its restaurants, I am often intrigued by the Italian dishes on the menu, their origin and evolution. The deep-dish pizza, for example, originated at Chicago's Pizzeria Uno, although I understand that some of the best can be found at Lou Malnati's and Giordano's. But this style of pizza surely has its roots in Sicily, and since some of the first and most numerous immigrants to Chicago were the Sicilians, it would follow that they brought their pizza-making style with them. Focaccia and pizza are eaten all over Italy. But in Sicily, as you walk the streets of the Ballero Market in Palermo, cart vendors beckon you with hot *sfincione,* a thick rectangular pizza, topped with tomato, dried oregano, and anchovies. Surely this is the pizza the Sicilian immigrants brought to Chicago.

Chicken Vesuvio seems to be another one of those Chicago dishes. It appears on most Italian American restaurant menus, and it seemed to be the Sunday dish for Chicago's Italian American immigrants. Vesuvio is the volcano shadowing Naples, so the dish most likely reflects the flavors of the Neapolitan immigrants—roast chicken and potatoes to which various vegetables can be added, from peas to mushrooms to fava beans to peppers, and even sausages. Roast chicken transcends all cultures, but this rendition seems to belong to Chicago.

Then there is the "Chicago Style Italian Beef Sandwich." I waited at Al's Beef to get a juicy taste on a recent visit, although the one I liked best is at Johnny's Italian Beef in Elmwood Park (where the line goes down the street). It would seem that this sandwich originated at large Italian American weddings. Beef was appreciated but too expensive, so sometimes roasted pieces of beef were sliced thin, tossed with lots of braised onions, peppers, celery, herbs, and spices, then stuffed into a long loaf of Italian bread and cut into pieces for the guests to enjoy. With a good glass of homemade wine and some traditional music, a great time was had by all.

Italian immigrants shopping at Angelo Caputo's marketplace in Chicago; Piazza diMaggio, across the street from the Hall of Fame

But the one recipe I was most surprised to find in Chicago was the breaded shrimp over pasta. On one of my trips to Sicily, I visited Anna Cornino in Custonaci, near Trapani. She was going to teach me how to make traditional couscous by hand, and make couscous we did. But as we prepared the couscous, it was nearing lunchtime, and Anna whipped up a quick plate of pasta with a simple tomato pesto and dressed it on top with small fried fish, whitebait, called *cento in bocca*. It was the first time I had had such a combination. Anna explained that local fishermen would sell all the best and biggest fish, and would bring home the small mixed bag of what they had left. Sometimes this was not enough for the whole family, so the wife usually made a plate of pasta and divided the fried fish on top of the pasta. The connection was now very clear: those immigrants in Chicago were also using the pasta as filler, flavored by the more expensive shrimp. Just like the Sicilian immigrants who brought the recipe with them, Chicago Italians were finding ways to honor old traditions in a delicious dish.

# Chicken Vesuvio

*Pollo alla Vesuvio*

This chicken dish is a signature Italian dish from Chicago. Just about every Italian restaurant in Chicago has some rendition of it. Traditionally made on Sundays, it is a whole chicken cut up in pieces with potatoes, peppers, peas, and lots of garlic and oregano. We have a similar chicken dish in our family, Grandma's "chicken and potatoes." At our house, it is everybody's favorite, and we do make it on most Sundays.

SERVES 6 TO 8

Vegetable oil, for browning

2 pounds russet potatoes, peeled, cut into lengthwise wedges

1 pound sweet Italian sausage, cut crosswise into 1-inch pieces

One 4½-pound chicken, cut into 14 serving pieces including back and neck (see note)

4 teaspoons kosher salt

5 tablespoons extra-virgin olive oil

6 garlic cloves, crushed and peeled

2 small onions, peeled, quartered at the root end

1 teaspoon dried oregano

1 cup dry white wine

1 cup chicken stock (see page 40)

2 red, yellow, or orange bell peppers, cut into thick strips

16 ounces frozen peas, thawed

Preheat the oven to 400 degrees F and prepare a large roasting pan.

Heat ½ inch vegetable oil in a skillet over medium heat. Add the potatoes and sausage, and brown on all sides, about 8 minutes. When browned, transfer the potatoes and sausage to the roasting pan.

Season the chicken all over with 2 teaspoons salt. Brown chicken on all sides in batches, about 8 to 10 minutes per batch. Transfer the breast pieces to the roasting pan, leaving the dark meat in the skillet.

Drain the vegetable oil from the skillet, and pour in 3 tablespoons olive oil and the crushed garlic. Once the garlic begins to sizzle, toss in the onions and oregano. Deglaze with the white wine. When the white wine has reduced by half, add the chicken stock.

Return to a boil, and then pour all the contents of the skillet into the roasting pan. Toss in the bell peppers and sprinkle everything with the remaining 2 teaspoons salt. Drizzle with the remaining 2 tablespoons olive oil.

Place in the oven, and roast 20 minutes; then scatter in the peas. Stir and return to oven, to roast until the chicken is tender and caramelized and only a thin layer of liquid remains in the bottom of the pan, about 30 to 40 minutes more, stirring occasionally during roasting. Serve family-style on a warm platter.

NOTE  To get fourteen pieces from the chicken, cut as follows: two wings, two drumsticks, two thighs, each breast half in two pieces, neck chopped in two pieces, back in two pieces.

# Chicken Trombino

*Pollo alla Trombino*

Ralph's claims to be the oldest Italian restaurant in Philadelphia, and it is still run by the original family. It was opened in 1900 by Francesco and Catherine Dispigno, emigrants from Naples, who named the restaurant after their son Ralph. A host of celebrities have eaten at Ralph's, and while we were eating there, a nearby couple told us they travel an hour each way once a month to come and eat there. The original mosaic-tile floor is beautiful, and eating in the upstairs room transports you back to the 1920s. Now Jimmy and Eddie Rubino, still part of the family, run the restaurant, and this chicken dish has been on the menu as long as they can remember.

SERVES 4 TO 6

Four 6-to-8-ounce boneless, skinless chicken breasts

1½ teaspoons kosher salt

All-purpose flour, for dredging

2 tablespoons unsalted butter

2 tablespoons extra-virgin olive oil

4 plum tomatoes, seeded and diced

8-ounce jar roasted red peppers, drained and sliced

1 teaspoon dried oregano

1 cup grated provola

2 tablespoons shredded fresh basil

Cut each chicken breast on a bias with a sharp chef's knife, making two slices out of each breast. Season chicken all over with ½ teaspoon salt. Spread the flour on a rimmed plate, then dredge chicken in flour and tap off excess.

Melt the butter and the olive oil in a large skillet over medium heat. When the butter is melted, add the chicken and cook until browned on one side, about 2 minutes. Flip the pieces, and brown the other side, about 2 minutes more.

When the chicken is browned, pour the tomatoes, roasted peppers, oregano, and remaining 1 teaspoon salt into the skillet. Bring to a simmer, and cook until the separate ingredients come together as a sauce, about 5 minutes.

Sprinkle the dish with the provola and shredded basil. Cover the skillet, and simmer just until the cheese melts and the chicken is cooked through, about 2 minutes more.

# Little Italy, in New York City

Ellis Island, or *l'isola delle lacrime* (island of tears), was the entry point for many Italian immigrants. Some ventured to the Midwest, and some made it all the way to the other coast. But there was also a group of Italian immigrants who made their homes on Mulberry Street, Arthur Avenue, and Monte San Giacomo (in Hoboken). New York City's Little Italy at its height had over a hundred thousand Italians living in the six-block radius. Today that number has dwindled to around ten thousand, with many second- and third-generation Italian Americans moving to the suburbs. As the Italians are becoming ever more part of mainstream America, the neighborhood is giving way to other new immigrant cultures.

The different blocks of Little Italy were settled almost regionally. Northern Italians were mostly in Greenwich Village; Sicilians, Calabrese, and Neapolitans were in Little Italy, but divided by block; Mulberry Street was predominantly Neapolitan. Icons such as Tony Bennett, Martin Scorsese, and Robert De Niro were all born here. Two of New York's oldest Roman Catholic churches are in Little Italy, Most Precious Blood and Old St. Patrick's, and Most Precious Blood is the home to the sanctuary of San Gennaro, which is celebrated every year in a festival.

As a young immigrant in the 1960s, I loved going to Little Italy for the Feast of San Gennaro. It reminded me of the *sagre,* local feasts, that are celebrated all over Italy, so coming to Little Italy to celebrate was like savoring a little piece of home. We always stopped at Ferrara Bakery for a cappuccino and a cannoli or baba au rhum. Today, when I go and shop at Lou Di Palo's, I still stop for a cappuccino at Ferrara Bakery, then visit with Lou and admire, of course, his great selections of cheeses and Italian specialties. Lou is a second-generation Italian who grew up on Mulberry Street, and he developed an intense knowledge and passion for Italian cheese. I don't think anyone in New York knows more about Italian cheese than Lou.

Now, with some good cheese in my shopping bag, my next stop is to visit Romana Raffetto at Raffetto's Pasta on West Houston Street. Raffetto's has been in business since 1906, and there you will most likely find Romana Raffetto scurrying around between the sauce pot and the pasta-rolling machine. Pasta and sauce are like a horse and carriage—you can't have one without the other. Right around the corner from Raffetto's is our restaurant Lupa, and down the block on MacDougal Street is Villa

At Villa Mosconi in Little Italy with Giovanni Ghezzi, Margharita Chiappa, and Pietro Mosconi

Mosconi, under the direction of Chef Pietro Mosconi. Next door to Villa Mosconi is one of the oldest Italian clubs, Tiro a Segno.

Farther down on Mulberry Street, so named after the mulberry trees that were once growing there, is the Torrisi Italian Specialties, a little restaurant opened by two young chefs, Mario Carbone—who worked for us at Del Posto—and Rich Torrisi, who worked at A Voce. Their premise is to cook Italian with all Italian American products. As Florence Fabricant has written about them in the *New York Times:* "Richard Torrisi and Mario Carbone are updating the meaning of Italian-American." On my last trip to Torrisi, we had some delicious roast heritage turkey, roasted cauliflowers with bread crumbs, and the tricolored almond cookies.

Every time we have visitors from Italy, a trip to Little Italy and Ellis Island is a must, and every time the ferry slips up to the pier at Ellis Island, I feel a tightness in my chest. Although my arrival as a young immigrant was at the then Idlewild Airport, I recall the fright in my mother's eyes, her vulnerability, and her sense of despair at that moment. I recall clinging to her, to combine our strengths, to brace for the unknown awaiting us. In retrospect now, I know that no place in the world could have embraced us and offered us the opportunity that America did, and I am certain that I am a very lucky woman. I am the product of two of the greatest cultures in the world, Italy and America.

# Brined Turkey Breast Torrisi

## *Petto di Tacchino in Salamoia alla Torrisi*

This was one of the recipes that I took away from my great lunch with Mario Carbone and Rich Torrisi of Torrisi Italian Specialties in New York's Little Italy. Turkey is, of course, an all-American product that was brought back to Europe after the discovery of the New World, and it is still not big on tables in Italy. But in this recipe, traditional technique and New World bird combine to make a delicious hybrid.

"Sous-vide," French for "without air," is a technique of cooking food sealed in a plastic bag. Such foods usually cook for a long time at a low temperature, about 140 degrees F. The integrity of the product is preserved, and, when vacuum-sealed, the food will last longer. To perform this technique properly, one needs a lot of expensive and cumbersome equipment. Some contemporary restaurant chefs use it, and with good results, but I certainly do not recommend it for home use.

Rich Torrisi and Mario Carbone of Torrisi Italian Specialties in New York City's Little Italy

The day before you want to cook the turkey breast, make the brine: Combine 2 gallons cold water with the salt, sugar, lemons, lemon juice, and bay leaves in a large pot. Bring to a boil just long enough to dissolve the salt and sugar, then remove from heat and let cool completely. Submerge the turkey breast in the brine, weighting it down with a plate. Refrigerate 24 hours while the turkey brines.

When you are ready to cook the turkey, drain and rinse it. Lay out a large sheet of doubled plastic wrap, and make a bed with the leek and celery in the center. Lay the turkey on top of the vegetable bed, and wrap the turkey snugly in the plastic wrap, using more if necessary to seal the package completely. Put the turkey breast in a gallon-sized resealable plastic bag. Seal most of the way, then slip a straw into the bag and suck out the excess air. Seal completely.

Put the wrapped and bagged turkey breast in a large pot, and add enough water to cover. Adjust the heat to maintain a constant temperature between 170 and 180 degrees F. Cook the turkey for 40 minutes; then puncture the plastic with a meat thermometer to insert it in the breast. The internal temperature in the breast meat should reach 165 degrees F when done.

While the turkey cooks, preheat oven to 375 degrees F. Place each garlic head on a square of foil, drizzle with olive oil, and wrap the foil to seal. Roast in oven until the garlic is tender throughout, about 30 to 40 minutes, depending on the size of the garlic heads. Remove from oven and let cool. Squeeze out the garlic cloves from the skin into a bowl, and mash with the honey, vinegar, salt, and 2 tablespoons hot water.

Increase the oven temperature to 425 degrees F. When the turkey has finished poaching and reached an internal temperature of 165 degrees F, place the package in an oiled roasting pan and cut open the bag and plastic wrap, letting the cooking juices flow into the pan, then remove the turkey from the bag and return it to the roasting pan. Brush the glaze onto its skin. Return the roasting pan to the oven, and roast until the skin is browned and crisp, about 20 minutes. Let rest 10 minutes before carving.

SERVES 8

FOR THE BRINE

1 cup kosher salt

¼ cup sugar

2 lemons, quartered and juiced

4 fresh bay leaves, or 6 dried bay leaves

FOR THE TURKEY AND GLAZE

5½-pound bone-in, skin-on whole turkey breast

1 leek, trimmed, quartered lengthwise

3 stalks celery, cut into 2-inch lengths

2 heads garlic

Extra-virgin olive oil, for drizzling

1 tablespoon honey

1 tablespoon good-quality balsamic vinegar

¼ teaspoon kosher salt

 # VEAL

# Veal Scaloppine in Lemon Sauce
## Scaloppine di Vitello al Limone

Veal piccata is a familiar dish in most Italian American restaurants across America: thin slices of veal briefly sautéed in butter with some lemon juice added to it. In this recipe, however, I added some capers, green olives, and thin slices of lemon. It brings much more body, flavor, and complexity to the dish. Chicken and turkey scaloppine are also delicious prepared this way.

**SERVES 4**

8 slices veal scaloppine (about 1½ pounds)

¼ teaspoon kosher salt

8 tablespoons (1 stick) unsalted butter

2 tablespoons extra-virgin olive oil

All-purpose flour, for dredging

4 garlic cloves, crushed and peeled

1 lemon, with rind, thinly sliced

½ cup pitted green olives, cut into strips

¼ cup drained tiny capers in brine

1 cup white wine

¼ cup lemon juice

3 tablespoons chopped fresh Italian parsley

Lay the veal out on a cutting board, and pound the slices with a meat mallet to an even ¼-inch thickness (or have your butcher do this for you). Season the veal with the salt.

Melt 4 tablespoons of the butter with the olive oil in a large skillet over medium heat. Spread the flour on a plate, and lightly dredge a batch of veal, tapping off the excess flour. Lay some of the veal in the skillet so the pieces are not touching. Let the veal caramelize on the edges, just a minute or two, then turn and caramelize the other side. Remove to a plate, and repeat with the remaining veal.

When all of the veal is out of the skillet, increase the heat to high and add the garlic and lemon slices. Turn the lemon slices to caramelize them all over, then toss in the olives and capers. Let the olives and capers sizzle for a minute, then pour the wine and lemon juice into the skillet. Bring the sauce to a rolling boil, then add 1 cup hot water. Boil the sauce until reduced by half, about 4 to 5 minutes; whisk in the remaining 4 tablespoons butter in pieces. Reduce heat so the sauce is just simmering, and slip the veal back in the pan. Simmer just to heat the veal through, a minute or two, taking care not to overcook.

Remove the veal slices to a warm platter. Stir the parsley into the sauce, and pour over the veal.

# Veal Scaloppine Marsala
*Scaloppine di Vitello al Marsala*

This is the quintessential Italian American dish: from the 1950s through the 1980s, every Italian restaurant had it on the menu. It is still one of America's favorite dishes and is easy to make. The important part of the recipe is to begin cooking the meat and mushrooms separately, then combine them at the end so the flavors blend.

Marsala is the special ingredient in this dish. Around the city of Marsala, Malvasia, a varietal of a very aromatic grape, grew in abundance. Wine has been made from this varietal for centuries, and the English took note of it and began importing it. The history of England and the New World needs no retelling, and this is most likely how Marsala made it across the pond. When the Sicilian immigrants settled in America, and rediscovered it, it was a natural reunion.

Melt 4 tablespoons of the butter with 2 tablespoons of the oil in a large, heavy skillet set over medium heat. Shake the flour onto a rimmed plate. Season the veal all over with the salt, and dredge lightly in the flour, tapping off the excess. Add the veal to the skillet, moving it around so it all fits, and cook until browned and caramelized on the edges, about 1 to 2 minutes per side. Remove the veal to a plate.

Increase the heat to medium-high, and add the remaining 2 tablespoons olive oil and the sage leaves to the skillet. Once the sage is sizzling, add the mushrooms and shallots. Add about 2 tablespoons of the Marsala to get the mushrooms cooking. Cook and stir until the mushrooms have released their liquid and all the liquid has cooked away, about 3 to 4 minutes. Pour in the rest of the Marsala and the stock. Bring to a rapid simmer, and cook until the sauce has reduced by half, then whisk in the remaining 2 tablespoons butter in pieces.

Return the veal to the sauce, and simmer until just cooked through, about 1 to 2 minutes. Stir in the chopped parsley and serve.

SERVES 4

6 tablespoons unsalted butter

¼ cup extra-virgin olive oil

All-purpose flour, for dredging

8 slices veal scaloppine (about 1½ pounds)

½ teaspoon kosher salt

6 large leaves fresh sage

1 pound mixed mushrooms (cremini, button, shiitake, etc.), thickly sliced

2 large shallots, finely chopped (about ½ cup)

½ cup Marsala

1 cup hot chicken stock (see page 40)

¼ cup chopped fresh Italian parsley

# Veal Saltimbocca

## *Saltimbocca di Vitello*

Veal saltimbocca, which literally translates as "jumps in the mouth," hails from Rome. It is rather simple, but simplicity is hard to achieve. In the late 1960s, when I worked in Italian restaurants to help pay for my college tuition, veal saltimbocca was always on the menu but never tasted like it did in Rome.

The important flavor ingredients here are the prosciutto and the fresh sage. The early immigrants were curing hams into prosciutto at home, which eventually developed into formal businesses, such as the Volpi & Co. in St. Louis, now known as Volpi Foods. In those days, fresh herbs were hard to find—unless you were Italian and grew them at home. By the time I opened Felidia in the 1980s, fresh herbs were coming to the supermarkets, and by the 1990s, *Prosciutto di Parma* began crossing the ocean, so now the saltimbocca has regained its true flavors. So, unless you use fresh sage, skip it.

SERVES 4

8 slices veal scaloppini (about 1½ pounds)

8 slices prosciutto (about 3 ounces)

12 large fresh sage leaves

¼ cup extra-virgin olive oil

4 garlic cloves, crushed and peeled

2 pounds fresh spinach, washed, stems removed

¾ teaspoon kosher salt

Flour, for dredging

5 tablespoons unsalted butter

¾ cup dry white wine

1 cup chicken stock (see page 40)

Pound the veal to an even ¼-inch thickness with a meat mallet. Cover each piece of veal with a slice of prosciutto, and lightly pound with the back of a knife, scoring the prosciutto so it is embedded in the veal. With a toothpick, pin a sage leaf onto each piece of veal.

Heat 2 tablespoons of the olive oil in a large skillet over medium-high heat. Toss in the crushed garlic; once the garlic is sizzling, add the spinach and season with ¼ teaspoon salt. Cover, and cook until the spinach has wilted, about 3 minutes. Uncover, and cook away any excess liquid, about 3 minutes more. Remove the spinach from the pan, and keep warm while you cook the veal.

Lightly flour the veal scaloppini. Wipe out the skillet, then, over medium-low heat, heat 2 tablespoons butter with the remaining olive oil. When melted, add the veal to the skillet, prosciutto-sage side down. Lightly brown both sides, about 1 minute per side. Remove the veal to a plate.

Wipe out the skillet, and set over medium-high flame. Toss in the remaining butter. When melted, add the remaining sage leaves. Once the sage is sizzling, pour in the wine. Bring to a boil, then add the stock and the remaining salt. Boil until the liquid has reduced by about half, about 5 minutes. Return the veal to the pan, and simmer until just cooked through, about 1 to 2 minutes. Remove the toothpicks, and serve over the spinach.

Veal Saltimbocca and Braised Cauliflower with Tomatoes

# Braised Veal Shank

## Osso Buco

In America, meat was plentiful, and combining good veal shanks with lots of vegetables and herbs and simmering it for hours results in fork-tender meat nestled in a complex and savory sauce. *Osso buco,* literally translated as "a bone with a hole," is a dish that originated in Milan. A favorite then, it still outsells many other meat choices on the menu at Becco, Lidia's KC, and Lidia's Pittsburgh.

Serve this dish with an espresso spoon—or, even better, a marrow spoon—so that your guests can scoop out the marrow as the ultimate delicacy.

SERVES 6

4 fresh bay leaves, or 6 dried bay leaves

1 large sprig fresh rosemary

3 cups chicken broth (see page 40), or more as needed

¼ cup extra-virgin olive oil

Six 2-to-3-inch-thick *osso buco* (veal shank cut in half, tied around the circumference)

1 teaspoon kosher salt

1 large onion, cut into 1-inch chunks

2 medium carrots, cut into 1-inch chunks

2 stalks celery, cut into 1-inch chunks

3 tablespoons tomato paste

1 cup dry white wine

6 whole cloves

2 small oranges, 1 peeled with a vegetable peeler, 1 zest grated

Tie the bay leaves and rosemary together with string. Pour the chicken broth into a small pot and keep warm over low heat.

Heat the olive oil in a large Dutch oven over medium heat. Season the *osso buco* with the salt. When the oil is hot, add the *osso buco* and brown on all sides, about 6 to 7 minutes in all. Remove browned *osso buco* to a plate.

Add the onion, carrots, and celery to the Dutch oven. Cook until the onion begins to soften and all of the vegetables are caramelized, about 5 minutes. Push aside the vegetables to clear a dry spot in the pan, and add the tomato paste. Let it toast for a minute or two, then stir it into the vegetables. Add the wine and the herb package. Bring to a boil, and cook until the wine is reduced by half, about 3 minutes. Drop in the cloves and the orange peel (reserve the zest from the other orange for later). Return the *osso buco* to the pot in one layer, and pour the chicken stock over the top until it is almost, but not quite, covering the *osso buco*. Adjust heat so the liquid is simmering, cover, and cook until the *osso buco* is tender, about 1½ hours.

Once the meat is tender, uncover, and remove the vegetable chunks to a platter. Put the *osso buco* on top of the vegetables. Discard the bay leaf/rosemary package. Bring the liquid in the Dutch oven to a boil, and cook down until saucy, about 4 to 5 minutes. Remove the strings from the *osso buco*. Pour the sauce through a strainer directly over the *osso buco* on the platter, pressing on any remaining vegetable solids with a wooden spoon. Sprinkle the orange zest over the top, and serve.

# Veal Milanese

*Scaloppine alla Milanese*

This dish is traditionally made with veal, but is also delicious when made with pork or chicken. However, the best way is with tender veal chops, pounded while still on the bone, then boned, breaded, and fried. Served on the bone is a bit more expensive than the boneless-leg cut, so, if you want to splurge, by all means buy 4 or 6 chops to make this recipe. In restaurants in Milano most likely you would be served Milanese on the bone.

Lay the veal out on a cutting board, and pound slices with a meat mallet to an even ¼-inch thickness (or have your butcher do this for you). Season the veal with ¼ teaspoon salt.

Whisk together the eggs, parsley, lemon zest, and a pinch of salt in a shallow bowl. Spread the flour and bread crumbs in two shallow bowls or rimmed plates. Lightly dredge the veal in flour and tap off the excess. Dip the veal in the beaten eggs, letting the excess drip back in the bowl, then coat the veal in bread crumbs.

Heat the vegetable oil and butter in a large skillet over medium heat. When the butter is melted and the oil is hot enough that the tip of a piece of veal sizzles on contact, add a batch of veal to the skillet. Cook until the veal is golden brown and crispy, about 2 minutes, then turn. Cook until the second side is browned and crispy and the veal is just cooked through, about 2 minutes more. Remove the veal, drain on paper towels, and repeat with the remaining veal. Season the hot cutlets with remaining salt.

Serve this dish topped with a green salad, including tomato and some fresh mozzarella, dressed with a squirt of lemon juice.

SERVES 4 TO 6

8 slices boneless veal (see headnote) (about 1½ pounds)

½ teaspoon kosher salt

4 large eggs

¼ cup chopped fresh parsley

Finely grated zest of 1 lemon

All-purpose flour, for dredging

2 cups fine dry bread crumbs

½ cup vegetable oil

4 tablespoons unsalted butter

 # BEEF

# Braised Beef Rolls

*Braciole di Manzo*

The *braciola,* stuffed beef rolled and braised, was and still is part of the Sunday pasta sauce tradition in many Italian American homes across America. If you travel through the Italian communities around America today and ask people, "What dish do you remember eating at home on Sunday?," the answer is often pasta with *braciole* and meatballs. Meat was far more available in America than back home in Italy, and adding it to a tomato sauce enhanced the ritual Sunday meal, when the whole family was assembled around the table.

A *braciola* is easy to make: once you have gathered all the ingredients and rolled them into a thin beef slice, it cooks in the tomato sauce for several hours, rendering a delicious pasta sauce to coat some rigatoni and fork-tender *braciole* to eat with braised escarole and olive-oil-mashed potatoes.

SERVES 6

1 cup milk

2 cups stale bread cubes

2 to 2½ pounds boneless bottom-round beef rump roast, trimmed of fat

½ cup chopped fresh Italian parsley

2 hard-boiled eggs, coarsely chopped

¼ cup pine nuts, toasted

5 tablespoons extra-virgin olive oil

Pour the milk over the bread cubes in a bowl, and let soak while you slice the beef.

Slice the beef into 2-to-3-ounce slices (ideally, you want twelve pieces). Pound the slices all over with a mallet to about ¼ to ⅛ inch thick. If slices tear, don't worry—you can patch as necessary, by overlapping the torn pieces of meat.

For the filling: Squeeze the excess milk from the bread, and put the bread in a large bowl. Add the parsley, eggs, pine nuts, 1 tablespoon olive oil, and 1 teaspoon salt to the bread bowl. Season with pepper.

Lay the pounded beef slices out flat on your work surface, and season with salt. Evenly divide the filling among the slices, approximately 2 to 3 tablespoons for each slice, then spread to within 1 inch of the edge on all slices. Put a piece of provola cheese lengthwise in the middle of each slice. Roll the slices lengthwise, and pin the rolls closed with toothpicks by pinching the meat.

Heat the remaining oil in a large Dutch oven over medium heat. Season the *braciole* with salt, and add to the pot to brown on all sides, about 2 to 3 minutes on each side, in batches if necessary. Remove the browned *braciole* to a plate, and toss the onion into the pot. Cook until the onion is softened, about 4 to 5 minutes, then add the garlic. Cook a minute or two, until the garlic is sizzling, then pour the white wine into the pot. Increase heat, bring to a boil, and cook until the wine is almost evaporated, about 4 to 5 minutes. Pour in the tomatoes. Slosh out the tomato cans with 1 cup hot water each and add that as well. Season with the oregano, peperoncino, and the remaining 2 teaspoons salt.

Return the sauce to a boil, return the beef rolls to the pot, and adjust the heat to maintain a steady simmer. Cover, and cook until the *braciole* are very tender, 1¼ to 1½ hours. If the sauce is too thin, remove the *braciole* to a plate and reduce the sauce over high heat until it thickens to a gravy consistency.

1 tablespoon kosher salt, plus more for seasoning

Freshly ground black pepper to taste

4 ounces mild provola cheese, cut into ¼-inch sticks (you will need 12 pieces)

1 medium onion, chopped (about 1½ cups)

4 garlic cloves, crushed and peeled

1 cup dry white wine

Two 28-ounce cans Italian plum tomatoes, preferably San Marzano, crushed by hand

1 teaspoon dried oregano

¼ teaspoon peperoncino flakes

Pan-Seared Steak with Pizzaiola Sauce

# Pan-Seared Steak with Pizzaiola Sauce

*Bistecca alla Pizzaiola*

What is important to remember about this dish is that the steak and the sauce never cook together. That way, all the meat juices remain in the steak; if you were to cook them together, the juices would seep out. Meanwhile, the pepper-and-mushroom sauce remains bright and fresh with the flavor of the tomatoes and vegetables.

SERVES 4

Heat the olive oil in a large skillet over medium-high heat. When the oil is hot, add the sliced garlic. Let the garlic sizzle a minute, then toss in the bell peppers and mushrooms. Season with 1 teaspoon of the salt and the oregano. Sauté until the mushrooms and peppers are caramelized on the edges, about 5 minutes.

Pour in the tomatoes, and slosh out the can with ½ cup hot water, adding that to the skillet as well. Bring to a simmer, and cook, uncovered, until the sauce is thickened and the peppers break down, about 12 to 15 minutes.

Season the steaks with the remaining ¼ teaspoon salt. Sear them in a large cast-iron skillet over high heat until done to your liking, about 4 minutes per side for medium rare. Let the steaks rest for a few minutes while the sauce finishes cooking.

To serve, put the steaks on plates and top with the pepper sauce. Serve immediately.

3 tablespoons extra-virgin olive oil

3 garlic cloves, sliced

1 red bell pepper, cut into 1-inch strips

1 yellow bell pepper, cut into 1-inch strips

2 cups sliced white button mushrooms

1¼ teaspoons kosher salt

½ teaspoon dried oregano

14-ounce can Italian plum tomatoes, preferably San Marzano, crushed by hand

Four 8-ounce bone-in shell steaks, about 1 inch thick

NOTE This recipe could also be made with a piece of beef tenderloin, seared and then sliced.

# Italian American Meatloaf

*Polpettone*

One would think that meatloaf is very American, but its origins are actually in a German colonial dish of minced pork mixed with cornmeal. Italians serve it a lot as well, and in this rendition the cultures blend deliciously with the addition of a *pestata*, a paste of carrots, celery, and onions. Not only does the meatloaf taste delicious, but it is foolproof, moist every time. The leftovers reheat as if just cooked, and Italians love to serve it with roasted potato wedges.

**SERVES 10 OR MORE**

2 cups cubes of country bread with crust

1 cup milk

2 medium carrots, cut into chunks

2 medium stalks celery, cut into chunks

1 medium onion, cut into chunks

1½ pounds ground beef

1½ pounds ground pork

1 bunch scallions, trimmed and chopped

1 cup grated Grana Padano or Parmigiano-Reggiano

1 cup marinara sauce (see page 108) or puréed canned tomatoes

½ cup chopped fresh Italian parsley

2 teaspoons kosher salt

1 teaspoon dried oregano

2 tablespoons extra-virgin olive oil

Preheat the oven to 375 degrees F.

Put the bread cubes in a medium bowl, and pour the milk over them. Let the bread soak until it is soft. Meanwhile, combine the carrots, celery, and onion in a food processor, and pulse to make a fine-textured paste or *pestata*.

When the bread is soft, squeeze out the excess milk and put the bread in a large mixing bowl. Mix the *pestata*, ground meats, scallions, grated cheese, marinara sauce, parsley, salt, and oregano with the bread, using your hands to distribute all of the ingredients evenly. Oil a 10-by-15-inch Pyrex or ceramic baking dish with the olive oil. Form the meat mixture into a loaf in the oiled pan.

Place in the oven, and bake until browned and cooked through (the center of the meatloaf should read 165 degrees F on an instant-read thermometer), about 1 hour and 15 minutes. Let cool for 10 minutes before slicing.

About dried oregano: I typically like fresh herbs, but in the case of oregano I prefer it dried. However, I do not like the jarred product: I always buy a bouquet of dried oregano, from either Italy or Greece. It comes wrapped in a plastic bag and is easy to handle. Just rub the oregano in the plastic between your hands and shake the loose leaves out from one side. Then wrap the bouquet to seal it, and store in a dry place for next time.

Oregano is great to flavor sauces, stuffing, in braised meats, and on pizza and focaccia. I even use it when I make myself sunny-side-up eggs with grated Grana Padano.

Back on Arthur Avenue: Salumi hanging at the
Calabria Pork Store; weighing meat on a
scale at Biancardi Meats

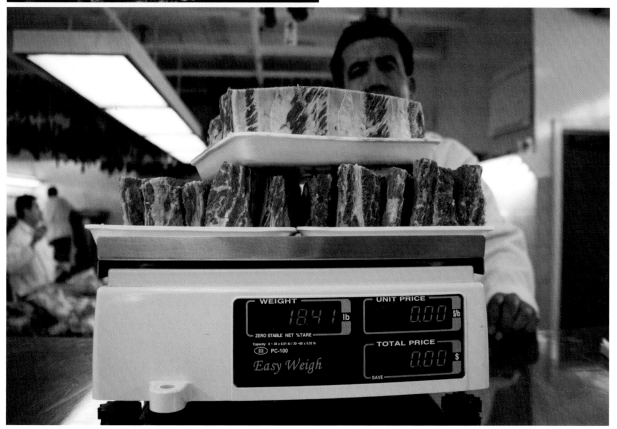

 # LAMB

# Italian Lamb Stew

*Stufato d'Agnello*

Italians eat a lot of lamb, especially in the spring and summer. I recall that on every major holiday I would always see the whole animal slowly turning on the spit, and it was indeed delicious. I particularly liked to nibble on the rib bones, and my second-favorite was part of the shoulder blade. But when there was no holiday, the slaughtered animals were butchered and sold and enjoyed as lamb shanks, chops, and stews. For this dish, either the boneless shoulder meat or boneless leg of lamb could be used, but the shoulder is more economical, and I am sure this cut is what the Italian immigrants used. In this slow cooking process, the flavors harmonize and the meat becomes fork-tender.

SERVES 8

4 pounds boneless lamb shoulder, trimmed, cut into 1-inch cubes (once trimmed, lamb will yield about 3 pounds cubes)

4 teaspoons kosher salt

All-purpose flour, for dredging

10 tablespoons extra-virgin olive oil

1 cup chopped celery

1 cup chopped onion

4 garlic cloves, crushed and peeled

2 cups dry red wine

2 carrots, peeled and cut into 1-inch chunks

Season the lamb with 2 teaspoons salt. Pour the flour into a rimmed dish. Dredge the lamb in flour, tapping off the excess. Heat 3 tablespoons of the olive oil in a large Dutch oven over medium heat. Add half of the lamb, and brown on all sides, about 6 to 7 minutes. Remove the cooked lamb to a plate, and repeat with the remaining lamb.

Meanwhile, combine 3 tablespoons of the oil, the celery, onion, and garlic in a food processor and pulse to make a fine-textured paste or *pestata*. When all of the lamb has browned and been removed, pour 4 more tablespoons of oil into the Dutch oven over medium-high heat, and scrape in the *pestata*. Cook, stirring, until the *pestata* dries out and begins to stick to the bottom of the pan, about 10 minutes. Return the lamb to the pot, and stir to coat the lamb with the *pestata*.

Pour the red wine over the lamb, and bring to a boil. Boil until the wine is reduced by about half. Add the carrots, rosemary, dried oregano, and tomatoes to the pot. Rinse out the tomato can with 1 cup of water and add that as well. Stir in the remaining 2 teaspoons salt.

Bring to a simmer, cover, and cook 1 hour. Plop in the potatoes, cover again, and cook until the potatoes are almost tender, about 20 to 30 minutes. Uncover, and add the bell peppers. Cook, uncovered, until the bell peppers are tender and the sauce has thickened, about 20 minutes more.

1 large sprig fresh rosemary

1 teaspoon dried oregano

28-ounce can Italian plum tomatoes, preferably San Marzano, crushed by hand

1 pound red potatoes, cut into 1-inch chunks

2 red bell peppers, cut into eighths

Jeremy, the young grandson of the Bonino family at LBJ Farms in Gilroy, California, takes a good nap.

Lamb with Roasted Peppers; Broccoli with Garlic and Anchovies

# Lamb with Roasted Peppers

*Spezzatino d'Agnello con Peperoni Arrostiti*

Peppers are a New World product, but they rapidly took hold in Italian soil, especially in the regions of Calabria, Basilicata, and Sicily, in southern Italy. Most of the early immigrants came from these regions and, missing many of their traditional products, found a friend in the peppers they found in America and used them abundantly. Peppers are used much more in Italian American cooking than in Italian cooking, and can be found in recipes such as sausage and peppers, peppers frittata, chicken cacciatore with peppers, veal and peppers, and, as it would follow, lamb with peppers. A sturdy two-foot pepper plant yields an abundant quantity of peppers, and was a favorite planting in the small backyard gardens of Italian immigrants.

**SERVES 8 OR MORE**

- 3 to 3½ pounds boneless lamb shoulder, trimmed, cut into 2-inch cubes
- 1 tablespoon kosher salt
- All-purpose flour, for dredging
- ¼ cup extra-virgin olive oil
- 3 tablespoons vegetable oil
- 2 medium onions, cut into 1-inch chunks
- 4 medium carrots, cut into 1-inch chunks
- 5 garlic cloves, chopped
- 2 fresh bay leaves, or 3 dried bay leaves
- 1 cup dry white wine
- 1 tablespoon dried oregano
- 2 tablespoons red-wine vinegar
- 4 roasted red bell peppers, jarred or freshly roasted, cut into 1-inch-thick strips

Season the lamb with 2 teaspoons salt. Spread flour on a plate, and dredge the lamb in flour, tapping off the excess. Heat the olive oil and vegetable oil in a large skillet or shallow Dutch oven over medium-high heat. Add the lamb, and brown on all sides, about 8 minutes. Remove the browned lamb to a plate.

Add the onions, carrots, and garlic to the skillet or Dutch oven. Once they are sizzling, reduce the heat to medium and toss in the bay leaves. Cook until the garlic is fragrant, about 1 minute. Pour ½ cup of the white wine into the pot so the garlic doesn't burn. Return the meat to the pot, sprinkle with the oregano, and let cook over gentle heat until the meat juices are released, then dried up again, about 5 minutes. Pour in the remaining ½ cup white wine, bring to a simmer, then cover and cook until lamb is tender, about 1 hour. Check occasionally to make sure the lamb is still cooking in liquid. If not, reduce the heat to keep the bottom of the pan from drying up.

When the lamb is tender, uncover and pour in the vinegar and the remaining teaspoon salt. Cook, uncovered, until the liquid is almost gone, about 5 minutes. Add the roasted-pepper strips, and cook until the flavors come together, about 5 minutes.

# ❦ PORK

# St. Louis, Missouri

I visit St. Louis often, to do events, go to conventions, and host dinners that showcase Bastianich wines. It is not too far from Kansas City, where we have our restaurant Lidia's, so when I visit the restaurant I make a trip to St. Louis as well. In St. Louis I have good friends in the Bommarito family: Tony Bommarito and his son, wine distributors, make sure that the Bastianich wines are available in St. Louis and, for that matter, in all of Missouri. Tony and his brother Vincent and family run Tony's restaurant, where I have had many a delicious meal, and Vincent, his wife, Martha, and I have been known to travel to Italy together to explore and find new Italian flavors and products to bring back to our restaurants. St. Louis has a great Italian heritage, and there are many good Italian restaurants to dine at. Some of my favorites are Cunetto House of Pasta, Trattoria Marcella, LoRusso's Cucina, Dominic's, Giovanni's on the Hill, Rigazzi's, and Charlie Gitto's.

My most recent trip was purely for research. We knew there was a strong Italian American community there, known as "The Hill," and Tanya and I were determined to get to know it. Armed with a detailed street map, we took a cab from downtown St. Louis and ended up on Marconi Avenue. The streets were lined with small houses, most of them with fenced-in yards and small porches. On our walk, I could almost hear the humming of conversation on those porches as it would have been in its Italianissimo days, 1900 to 1950.

And indeed I did hear a tender voice calling, "Lidia . . . Lidia, is that you, Lidia?" Rocking on a small chair was a woman with a wide-brimmed straw hat, gray strands of hair streaming out to frame her kind, gentle face with its welcoming smile. A large pin of the Madonna adorned the left shoulder of her blue sweater. A black Labrador began barking and wagging his tail as she addressed us. "Lidia, I have been watching you for years. Come!" Slowly we approached and climbed onto the porch. As we talked, I learned that Anna Feronato, seventy-nine, had lived with her parents, Gilda and Domenico, on The Hill. They came to the United States from Vicenza, in the

Veneto region of Italy. Most of the immigrants on The Hill were from Lombardy and Sicily.

She was born and raised in the small house across the street, which she pointed out to us. "It had two rooms, and we were five kids. I slept with my sister until the day she got married, and when she left, I felt like a piece of me had left with her. We all grew up to be good people, and in turn raise good families. The shoemaker lived two houses down, the baker three houses up, and the street was always full of children playing."

The church bells rang as we talked, the sound coming from not too far away. Anna informed us it was the bells of St. Ambrose Church, the church built by the immigrants—the center of the community, where everybody gathered to pray, to celebrate, to be grateful, and to help new immigrants. A bronze statue of an immigrant family graces the entrance to the church now. Ah, now it's clear—St. Ambrosio, the patron saint of Milano, the capital of Lombardy, always longing for home.

Let's meet in St. Louis!

We said goodbye to Anna, and since it was lunchtime, Tanya and I headed for the oldest Italian restaurant on The Hill, Rigazzi's, just down the road from Anna's house. It was on their menu— among "Italian-Stuffed Pork Chops," "Pasta 3 ways—Ziti, Ravioli, and Cavatelli" with a slice of garlic bread—that we encountered the "Parmiciano" sandwich. It was a delicious tender veal cutlet topped with savory tomato sauce and melted mozzarella (see page 74). However, one major observation: the cutlet was made of chopped veal, then breaded and fried. It was a first for me—a cutlet made of chopped meat?

It all became clear a few months later, when I went to Memphis to do a dinner and a book signing at a fund-raising event for the Brooks Museum of Art. The morning before the event, Thayne and Anne Muller, the chairs of the event, took me to breakfast. The best breakfast in Memphis was to be had at the Cupboard, which the Cavallo family has been running for generations. We had grits and sausages, country-ham steak with red-eye gravy, biscuits with white gravy, and a country-fried steak. All was delicious, but what intrigued me most was the fried steak—chopped beef made into a flat patty, then breaded and fried. As they explained it, country-fried steak is an old tradition in the South.

St. Louis came back to mind. Those Italian immigrants must have experienced the country-fried steak somewhere, and ingeniously used the technique of chopping less expensive and tougher cuts of veal to turn it into a "veal cutlet." Ingenious indeed, and most likely how the "Parmiciano" came to be.

I found the story of the St. Louis pizza quite interesting, so I had to go to Imo's

Pizza, opened in 1964 by Ed and Margie Imo, where supposedly this pizza was born. It was indeed different from any pizza I had had before: here the pizza crust has a texture between a cracker and shortbread (see page 87). Piled on top is a unique cheese mixture, a response to the memory of the milky-velvety mozzarella cheese found on pizza in Italy. Legend has it that the original owner of Imo's, Ed, used to lay tile for a living and so was accustomed to cutting things into squares—thus the distinctive shape of the slice.

Another Italian family institution in St. Louis is Volpi—"the taste of Italy since 1902"—producers of prosciutto, salami, and cured meats. It was important to immigrants to keep a traditional Italian table. How could they set up an Italian table for Sunday dinner without prosciutto? Immigrant artisans who had the talent, like the Volpi family, opened small businesses and turned them into national and international conglomerates. The Volpis hailed from around Modena, the epicenter of Italian prosciutto curing, where *Prosciutto di Parma* comes from, and knew the tradition of curing prosciutto well.

When I was a child, every November, almost like a ritual, my family saw to the slaughter of the pig that my grandmother had been feeding all year. It was a time to celebrate, because that one two-hundred-kilogram animal would provide the means to feed the entire family for the next year. We made prosciutto out of the two hind legs, *spaletta* (a skinnier, less prized version of prosciutto) out of the two front legs, pancetta from the belly, and *ombolo* (cured filet preserved in rendered fat, along with the dried sausages, to remain moist). Whenever my grandmother got cooking, she would dig into the solid rendered fat and fish out a fat-covered piece of the cured meat; with that she would begin browning her *soffritto,* which became the base for a sauce or a soup. I especially liked it when she would cut up the *ombolo* or sausages in small pieces, lightly brown them in the rendered fat, and then throw in a few whisked eggs just gathered from the chicken coop and serve it with a slice of her country bread. Life was good. . . .

Every bit of the animal was used. We made *sanguinaccio* (blood sausage), regular sausages, *musetto* (head cheese), cured hoofs, ears. Even the tail was cured, and the bladder, after some drying out, was turned into a soccer ball for the boys. So I understand how prosciutto is essential to the Italian family table, and how the Volpi family prospered with their products. Today *Prosciutto di Parma,* as well as the prosciutto from San Daniele di Friuli, the region I hail from, is imported and readily available in the United States. But the Volpi family continues to do well and produce diversified cured-meat products in St. Louis.

# Sausage and Peppers

*Salsiccia e Peperoni*

I am sure all of you have had some version of sausage and peppers, but this one is easy to make, and the sausages remain juicy. The idea is to cook the sausages and vegetables separately, and then combine them at the end. Even though sausage and peppers seem to be quintessentially Italian, peppers are a New World food and were introduced to Italy only after the discovery of the Americas. Italians quickly made them their own and incorporated them on their table. So, when they came to America as immigrants, peppers were abundant and used with excess in many of the Italian American dishes. They are now ubiquitous at every Italian street fair.

SERVES 6 TO 8

2 tablespoons extra-virgin olive oil

12 sweet Italian sausage links (about 3 pounds)

8 garlic cloves, crushed and peeled

4 hot pickled cherry peppers, stemmed, halved, and seeded (leave some of the seeds in if you like the heat)

3 small onions, peeled, cut into wedges attached at the root end

1 pound mixed mushrooms, halved (button, cremini, shiitake)

3 red, yellow, or orange bell peppers, quartered, or cut into sixths if large

½ teaspoon kosher salt

Heat the olive oil in a large skillet over medium heat. Add the sausage, then cover and cook, turning occasionally, to brown all sides, about 10 minutes in all. Uncover, add the crushed garlic and cherry peppers, cover, and cook until the sausages are cooked all the way through, about 10 minutes more. Remove sausages to a plate.

Add the onion wedges and cover the skillet. Cook, tossing occasionally, until the onions begin to caramelize on the edges, about 5 minutes. Add the mushrooms and bell peppers, season with the salt, stir, and cover. Cook, stirring occasionally, until all of the vegetables are tender, about 10 minutes more. Uncover, increase heat to get the pan juices simmering, and cook until the juices have reduced and glazed the vegetables, about 10 minutes.

Return the sausages to the skillet. Cook and toss to heat the sausages through and combine flavors, about 3 minutes more.

Pork Chops Capricciosa

# Pork Chops Capricciosa

*Costolette di Maiale alla Capricciosa*

This is one of those one pot meals that bring spice and a lot of flavor to the table. It is a traditional method of cooking and combining ingredients, especially in southern Italy, and many restaurants have it on their menus, especially those in the Little Italys across America. This method of adding the cherry peppers, potatoes, and vinegar can be used with chicken or rabbit, too. The spice gives the dish its "capricious" name.

Season the pork chops all over with 1 teaspoon salt. Spread the flour on a plate, and dredge the chops in flour, tapping off the excess.

Heat the oil and butter in a large skillet. When the butter melts, slide in the chops and brown on one side, about 3 to 4 minutes over medium heat. Turn the chops, and plop the garlic cloves in the spaces between them in the pan. When the garlic starts to sizzle, drop in the pickled cherry peppers, and let sizzle until the chops are browned on the second side, another 3 to 4 minutes.

When the chops are browned, push them to one side of the skillet and add the potatoes. Season the potatoes with 1 teaspoon of the salt, and sprinkle in the rosemary needles and the red onions. Cover the skillet, and cook, gently turning everything occasionally, until the onions and potatoes are almost tender, about 12 to 15 minutes.

Pour the vinegar into the skillet. Cook, covered, until the potatoes and onions are tender and the chops are cooked through, about 5 minutes more. Uncover, and season with the remaining ½ teaspoon salt. If the sauce is too liquid, remove chops to a plate, increase heat to high, and boil until the sauce is thickened to your liking. Pour the sauce over the chops.

**SERVES 6**

Six 8-ounce bone-in pork loin chops, about 1 to 1½ inches thick

2½ teaspoons kosher salt

All-purpose flour, for dredging

2 tablespoons extra-virgin olive oil

2 tablespoons unsalted butter

4 garlic cloves, crushed and peeled

6 pickled hot cherry peppers, halved and seeded (or leave some seeds in for more heat)

1½ pounds russet potatoes, peeled and cut into 2-inch chunks

2 sprigs fresh rosemary

2 red onions, peeled and cut into eighths

½ cup white-wine vinegar

# Pork Rolls with Sun-Dried Tomatoes and Prosciutto

*Involtini di Maiale con Prosciutto e Pomodori Secchi*

Pork meat, which is nutritional and economical, is used a lot in Italy. Using the tenderloin for this dish guarantees a tender result, but one can use boneless shoulder or leg meat instead, cutting it into thin slices. You can also make this dish with chicken breast or boneless chicken legs. The sun-dried tomatoes bring a lot of flavor to the dish; I use them whole, or sometimes purée them in a processor and spread the paste on the meat, but in this recipe I slice them.

SERVES 6

2 pork tenderloins (about 2 pounds total)

½ teaspoon kosher salt

12 oil-packed sun-dried tomatoes, drained, sliced into ½-inch pieces

4 ounces prosciutto, thinly sliced

2 tablespoons unsalted butter

2 tablespoons extra-virgin olive oil

All-purpose flour, for dredging

6 to 8 large fresh sage leaves

20 ounces cremini mushrooms, thickly sliced

Cut each pork tenderloin crosswise, on the bias, into six equal slices—twelve slices in all. Pound each piece of pork to an even thickness of about ½ inch, using a meat mallet. Season the pork on both sides with the salt.

Lay the pork slices flat on your work surface, and evenly place the sliced sun-dried tomatoes on top. Layer on the sliced prosciutto, cutting or tearing it to fit on the pork slices without draping over the sides. Roll up the pork lengthwise, enclosing the filling, and secure with toothpicks.

Melt the butter and the oil in a large skillet over medium-high heat. Pour the flour onto a plate. Dredge the pork rolls lightly in the flour, tapping off the excess. Sear the pork in the skillet on all sides, about 8 to 10 minutes in all, then push the pork to one side of the pan and toss in the sage leaves. Once the sage is sizzling, add the mushrooms, and cook until they are starting to brown, about 3 to 4 minutes. Redistribute the pork rolls evenly in the pan with the mushrooms, then cover the skillet and lower the heat. Simmer until the mushrooms have given off their juices and the pork is tender, about 10 to 12 minutes.

Domenico Susi at Sulmona Meat Market in Boston

# Pork or Chicken Rolls with Fontina and Asparagus

*Involtini di Maiale o Pollo con Fontina ed Asparagi*

Rollatini are a popular dish in Italy. They can be made with chicken, veal, or pork, and the stuffing can be just about anything you like, but do include cheese. The delight of rollatini is the oozing cheese when you cut into them. So, whatever you do, do not skimp on the cheese.

This dish was very popular on the menus of Italian American restaurants in the sixties and seventies. Fontina has great melting qualities; when it is not readily available, Muenster cheese is often substituted.

SERVES 6

1½ teaspoons kosher salt, plus more for pot

12 medium asparagus spears

1 cup chicken stock (see page 40)

¼ cup dried porcini

2½ pounds boneless pork loin, trimmed

2 plum tomatoes, seeded and sliced into thin strips

8 ounces Italian fontina, cut into thin strips

1 tablespoon chopped fresh Italian parsley

All-purpose flour, for dredging the pork

6 tablespoons unsalted butter

2 tablespoons extra-virgin olive oil

8 fresh sage leaves

1 pound mixed mushrooms, sliced (button, cremini, shiitake, chanterelles, etc.)

1 cup dry white wine

Preheat oven to 450 degrees F.

Bring a medium pot of salted water to boil. Slip in the asparagus, and blanch until crisp-tender, about 3 minutes. Run the asparagus under cold water and pat dry. Bring the chicken stock to simmer in a small pot, then add the dried porcini and remove from heat. Let soak.

Slice the pork crosswise into twelve slices. Pound the pork slices to an even ½-inch thickness with a meat mallet. Season the pork with ½ teaspoon salt. Lay the pork on your work surface, and evenly divide the tomato strips on top, lining them along the longer side of the pork slice. Put an asparagus spear on each slice, and cut to fit on the meat. Divide the fontina evenly among the pork slices, and sprinkle with the parsley. Roll up the pork snugly around the asparagus, tomato, and cheese, tucking the ends in, to enclose the filling. Close each roll with a toothpick or two.

Drain the porcini from the broth, reserving the soaking liquid, and coarsely chop. Spread the flour on a rimmed plate. Dredge the pork rolls in the flour, tapping off the excess. Heat 3 tablespoons of the butter and the oil in a large Dutch oven over medium heat. When the butter is melted, add the pork rolls and brown on all sides, about 5 to 6 minutes. Remove the browned rolls to a plate.

Toss the sage leaves into the Dutch oven. When the sage is sizzling, add the sliced fresh mushrooms and chopped porcini. Season with the remaining 1 teaspoon salt, and sauté until the mushrooms are browned and softened, about 6 minutes. Pour the white wine into the Dutch oven with the remaining 3 tablespoons butter. Bring to a boil, and let the wine reduce by half, about 2 minutes; then pour in the porcini soaking liquid. Bake the pork, uncovered, until cooked through, about 18 to 20 minutes. If the pork is cooked but the sauce is too thin, remove the pork to a plate and reduce the sauce on the stovetop. Remove toothpicks before serving.

Wild asparagus, like these from the market in Pula in Croatia, are perfect for this dish.

# RUBS, MARINADES, AND GLAZES

## Wild Fennel Rub

*Profumo al Finocchio Selvatico*

In Italy, wild fennel grows literally wild, all over the place, especially in the south of the peninsula. During my travels across America, I also found it abundant as well, wild and cultivated, but the wild fennel grows especially aromatic in California. You can buy wild-fennel seeds to make this recipe, but you can just as well harvest them in the wild by picking the dried flower tops that harbor the fennel seeds in late summer. The anise-licorice flavor brings freshness to any meat when used as a rub.

THIS MAKES ENOUGH FOR 2 MEDIUM-SIZED CHICKENS, OR SEVERAL POUNDS OF CHICKEN PARTS OR PORK CHOPS

4 tablespoons wild-fennel seeds, or 3 tablespoons wild-fennel powder

Finely grated zest and juice of 1 lemon

6 garlic cloves

½ cup olive oil

If using fennel seeds, grind to a powder in a spice grinder.

Combine the fennel powder, lemon juice, zest, and garlic in a mini–food processor, and process to a smooth paste. Drizzle in the olive oil with the machine running to make an emulsified paste.

NOTE  Rub the meat with the mixture and let marinate for 2 to 3 hours before cooking.

Wild fennel growing at Andy Boy Farms in California

# Beer Marinade for Chicken or Pork Roast

*Marinata di Birra per Pollo o Maiale*

I like to use a light beer, but heavier and darker beer adds more complexity.

MAKES ABOUT 2 CUPS,
ENOUGH FOR 3 TO 4 POUNDS
OF CHICKEN OR PORK ROAST

1½ cups beer

2 tablespoons brown sugar

1 tablespoon balsamic vinegar

1 teaspoon peperoncino flakes, ground to a powder

3 garlic cloves, sliced

2 teaspoons kosher salt

4 fresh bay leaves, or 6 dried bay leaves

½ teaspoon ground cloves

Stir all the ingredients together in a bowl until mixed well.

Set the meat in a plastic bag, and pour in the marinade. Seal the bag, set in a bowl, and refrigerate overnight. Dump the meat and marinade into a baking pan, and bake as usual.

Because of the ever-evolving ethnic cultures, Polcari's in Boston has expanded its range to include spices from all around the world.

# Dry Porcini Rub

*Profumo di Porcini Secchi per la Carne*

This rub is great for steaks, roasts, rotisserie chicken, lamb, and even hamburgers. Make sure the meat is patted dry before applying the rub. It is great on the grill or roasted in the oven. When added to hamburgers it adds flavor and also keeps them moist.

Toss all the ingredients together in a bowl. Pat the meat dry, and then cover it well with the rub. Keep in the refrigerator overnight, then grill or roast as desired.

MAKES ABOUT 1½ CUPS

½ cup sugar

2 tablespoons celery salt

2 tablespoons finely ground black pepper

1 cup porcini powder

# Marinade for Chicken

*Marinata per Pollo*

This marinade works best when the chicken is cut up in pieces; I also use it to marinate lamb shoulder or lamb leg cut into pieces.

Toss all the ingredients together in a ziplock bag large enough to hold the chicken pieces. Add the chicken pieces, and toss well to cover, then let marinate for 4 to 5 hours. Roast the chicken with the marinade.

MAKES ENOUGH FOR 3 TO 4 POUNDS OF CHICKEN

5 garlic cloves, sliced

4 tablespoons fresh rosemary needles

½ cup extra-virgin olive oil

4 tablespoons red-wine vinegar

Kosher salt and black pepper to taste

# Moist Rosemary Rub for Chicken, Steak, or Lamb

*Stroffino Umido per Pollo, Bistecca, o Agnello*

Make sure the meat is patted dry before applying the rub. This rub is great to flavor roasted potatoes as well. Toss 2 or 3 tablespoons of it with cut-up potatoes in a roasting pan, and roast as usual.

MAKES ENOUGH RUB FOR
APPROXIMATELY 3 TO
4 POUNDS OF MEAT

2 tablespoons finely ground black pepper

2 tablespoons kosher salt

6 tablespoons fresh rosemary needles

8 garlic cloves, diced

½ cup extra-virgin olive oil

Combine all the ingredients in a blender, and pulse into a coarse paste. Rub the meat with the paste, let sit for 1 hour, then grill or roast—whichever you prefer.

# Pork Marinade

*Marinata per Maiale*

This marinade is great with all cuts of pork: loin, butt, ribs, fresh ham, or chops.

Combine all the ingredients in a plastic bag, and mix well. Add pork and toss to cover the meat. Set in a bowl and let sit overnight. Grill or roast the meat.

MAKES ENOUGH FOR 3 TO
4 POUNDS OF PORK

⅛ teaspoon freshly ground black pepper

1 teaspoon kosher salt

½ cup balsamic vinegar

1 tablespoon honey

6 fresh sage leaves, shredded

4 garlic cloves, sliced

2 tablespoons freshly grated horseradish

½ cup pomegranate juice

Blueberry Frangipane Tart and Italian Rum Cake

# Desserts

# Ricotta Cookies

*Biscotti di Ricotta*

These cookies are moist and delicious and simple to assemble. In the Italian cuisine, ricotta seems to be able to resurface deliciously in every course. Since it is a by-product of making cheese, the shepherds had plenty of ricotta. Hence, many desserts are still made from it, like these delicious cookies.

MAKES ABOUT 3½ DOZEN

2¼ cups all-purpose flour

1 teaspoon baking powder

Pinch kosher salt

1 cup granulated sugar

½ cup (1 stick) unsalted butter, at room temperature

2 large eggs

8 ounces fresh ricotta, drained

½ teaspoon vanilla extract

FOR THE GLAZE

2 teaspoons lemon zest, plus ¼ cup lemon juice

2 cups confectioners' sugar, sifted

Preheat oven to 325 degrees F. Sift together flour, baking powder, and salt into a bowl, and set aside.

Line two baking sheets with parchment paper.

Cream the sugar and butter in a mixer fitted with the paddle attachment on high speed until light and fluffy, about 2 minutes. Reduce the speed to medium, and crack in the eggs one at a time, beating well between additions. Plop in the ricotta, vanilla, and lemon zest, and beat to combine. Add the flour mix, and beat on low until just combined, but do not overmix.

Drop the dough in heaping tablespoons onto the baking sheets. Place in oven, and bake, rotating pans halfway through the baking time, until the cookies are puffed, golden, and cooked all the way through, about 20 to 22 minutes. Remove from oven, and cool on wire racks.

When the cookies are completely cool, make the glaze. In a bowl, whisk together the confectioners' sugar and lemon juice to make a smooth glaze. Adjust the consistency with a little water or more confectioners' sugar to make the glaze thick enough to stick to the cookies when dipped. Hold each cookie with two fingers, then dip the top of the cookie in the glaze and let dry on racks until all are done. Let dry for 2 hours before storing.

# Almond Pine Nut Cookies

*Amaretti con Pinoli*

This is one of the most classic Italian American cookies, and it is one of the easiest to make. In Italian American culture, these are simply known as pinoli cookies, the word "pinoli" referring to the pine nuts that top the cookies, a distinct Sicilian twist.

The personal element in making this cookie is to ask yourself if you like it chewy or crumbly crisp—the difference is all in the baking time. With the timing given below, they will be a bit chewy, but of course it depends on how big you make them. Oh, so many variables in cooking!

Preheat oven to 350 degrees F. Line two baking sheets with parchment.

Crumble the almond paste into the work bowl of a food processor and process until the paste is in fine crumbs. Sprinkle in the sugar with the motor running. Once the sugar is incorporated, add the egg whites and orange zest. Process to make a smooth dough, about 20 to 30 seconds.

Spread the pine nuts on a plate. Form the dough into 2-tablespoon-sized balls by rolling it between the palms of your hands, then roll the dough in the pine nuts until coated, then place on baking sheets. Bake until lightly golden and springy to the touch, about 13 to 15 minutes. Let cool on baking sheets for about 5 minutes, then transfer the cookies to cooling racks to cool completely.

**MAKES ABOUT 30 COOKIES**

Two 7-ounce tubes almond paste

1 cup sugar

2 large egg whites

Finely grated zest of 1 orange

1½ cups whole pine nuts

Easter egg wreaths adorn windows at Lulu's Sweet Shop in Boston's North End during the Easter holiday season.

# Rainbow Cookies

*Dolcini Tre Colori*

There are many traditional Italian almond-paste cookies, but rainbow cookies seem to have been created in America by Italian American immigrants to honor the colors of the Italian flag. The recipe requires patience, but it is not difficult. As with most baking recipes, follow the instructions carefully and you will be rewarded with cookies that everybody loves and that keep moist for more than a week. You can find them in Italian bakeries year-round, but they are especially popular at Christmastime.

MAKES ABOUT 3 DOZEN

2½ sticks unsalted butter, softened, cut into pieces, plus more for the pans

2 cups all-purpose flour, plus more for the pans

8 ounces almond paste

1 cup sugar

4 large eggs, separated

½ teaspoon kosher salt

1 teaspoon red food coloring (gel or paste preferred)

1 teaspoon green food coloring (gel or paste preferred)

Two 15-ounce jars smooth (not chunky) apricot jam

1½ pounds bittersweet chocolate, chopped

Preheat the oven to 350 degrees F. Butter and flour three 15-by-10-inch rimmed sheet pans, and line the bottoms of the pans with parchment paper.

Combine the almond paste and all but 2 tablespoons of the sugar in an electric mixer fitted with the paddle attachment. Mix on medium speed until you have fine crumbles. Add the butter, a few pieces at a time, and pulse until well mixed. Plop in the egg yolks, one at a time, and mix until the batter is smooth. Sprinkle in the salt, and mix. Sift in the flour, and mix until just combined.

The rainbow cookies at Torrisi Italian Specialties in New York City's Little Italy

Whisk egg whites in a bowl until foamy. While whisking, slowly add the remaining 2 tablespoons sugar, and whisk until firm peaks form. Fold about a third of the egg whites into the batter to lighten it, then gently fold in remaining egg whites.

Divide the batter evenly into three bowls. Leave one bowl plain, without any coloring. Add the red food coloring to one bowl, stirring to make a deep-salmon color. Add the green food coloring to the last bowl, stirring to make a medium-green color. Spread batter into each of the prepared pans with a spatula. Bake, rotating pans to opposite racks, until the cakes are cooked through and just beginning to brown around the edges, about 8 to 10 minutes. Remove from oven, let the cakes cool completely on wire racks, then remove from pans.

Trim each of the layers to even out the thickness of the cakes. Put the green cake layer back, cut side up, into one of the lined pans. Spread one jar of jam over the cake, almost all the way to the edges. Place the plain layer of cake on top of the jam. Spread the remaining jar of jam almost all the way to the edges of the plain layer. Place the red layer on top of the jam, cut side up. Wrap the entire cake in plastic, and top with another pan, weighted with cans. Chill in the refrigerator 4 hours or overnight.

Melt chocolate in a double boiler. Unwrap the cake, and place on a wire rack over a rimmed baking sheet. Pour and spread the chocolate over the top of the cake, using a spatula to guide the chocolate over the top and down the sides of the cake. If the kitchen is cool, let the chocolate harden that way; if it is warm, clear a space in the refrigerator to place the cake, and let the chocolate harden. When the chocolate is about halfway set, gently rake the topping with the tines of a fork or a dough scraper with dentals, starting from the end of the chocolate covering all the the way to the other end, slightly undulating the lines as you move along. Repeat until all of the chocolate has indented stripes. Let the chocolate set completely.

Using a serrated knife, cut the set and decorated layers into three dozen rectangles, using the outer sides to form perfectly cut rectangles.

# St. Joseph's Fig Cookies

*Biscotti ai Fichi di San Giuseppe*

As much as Italians would like to claim the fig as their own, it has deep origins somewhere in Mesopotamia. Then it made its way into the Middle East and the rest of the world. The Egyptians adored the fig and praised it as a medicinal and delicious fruit. Fig breads and sweets were made way before the Italians started, but you cannot take away the importance the fig cookie has on St. Joseph's Day for the Italian culture. As the legend goes, during a year of drought and famine in Sicily, people would gather and pray to St. Joseph for help. St. Joseph responded by sending heavy rains. To this day Sicilians respond by making the St. Joseph's table full of offerings, and among them must be the St. Joseph's fig cookies.

MAKES ABOUT 4½ DOZEN

½ cup honey

6 tablespoons grappa or brandy

4 teaspoons orange juice

2 cups diced dried black figs

3¾ cups all-purpose flour

½ cup granulated sugar

1½ teaspoons baking powder

¼ teaspoon kosher salt

2 large eggs

6 tablespoons milk

2 teaspoons lemon zest

¼ teaspoon ground cinnamon

½ cup walnut pieces

FOR THE GLAZE

1½ cups confectioners' sugar, or as needed

3 tablespoons milk, or as needed

Bring the honey, grappa, and orange juice to a boil in a saucepan. Add the figs, and bring to a simmer. Simmer until the figs are plumped, about 2 to 3 minutes. Remove from heat, and let cool thoroughly while you make the dough.

Combine the flour, sugar, baking powder, and salt in a food processor. Beat together the eggs and milk in a small bowl. Pour the egg-milk mixture into the dry ingredients with the processor running, and pulse until the dough forms a ball, about 15 to 20 seconds. Knead the dough on the counter once or twice, then wrap in plastic wrap and let it rest in the refrigerator at least 1 hour or until firm.

When the fig filling is cool, scrape it into a food processor and sprinkle in the lemon zest and cinnamon, processing all to make a smooth paste. Then add the walnuts, and pulse a few more times, leaving the nuts slightly chunky. Transfer the filling to a bowl, and freeze until firm, about ½ hour.

Preheat the oven to 350 degrees F. Divide the dough in half, and roll one half, between sheets of parchment paper, into a rectangle about 16 by 7 inches. Cut the rectangle in half to make two long strips. With the palms of your hands, roll a quarter of the filling into a log and set it down on the center of one strip. With a pastry brush, lightly wet one long edge of the strip, then, using the parchment paper underneath, begin to roll the dough until you have covered the filling and the two ends of the dough meet. Press gently and seal the log. Roll the seam underneath, and flatten the top slightly with the palm of your hand. Repeat with the remaining dough and filling; you will now have four long logs with filling in the center.

Cut the logs into 1-inch lengths using a wet knife, and place in the same position on parchment-lined baking sheets. Place in oven and bake until golden, about 15 to 20 minutes. Transfer the cookies to a wire rack and cool completely.

To glaze cookies: Sift the confectioners' sugar into a bowl, and whisk in the milk to make a smooth glaze. Dip a cookie into the glaze; it should stick to the cookie in a thin layer. If not, adjust the consistency of the glaze with more milk if too dense or confectioners' sugar if too loose.

Let the glazed cookies dry on wire racks.

St. Joseph's Fig Cookies

# Kansas City, Missouri

When we decided to open Lidia's in Kansas City in 1998, in the Freight House, in the Crossroads Arts District, near Crown Center, it was our first venture outside of New York City. I get asked all the time: why Kansas City? It is smack in the middle of America, and, after all, we wanted to share our product, traditional Italian food, with America beyond New York. Little did we realize how effective the Italian immigrants before us had been in bringing Italian culture and food to Kansas City.

Columbus Park served as Kansas City's Italian neighborhood; it is not far from the city center, with the Missouri River defining one of the neighborhood's boundaries. Columbus Park was the area in which many immigrants got off the riverboat; many Italian immigrants came to Kansas City between 1890 and 1920 to work on the railroad and in the meat-packing industries, and Columbus Park became the Italian ethnic neighborhood, full of mainly Sicilian immigrants.

I wanted to know the history of the Italians before me in Kansas City, so, on a misty March morning, Tanya and I went to Columbus Park to see what Italian heritage was still there. We were told to visit Scimeca's Italian Sausage Co., which had been making sausages for over seventy-five years, and La Rocca Grocery. Mike greeted us at La Rocca's, but it is Joseph La Rocca who runs the shop, with his two nephews Mike and Frank. One could see, from all the black-and-white pictures on the wall, that the store had a family story to tell. The story was of Italy, of Italian food products needed by the immigrants, and now by stores and restaurants selling and cooking Italian.

The La Roccas were very generous with their time and information, so much so that Mike walked us two blocks over to the Holy Rosary Church, which is the epicenter of all things Italian in the neighborhood. The ladies of the church still put on quite an altar for St. Joseph's Day, and, as luck would have it, we were visiting in March, a few days before St Joseph's. When Mike La Rocca took us to the Holy Rosary Church, he showed us the basement, where about fifty of the local Italian women and men were busy baking, icing, and molding the cakes and cookies that would decorate St. Joseph's altar. We could have been in Sicily, the setting was so real and intense.

On the way back, we passed La Sala's Deli, started in 1921, which is still making

Union Station in Kansas City, Missouri; the inside dining room at Lidia's Kansas City

po' boy sandwiches today. The roads are lined with small two-story homes, very similar to the homes in many other Little Italys across America. All have the essential porch for the evening *chiachierata,* for which families and friends gather. The Italians are well incorporated in the matrix that is Kansas City. The Mirabiles are a long-established family in the restaurant business in Kansas City; even before we opened a restaurant there, I recall traveling with Mrs. and Mr. Jasper Mirabile, Sr., to Italy, with Gruppo Ristoratori Italiani. He was a chef dedicated to his Italian roots, always curious, and wanting to bring the regional food of Italy back to his restaurant, Jasper's. His son Jasper Jr. now carries on the legacy of his Italian father and continues to run Jasper's, a great Italian restaurant.

The Parisi Brothers line have supplied the Kansas City area with traditional Italian products for generations. They distribute Lidia's Pasta and Lidia's Sauce in the Midwest, and have hundreds of thousands of pounds of Italian cheese aging in the Kansas City caves.

The Garozzos are a family that I know less well, but they have done Italy proud with their Italian restaurants in Kansas City. And the American Italian Pasta Company, North America's largest producer of dry pasta, is based in Kansas City, in the heart of the Midwest, where there is plenty of grain to make pasta.

# Orange Cookies

*Biscotti all'Arancia*

These traditional Italian cookies are as easy as it gets, and everybody loves them. The citrus flavoring renders them inviting, and most likely you have had them at Italian family celebrations such as weddings, confirmations, and baptisms. Not too sweet, these cookies will keep for a week or two in a cookie container.

Sift together the flour, baking powder, and salt into a bowl. Cream the butter and sugar in a mixer fitted with the paddle attachment on medium speed until light and fluffy, about 2 minutes. Crack in the eggs, one at a time, beating well between additions. Pour in the vanilla, the juices, and the zest, and beat to combine. Turn the mixer off, pour in the flour mixture, and mix on low just to combine. Wrap the dough in plastic, and let rest in refrigerator 1 hour.

Roll the dough into four logs, about 1½ inches in diameter and 10 to 12 inches long. Chill or freeze the logs for 20 minutes, until firm enough to cut without losing their shape.

Preheat the oven to 350 degrees F. Cut the logs into ½-inch rounds, and place on parchment-lined baking sheets. Place in oven, and bake until the cookies are golden, about 15 minutes. Remove, and cool the cookies completely on wire racks.

To glaze the cookies: Sift confectioners' sugar into a bowl, and whisk in the orange juice to make a smooth glaze. Dip a cookie in the glaze; it should stick to the cookie in a thin layer. If not, adjust the consistency of glaze with more juice or confectioners' sugar. Dip the top of the baked cookies in glaze, and let dry on wire racks.

MAKES ABOUT 6½ DOZEN

3 cups all-purpose flour

2 teaspoons baking powder

¼ teaspoon kosher salt

1½ sticks unsalted butter, at room temperature

½ cup plus 1 tablespoon granulated sugar

3 large eggs

1 teaspoon vanilla extract

2 tablespoons orange juice

2 tablespoons lemon juice

1 tablespoon orange zest

FOR THE GLAZE

2½ cups confectioners' sugar, or as needed

¼ cup orange juice, or as needed

Maria Merola of Maria's Pastry Shop in Boston gets ready for the holidays.

# Fried Sweet Dough

## *Zeppole*

Every region of Italy makes some form of these fried dough pastries called *zeppole*. They can be sweet or savory, with goodies embedded in the dough or stuffed after frying. *Zeppole* are especially prepared for St. Joseph's Day (March 19), during Lent, for the Christmas Vigilia (Eve), and on holidays. When sweet, they are usually dusted with powdered sugar and served hot. You can find them in every Little Italy in the United States around the holidays.

Heat the vegetable oil in a wide saucepan to 350 degrees F. (The oil should be an inch or two deep.)

For the filling: Whisk together the ricotta, mascarpone, amaretto, and confectioners' sugar in a bowl until smooth. Stir in the candied peel and chocolate. Refrigerate the filling while you make the *zeppole.*

Combine 1 cup water, the butter, sugar, and salt in a medium saucepan over medium heat. Bring to a boil, stirring to melt the butter. While stirring, add the flour and zest all at once. Cook, stirring constantly, until the dough dries out and pulls away from the sides of the pan. Remove from heat, and add the eggs one at a time, stirring vigorously to incorporate one before adding the next, until the dough is completely smooth.

Drop a batch of *zeppole* in 2-tablespoon dollops (a small ice-cream scoop is perfect for this) into the oil, making sure you don't crowd them in the pan, because they will grow in size. Fry the *zeppole,* turning on all sides, until light and golden brown all over, about 5 minutes per batch. Drain on paper towels, and repeat with the remaining dough.

To serve, when cold cut the *zeppole* in half with a serrated knife and with a pastry bag pipe the filling onto the bottom half. Cover and dust with additional confectioners' sugar if desired.

### MAKES ABOUT 1½ DOZEN

6 cups vegetable oil, or as needed, for frying

FOR THE FILLING

2 cups fresh ricotta, drained

1 cup mascarpone

3 tablespoons amaretto

½ cup confectioners' sugar, sifted, plus more for dusting

2 tablespoons finely chopped candied lemon peel

2 tablespoons finely chopped candied citron or orange peel

2 tablespoons finely chopped bittersweet chocolate or mini–chocolate chips

FOR THE DOUGH

4 tablespoons unsalted butter

1 tablespoon granulated sugar

½ teaspoon kosher salt

1 cup all-purpose flour, sifted

Finely grated zest of 1 lemon

4 large eggs, at room temperature

# Fried Sweet Dough Balls with Honey
*Struffoli*

Fried dough balls rolled in honey, collected in a mound and topped with sprinkles, is a typical Christmas vision at Italian American bakeries across the United States. What I found fascinating is that even though the cookies and prepared food are very good, it is all about memories and traditions. *Struffoli* seem to be a big part of that Italian American memory.

SERVES 8 TO 10

4 cups all-purpose flour

½ cup plus 1 tablespoon sugar

Finely grated zest of 1 lemon

Finely grated zest of 1 orange

¼ teaspoon ground cinnamon

Pinch kosher salt

4 large eggs

1 teaspoon vanilla extract

2 tablespoons unsalted butter, cut into small pieces

2 cups honey

Vegetable oil, for frying

Sprinkles, for garnish

Pulse together the flour, 1 tablespoon sugar, the lemon zest, orange zest, cinnamon, and salt in a food processor. Whisk together the eggs and vanilla in a separate bowl. Pour the egg mixture into the food processor with the motor running, and then drop in the butter pieces. Process until a smooth dough forms, about 30 seconds. Knead the dough on the counter a few times, then wrap in plastic and let rest at room temperature for 1 hour.

Make the syrup: Combine the honey, the remaining ½ cup sugar, and ⅓ cup water in a medium skillet over medium heat. Bring to a boil, and cook until syrupy, about 6 to 7 minutes.

In the meantime, heat 1 inch of vegetable oil in a pot or straight-sided skillet to about 365 degrees F, or until a piece of dough sizzles on contact. Pinch off a golf-ball-sized piece of dough, and roll into a rope about ½ inch wide. Cut the rope of dough into pieces the size of a hazelnut and roll into balls. Repeat until all the dough is used.

Fry the *struffoli* in batches until puffed and deep golden, about 3 to 4 minutes per batch. Drain on a paper-towel-lined baking sheet, and repeat with the remaining *struffoli*.

Toss the *struffoli* in the hot honey syrup, in batches, as many at a time as you can fit without crowding. Roll the *struffoli* in the syrup until well coated, then scoop them up with a slotted spoon or strainer, and drain off the excess syrup. Stack the *struffoli* in layers on a plate to form a cone, sprinkling each layer with the sprinkles as you stack. Repeat until all the *struffoli* are coated in the honey syrup and covered in sprinkles. Drizzle the completed stack of struffoli with any remaining syrup, if you wish.

# Southern New Jersey

Just a short ride from New York City, Hammonton, New Jersey, is a town which has one of the densest concentrations of Italians in the United States as well as being the blueberry capital of America. With a population of about thirteen thousand, 55 percent are of Italian heritage. Italian immigrants were skilled at agriculture and knew well how berry bushes grew. Blueberry farming in Hammonton offered jobs and the Italian immigrants came.

The Italian immigrant farmers came to New Jersey mostly from southern Italy and from Sicily. These pioneers arrived in southern New Jersey looking for homes not too far from the sea, where the climate was congenial and the land was cheap. Until 1850, the Pine Barrens of New Jersey were looked upon as wasteland, not good farming land for dairymen or the grain grower. But the sandy soil was perfect for growing berries. Although blueberries are not a fruit that was used in Italy, wild or cultivated berries are a big part of the Italian table. As a child, I collected wild blackberries from the thorny bushes in the forest and climbed the mulberry tree to harvest its delicate fruit. So, when I found myself in the midst of the blueberry bushes at Indian Brand Farms, I had my hands full in no time and ate my fill, since I love blueberries. Indian Brand Farms was established in 1895 by Michael DiMeo, who emigrated from Sulmona, in Abruzzo. It is still run by the brother-and-sister team Billy DiMeo and Ann DiMeo Montellite, and their family welcomed us warmly with a tableful of blueberries prepared in many ways, from bowls of blueberry jam, to blueberry cobbler, to a blueberry tart, scones, and ice cream (topped by blueberry crème fraîche). Even the plates had blueberries painted on them.

Billy DiMeo and sister Ann Montellite at their home in Hammonton, New Jersey—the blueberry capital of the world!

Not too far away, in Woolwich Township, we visited the Maugeri Farms, known as one of the largest Italian family-operated farms in New Jersey. Sure enough, when we arrived the whole family, three generations, were waiting for us with a tableful of food. Mamma Anna Maugeri served Tanya and me a wonderful lunch of roasted peppers, eggplant parmigiana, asparagus fritters, and tomato-and-cucumber salad, all just picked that morning, as well as some chicken cutlets thrown in for good measure. It felt like a homecoming, a welcome such as my mother would prepare.

But we came to the Garden State to see the beautiful vegetables, and Joe Maugeri, Jr., took us to see the never-ending fields of wonderful salad tomatoes, which extended to another endless field of plum and Roma tomatoes. Then came the yellow bursts of zucchini flowers, and certainly underneath those flowers were the crispy zucchini; then the shiny purple eggplants and peppers—and on and on the fields went. This vibrant family farm was started in 1922 by Salvatore Maugeri, and the business today, now over six hundred acres, is operated by brothers Sam and Joe Jr., all under the watchful eye of Mamma Anna.

When I first came to the United States as a young immigrant in 1958, the Catholic Relief Services, which brought us here, found a home for us in North Bergen, New Jersey. My American roots first took hold in New Jersey, and I feel quite at home here. And I thank my following in New Jersey, for whenever I do an event or a book signing here now, the response is tremendous.

With brothers Joe Jr. and Sam Maugeri, along with the matriarch Anna Maugeri, while visiting the Maugeri farm in southern New Jersey

# Blueberry Cobbler

*Crostata Coperta di Mirtilli*

Neither blueberries nor cobblers are Italian, but one of the largest and oldest blueberry farms in what is called the blueberry capital of the world is Indian Brand Farms, run by the DiMeo family of New Jersey. I had a wonderful blueberry cobbler when I visited, and my version of that recipe is simple and delicious.

Preheat oven to 400 degrees F.

Whisk together the sugar, lemon juice, and ⅓ cup water in a 9-inch deep-dish pie plate. Whisk in the cornstarch until smooth. Add the blueberries and bananas, and toss to coat.

Pulse to combine the flour, sugar, baking powder, and salt in a food processor. Drop in the butter pieces and almond slices, and pulse five or six times, until the dough looks like coarse crumbs. Drizzle in ⅓ cup cold water, and pulse just until the dough comes together. Dollop the dough in heaping spoonfuls over the blueberry mixture.

Place in oven, and bake until the blueberries are bubbling and the topping is cooked all of the way through and golden brown, about 35 to 40 minutes. Serve warm.

SERVES 6 TO 8

FOR THE FILLING

1 cup sugar

Juice of 1 lemon

3 tablespoons cornstarch

2 pints blueberries

2 bananas, peeled and sliced ½ inch thick

FOR THE TOPPING

1½ cups all-purpose flour

¾ cup sugar

1½ teaspoons baking powder

Pinch kosher salt

1½ sticks unsalted butter, cold, cut into small pieces

½ cup sliced almonds

Perfect blueberries, ripe for picking, at Indian Brand Farms in Hammonton, New Jersey

# Blueberry Frangipane Tart

*Crostata di Frangipane con Mirtilli*

The *crostata,* or tart, is as common in Italy as pie is in America. It is one of the best ways to showcase seasonal fruit as a dessert. Once the crust is made for the filling, add some marzipan and some plump, juicy seasonal blueberries. There is no need to add cornstarch to bind the juice of the berries—they will nestle into the marzipan.

SERVES 8 OR MORE

FOR THE CRUST

1¼ cups all-purpose flour

⅓ cup sugar

¼ teaspoon kosher salt

1 stick unsalted butter, cold, cut into small pieces

FOR THE FILLING

10-ounce can almond paste

½ cup sugar

2 large eggs

2 tablespoons all-purpose flour

1 pint blueberries

¼ cup pine nuts, lightly toasted

For the crust: Pulse to combine the flour, sugar, and salt in the work bowl of a food processor. Drop in the butter pieces, and pulse just until the dough comes together in clumps, about ten to fifteen pulses. Press the dough into the bottom and up the sides of a 9-inch tart pan. Let the crust rest in the refrigerator for 30 minutes.

Preheat the oven to 325 degrees F. Combine the almond paste and sugar in the same food-processor bowl (no need to wash it). Process until you have fine crumbs, then crack in the eggs and sprinkle in flour. Process until smooth.

Spread the almond filling in an even layer in the chilled tart shell. Top with the blueberries, and sprinkle with the pine nuts. Bake until the crust is deep golden brown and the filling is set, about 1 hour to 1 hour and 20 minutes.

Holding the freshly picked plump blueberries in the fields of Indian Brand Farms in Hammonton, New Jersey

# Boston's North End

Maybe Paul Revere should have shouted, "The Italians are coming!" instead of the British. He might have done so had he known that, at the area's peak in 1930, forty-four thousand Italian immigrants would be in the area, less than one square mile, known as the North End. The first Italian immigrants came in the 1860s from Genoa and settled in a three-block area off Fulton Street. The Genoese were followed by the Campanians, followed by the Sicilians, the Avellinese, the Neapolitans, and the Abruzzesi. *Paesani* tended to stick together even within the North End, creating micro-neighborhoods based on Italian regionality.

The North End is Boston's oldest neighborhood. In colonial days, it was an affluent area, and shipbuilders and merchants had businesses near the wharf. Eventually, the Bostonians opted for larger living quarters, and the houses became walk-up tenements for Irish, then Jewish, and then Italian immigrants. The Italians began as laborers at the port: peddlers, fishermen, and dockworkers. But by 1920, the North End had twenty-eight Italian physicians, six Italian dentists, eight Italian funeral homes, and, along just one block of Hanover Street, four or five Italian barbershops.

Most businesses were family run and owned, and many of them turned into success stories. Pietro Pastene, for instance, started a food store in the North End in 1874 which would later become the New York–based Pastene Corporation. Boston Macaroni Company, headed by John Ponte, began operations in 1890, and the Prince Macaroni Company started by three Sicilian friends—LaMarca, Seminara, and Cantella. "Wednesday is Prince Spaghetti Day" became a famous slogan in the late 1960s.

With many of its cobblestone streets still intact, and most of its merchants still of Italian descent, the North End has become a place to go for good Italian meals, pastries, or specialties, and a tourist destination for those visiting Boston. Of the Little Italys I have visited in the United States, the North End of Boston and Arthur Avenue in New York City are among the most vibrant remaining. The North End still retains the nostalgic old-neighborhood feel, but offers all the elements for a contemporary Italian lifestyle. I go to Boston often because of business, since my station, WGBH, is in Brighton. I used to go periodically to visit with Julia Child when she lived in Cambridge. My

Owner Jeff Cirace of Cirace & Son by
the wall of amari

son Joseph attended Boston College. For four years we would visit him and enjoy the city, and I would take him and his schoolmates by the dozen to lunches and dinners. Durgin-Park, in Quincy Market, was a stop for oversized prime ribs, but a visit to the North End was on the agenda every time.

Sometimes it was for a cannoli or *sfogliatella* at Maria's Pastry Shop, and feisty Maria Merola would always be there to charm us. Other times we would pick up Italian sandwiches at Salumeria Italiana, on Richmond Street, a quaint specialty store where one can still find everything Italian and delicious. The selection of Italian restaurants is endless in the North End: many of the old neighborhood grocery stores, fruit vendors, clothiers, and cobblers have disappeared and have been replaced by restaurants. The neighborhood today is still composed of more than 41 percent Italian Americans, and the *lingua franca* in the neighborhood is still Italian.

On a recent visit on a rainy day in May, Tanya and I wanted to visit Jeff Cirace at Cirace & Son. This 104-year-old wine and liquor store, which has always been in the Cirace family, carries more than three hundred different labels of grappa. A whole wall is dedicated to Italian amari, and Jeff prides himself on the limoncello that is made in Italy just for his store. His Italian-wine selection is extensive as well, all from good producers, and I was delighted to see the Bastianich Vespa on the shelves. Jeff is a man passionate about his profession, and although the "& Son" is on the door of this charming store, he made sure to tell me that his daughter, an attorney, just moved above the store, in the house where his grandparents lived, and wants to carry on the tradition.

Keeping with tradition, we went to visit the Sulmona Meat Market on Parmenter Street. Domenico Susi, the owner, was behind the counter on that rainy morning. He bought the store from the original owners in the 1960s, and now he and his son run the family business, making more than 120 pounds of hand-tied sausages a day, for which they continue to win awards. Business is good, but he laments that there used to be fifteen butchers in the North End and now there are only two.

It was pouring, and time for a cappuccino, so we made it to Modern Pastry, on Hanover Street. We ordered cappuccino, an *ampolina* (a stuffed pastry that looks like a

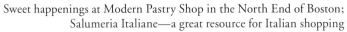

Sweet happenings at Modern Pastry Shop in the North End of Boston;
Salumeria Italiane—a great resource for Italian shopping

lobster tail), and a piece of their famous ricotta pie. Soon enough John Picariello, who runs the shop with his father, Giovanni, came over eagerly to share his family story. There are six generations of pastry chefs in the family, and as John sat at our table to continue the story, more and more pastries arrived, and we were obliged to keep tasting as we listened to their Italian story in Boston's North End.

# Butter Rum Cake

*Ciambellone al Rum*

I guess you could consider this one of many Bundt cakes, but it is different indeed. Though it is shaped and baked in a Bundt pan, the almond slices and the abundant soaking in rum syrup make it Italian American, as it has been made for generations at the Scialo Bros. Bakery in Providence, Rhode Island. Second-generation daughter Carol Gaeta still mans the store, and on the morning when we appeared unannounced, a happy couple, mother and father of the bride, were picking up all the traditional cookies and cakes to be set out at the wedding reception that evening. Italian Americans from Rhode Island, now living in Chicago, they wanted to celebrate this momentous occasion in their family's Italian American style in their native state.

Once the excited mother of the bride had packed all her goodies in the car and left, we had an opportunity to chat with Carol. She took us in the back, where baking sheets full of the butter-rum cake were lined up for soaking. Carol was generous enough to let us taste it, and gave us this delicious recipe to share with you.

**SERVES 10 TO 12**

FOR THE CAKE

2 sticks unsalted butter, at room temperature, plus more for buttering the pan

6 ounces almond slices, finely ground in a food processor, plus 2 ounces almond slices, toasted

4 cups all-purpose flour

1 tablespoon baking powder

½ teaspoon kosher salt

2 cups sugar

3 large eggs

6 large egg yolks

Zest of 1 large lemon

⅓ cup milk

Preheat the oven to 350 degrees F. Brush the inside of a 12-cup-capacity nonstick Bundt pan with softened butter, and coat the pan with the 2 ounces of toasted almond slices. Stir together the flour, ground almonds, baking powder, and salt in a bowl.

Cream the two sticks of butter and the sugar in a mixer fitted with the paddle attachment on medium-high speed until light and fluffy, about 2 to 3 minutes. Add the eggs and yolks a few at a time, letting them get incorporated before adding more. When all the eggs and yolks have been added, add the lemon zest and beat on high for 1 minute. Pour in half of the flour with the mixer on low speed. Once the flour is incorporated, pour in the milk. Finish with the remaining flour, and mix just until you have a smooth batter.

Pour the batter into the prepared pan, and bake until a tester inserted in the center of the cake comes out clean, about 1 hour to 1 hour and 10 minutes. Cool the pan on a rack for 15 minutes. Loosen the sides of the cake with a paring knife, and invert onto the rack.

Make the syrup while the cake is still warm: Combine 2 cups water, the sugar, and the rum in a small saucepan. Bring to a boil, and cook

With Carol Scialo Gaeta at Scialo Bros. Bakery in Providence, Rhode Island; Carol's famous butter rum cakes

down by about a quarter, or until you have a thin syrup. Transfer the warm cake to a rimmed plate or baking sheet. Brush the cake with the syrup, letting the cake soak up the syrup for a few minutes between brushings, until all the syrup is used.

FOR THE SYRUP
¾ cup sugar

½ cup dark rum

# Boston Cream Cake

*Dolcino di Boston alla Crema Pasticcera*

Boston cream cakes do not sound Italian, but this recipe was given to me by Italians. At Scialo Brothers Bakery in Rhode Island, we found trays upon trays of little chocolate-covered spheres. I thought they were some version of a *cassata* (a Sicilian domelike cake stuffed with ricotta cream—see page 318), but instead they were individual Boston cream pies. The French chef Sanzian, who worked at the Parker House Hotel (now the Omni Parker House) in Boston is credited with having invented the Boston cream pie. Italian or not, these were delicious.

MAKES 12

FOR THE PASTRY CREAM

½ cup sugar

4 teaspoons cornstarch

Pinch kosher salt

2 cups milk

2 large eggs

FOR THE CAKES

1½ cups all-purpose flour

1½ teaspoons baking powder

½ teaspoon baking soda

⅛ teaspoon kosher salt

6 tablespoons unsalted butter, softened

¾ cup sugar

2 large eggs

1 tablespoon extra-virgin olive oil

1 teaspoon vanilla extract

1 tablespoon orange zest

¾ cup freshly squeezed orange juice

Make the pastry cream: Whisk together the sugar, cornstarch, and salt in a medium pot. While whisking, pour in the milk. Set the pot over medium-low heat, and heat the mixture to just below boiling. Meanwhile, whisk the eggs in a large bowl. Remove the pot from heat, and pour the milk slowly into the eggs, whisking constantly, to temper the eggs. Pour the mixture back into the saucepan, and stir constantly over medium-low heat until the mixture thickens and just begins to simmer. Immediately scrape the mixture into a clean bowl. Let it cool slightly, then cover the surface of the pastry cream with plastic wrap. Refrigerate several hours or overnight, until chilled and thickened.

Make the cakes: Preheat the oven to 350 degrees F. Line a twelve-unit cupcake pan with paper liners. Sift together the flour, baking powder, baking soda, and salt onto a piece of parchment.

Cream the butter and sugar in a mixer fitted with the paddle attachment on medium-high speed until light and fluffy, about 2 minutes. Crack in the eggs, one at a time, mixing well between additions. Stir in the olive oil, vanilla, and zest. Beat on high speed for 2 minutes, to lighten and smooth the batter. Mix in the flour in three additions on low speed, alternating with the orange juice, beginning and ending with the flour. Once everything has been added, beat the batter on high speed for about 20 seconds.

Divide the batter evenly among the cupcake liners. Bake until a toothpick inserted in the center of a cupcake comes out clean, about

20 to 25 minutes. Remove the cupcakes from pan, and cool completely on a wire rack.

Make the glaze: Combine the corn syrup, rum, salt, and 2 tablespoons water in a small pot. Bring to a boil, and simmer until slightly thickened, about 2 minutes. Put the chopped chocolate in a heat-proof bowl, and pour the syrup over the chocolate. Stir until the glaze is smooth and shiny and all of the chocolate is melted. Let cool until thickened and just warm to the touch.

To assemble the cakes: Remove the cupcake liners from the cakes. Split the cakes at the base of the cap with a serrated knife.

To finish: Invert one cake, and place the cake cap on a plate, cut side up. Spoon the pastry cream onto the cake top, then top with inverted cake bottom, like an upside-down mushroom. Spoon the hot chocolate glaze onto the base facing you, letting the glaze run down the sides of the cake, spooning on more if necessary. Repeat with the remaining filled cakes.

FOR THE GLAZE

⅔ cup light corn syrup

2 tablespoons dark rum

Pinch kosher salt

8 ounces semisweet chocolate, finely chopped

Boston Cream Cakes

# Pick Me Up
## *Tiramisù*

This is a Cinderella dessert story. From simple leftovers—some coffee, leftover cake or cookies, an enrichment of cream or mascarpone—a prince of a dessert is born. Tiramisù is an Italian creation but its popularity in America began in San Francisco, and today it is as beloved in the United States as it is in Italy. In Italy this kind of dessert is categorized as *dolce al cucchiaio* (desserts to be eaten with a spoon), as is *zuppa inglese*.

Tiramisù can be made in advance, keeps well, is great to serve big numbers, and can even be frozen and remain delicious.

Italian American boys meet at Venda Ravioli, in DePasquale Plaza in the heart of Federal Hill in Providence, Rhode Island, for their mid-morning pick-me-up.

Melt the chocolate in a double boiler over simmering water, and keep it warm in the double boiler.

Meanwhile, whisk the cream in an electric mixer fitted with the whisk attachment until it just holds soft peaks. (Don't overwhip, because you will be whisking it again with the mascarpone, and you don't want to make butter!)

Whisk the mascarpone in a separate bowl with the mixer on medium speed until smooth. Sift in the confectioners' sugar and whisk until smooth. Whisk the whipped cream into the mascarpone until they are just combined. Refrigerate if not using right away.

Combine the espresso and granulated sugar in a medium saucepan set over low heat. Cook until the sugar has dissolved, then stir in the coffee liqueur. Remove from heat, and stir in about two-thirds of the melted chocolate. Pour the chocolate-espresso mixture into a large shallow pan, big enough to soak half the savoiardi at one time. Add half of the savoiardi to the soaking liquid, and soak, turning to coat all sides, until almost soaked through, about 1 minute.

Arrange the savoiardi in two rows in the bottom of an 9-by-13-inch (3-quart) Pyrex dish or ceramic dish to make a tight bottom layer, breaking as necessary to patch empty spaces. Drizzle with a third of the remaining warm melted chocolate. Spread half of the mascarpone in an even layer over the top of the cookies.

Soak the remaining twenty-four savoiardi in the remaining soaking liquid. (You should have used up most of the soaking liquid by this point.) Arrange the soaked savoiardi on top of the mascarpone, just as you did the first layer, and drizzle with another third of the warm melted chocolate.

Spread the remaining mascarpone in an even layer over top. Pour the remaining melted chocolate on top. Use a toothpick or paring knife to make lines at 2-inch intervals connecting the long sides of the pan. Now make perpendicular lines through the chocolate to create a crosshatch pattern. Chill the tiramisù at least 4 hours or up to overnight before cutting into squares to serve.

SERVES 10 OR MORE

1 pound bittersweet chocolate, chopped

2 cups heavy cream

2 cups mascarpone, at room temperature

1 cup confectioners' sugar

2 cups freshly brewed espresso

½ cup granulated sugar

½ cup coffee liqueur

48 savoiardi cookies (ladyfingers)

# Italian Rum Cake

## *Zuppa Inglese*

This moist, creamy, and flavorful dessert, *zuppa inglese* ("English soup"), has its roots in the English trifle and it was thought that it first appeared during World War II, when British soldiers were stationed in Italy with only meager custard rations. However, the recipe appears in Pellegrino Artusi's book, published in 1891, before any Allied forces had been stationed in Italy. Other theories reach as far back as the Renaissance.

*Zuppa inglese* is traditionally made with sponge cake, but I use savoiardi (ladyfinger) cookies, as are used in tiramisù, hence making the assembly much quicker. This dessert was a staple of every Italian American restaurant, and every Italian bakery made a version of it.

SERVES 8 OR MORE

2 cups whole milk

1¾ cups sugar

4 teaspoons cornstarch

Pinch kosher salt

3 large eggs

2 ounces bittersweet chocolate, finely chopped

⅓ cup diced candied orange peel

¼ cup rum

2 cups heavy cream, chilled

⅛ teaspoon ground cinnamon

36 savoiardi cookies (ladyfingers)

For the pastry cream: Pour the milk into a medium saucepan set over low heat. Whisk in ½ cup sugar, the cornstarch, and pinch of salt, and bring the milk to a simmer, just to dissolve the sugar.

Whisk eggs in a medium bowl. While whisking, slowly pour the hot milk into the eggs to temper them, then pour the mixture back into the saucepan. Return the saucepan to medium-low heat, and cook, stirring and whisking, until the mixture just simmers and thickens. Immediately remove from the heat and scrape into a bowl to cool. Mix in the chocolate and orange peel. Refrigerate until chilled and thickened, at least 1 hour.

For the sugar syrup: Bring 3 cups water and 1 cup of the sugar to a boil in a saucepan. Boil until reduced by about a quarter. Remove from heat, stir in the rum, and let cool completely.

When you are ready to assemble the zuppa, whip the cream and remaining ¼ cup sugar to form soft peaks. Fold half of the whipped cream, along with the cinnamon, into the chilled pastry cream.

Make a flat layer with half of the savoiardi in a 9-by-13-inch Pyrex or ceramic dish. Brush with half of the sugar syrup to moisten, then spread half of the pastry cream on top. Top with another layer of savoiardi, and brush on the remaining syrup. Spread the rest of the pastry cream over top in an even layer, then spread with the whipped cream. If you have any savoiardi left, crumble them over the top. Chill several hours, or overnight, to let the flavors blend before serving.

# Italian Cheesecake

*Torta di Ricotta*

Italian cheesecake is one of the easiest Italian desserts to make, and, yes, one can add raisins, orange, or pine nuts. But I recall my grandmother's simple version, made from goat's-milk ricotta with minimal sugar, and it was delicious. In America, the cream-cheese version, of much smoother consistency, is common, but an Italian will willingly partake of the crumbly consistency of ricotta cheesecake, any time.

Preheat oven to 350 degrees F. Brush an 8-inch springform pan with butter on the bottom and sides. Coat the bottom and sides with amaretto crumbs, tapping out the excess. Put the raisins in a small bowl, and pour the rum over them. Let soak while you make the filling.

Beat the eggs, sugar, and salt in a mixer fitted with the whisk attachment on high speed until it is foamy and the sugar has dissolved and no longer feels grainy, about 2 minutes. Plop in the ricotta, mascarpone, and citrus zests. Strain into the batter the rum in which the raisins soaked, and mix on medium until smooth and fluffy, about another 2 minutes. Now fold in the raisins and pine nuts with a spatula.

Put the springform pan on a baking sheet, and pour the batter into the pan, smoothing the top with a spatula. Bake until the edges are set and light golden, but the center is still a bit jiggly, about 1 hour and 15 minutes. Cool completely on a wire rack before removing from pan and serving.

SERVES 10 TO 12

2 tablespoons unsalted butter, softened

½ cup amaretto cookie crumbs (from about 4 or 5 amaretti)

½ cup golden raisins

3 tablespoons dark rum

5 large eggs

1 cup sugar

½ teaspoon kosher salt

4 cups drained fresh ricotta, at room temperature

1 cup mascarpone, at room temperature

Finely grated zest of 1 lemon

Finely grated zest of 1 orange

½ cup pine nuts, toasted

Italian Cheesecake

# Cappuccino Cake

*Dolce di Gelato al Caffè*

I picked up this simple, delicious, and very Italian cake on a visit to Angelo Brocato's ice cream and confectionery in New Orleans. I am sure you will want to make this dessert over and over again. If you are going to freeze it, keep the taste fresh by wrapping it tightly in plastic.

SERVES 8 TO 10

FOR THE CRUST

12 chocolate graham-cracker sheets, crushed (about 2⅓ cups)

3 tablespoons sugar

2 tablespoons espresso powder

Pinch kosher salt

5 tablespoons unsalted butter, melted and cooled

FOR THE FILLING

1 quart coffee ice cream

2 cups heavy cream

2 tablespoons sugar

1 cup sour cream

Preheat the oven to 350 degrees F.

Grind together the graham crackers, sugar, espresso powder, and salt in a food processor to make fine crumbs. Add the melted butter with the processor running, and pulse just to combine. Press the crumbs into the bottom and up the sides of a buttered 8-inch pie plate, making sure the crumbs are evenly distributed. Bake the crust until crispy, about 10 to 12 minutes, then cool completely before filling.

Remove the ice cream from freezer to soften a bit while you make the whipped cream. Whip the cream and sugar in a mixer fitted with the whisk attachment, to form soft peaks. Add the sour cream, and whisk until just combined.

Spread the ice cream in an even layer over the crust. Dollop the whipped-cream mixture on top, and spread upward to a dome shape. Freeze overnight, or until the cream is frozen. To serve, cut with a sharp knife dipped in hot water.

Michelina Brocato serving up gelato and cappuccino cake at Angelo Brocato's in New Orleans

# Italian Ice Cream Cake

## *Cassata*

*Incassare* in Italian means "to put in a box," and in this case the boxing consists of flavored ricotta in a light sponge cake, often decorated with candied fruits and chocolate. It is a dessert that, once filled and sealed, keeps well for a few days. That is why Italian American restaurants had it on the menu: low maintenance with good flavors. This versatile dessert can be filled with various flavors of ice cream, so try substituting that in place of the ricotta filling (in which case you will have to keep the cake in the freezer). Sicilian in origin, *cassata* is most easily found in areas of America that experienced a large influx of Sicilian immigrants, such as New Orleans.

### SERVES 8 OR MORE

#### FOR THE CAKE

Butter, softened, for the cake pan

1 cup all-purpose flour, plus more for the cake pan

½ teaspoon baking powder

6 large eggs

¾ cup granulated sugar

Zest of 1 small orange

#### FOR THE FILLING

1½ teaspoons gelatin powder

3 cups fresh ricotta, drained

1 cup confectioners' sugar

¼ cup finely chopped bittersweet chocolate

¼ cup finely chopped candied lemon peel

#### FOR THE SYRUP

5 tablespoons granulated sugar

2 tablespoons Grand Marnier

For the cake: Preheat the oven to 350 degrees F. Butter and flour the bottom and sides of a 9-inch springform pan. Sift together the flour and baking powder in a bowl.

Whisk the eggs in a mixer fitted with the whisk attachment on high speed until very light and fluffy, about 5 to 6 minutes. With the mixer on medium, slowly pour in the sugar, and mix until thick and glossy, about 1 to 2 minutes, then stir in the orange zest. Fold in the sifted flour with a spatula just until incorporated—don't overmix. Pour the batter into the prepared pan, and bake until a cake tester inserted in the center comes out clean, about 20 minutes. Let the cake cool on a wire rack, then run a knife around the sides of the pan to loosen and unmold.

For the filling: Dissolve the gelatin in 2 tablespoons hot water in a small bowl. Beat the ricotta and confectioners' sugar in a mixer fitted with the paddle attachment on medium speed until smooth, about 2 minutes. Scrape in the dissolved gelatin and mix to distribute. Stir in the chocolate and lemon peel with a spatula.

For the syrup: Bring the sugar to a boil with 1 cup water in a small pot. Boil until reduced by about a quarter, about 2 to 3 minutes. Remove from heat, and stir in the Grand Marnier. Let cool slightly.

To assemble: Line the inside of a 9-inch-diameter bowl with plastic wrap, letting several inches of excess wrap drape down the outside.

Cut the cake into three circular layers of equal thickness, using a serrated knife. Line the bottom of bowl with one cake slice, pressing to fit, and brush with some of the syrup to soak it evenly. Fill half of the cavity of the bowl lined with the cake with some of the filling. Fit another cake layer on top of the filling, pressing to fit snugly to the sides of the bowl, then brush with more syrup. Continue to fill the cavity with the remaining filling, and fit the final layer flat on top. Soak the last layer with the remaining syrup. Fold the excess plastic wrap over the top, and weight top with a heavy plate. Chill overnight, or until the filling is set; if filled with ice cream, set in the freezer.

For the glaze: Sift the confectioners' sugar into a large bowl, and whisk in the lemon juice to make a smooth, spreadable glaze. If necessary, add a little more confectioners' sugar or some water to get the correct consistency.

Remove the cake from the bowl and unwrap. Invert with dome up on a cake plate or stand. Spread the glaze over the top of cake, and let it slide down the sides, guiding it with a spatula to cover the cake completely. Let the glaze set at room temperature before serving.

FOR THE GLAZE

1½ cups confectioners' sugar, plus more if needed

3 tablespoons lemon juice

# Lemon Granita

*Granita al Limone*

Lemon ice is simple and delicious and very Italian. This recipe was given to me by Maria at Carm's in Chicago. It was not too sweet, with a nice tartness, and a bit slushy when she served it to me; I loved it.

**SERVES 12**

4 cups water

1 cup sugar

¾ cup lemon juice (about 2 lemons)

Pour the water and sugar into a small saucepan, and bring to a boil. Boil until the sugar is completely dissolved. Remove from heat, and stir in the lemon juice. Let cool slightly.

Pour into twelve 8-ounce plastic or paper cups, and freeze overnight or until solid. For a granular ice another option is to put the lemon mixture in a wide ceramic baking pan and set it in the freezer, scraping and mixing it every half hour as it solidifies. When all the liquid has solidified into loose crystals it is ready to serve. Spoon into decorative glasses.

Maria de Vivo at Carm's in Chicago serves me an absolutely delicious, mouth-puckering lemon ice.

Lemon Granita (top), Prickly Pear Granita (left), and Spumoni (right)

# Prickly Pear Granita

*Granita al Fico d'India*

Prickly pears—or *fichi d'India,* as they are called in Italy—grow wild and abundant in Sicily and are eaten simply as a fruit, as a salad, or churned into a dessert, as in this recipe for granita. In the Southwestern United States, the prickly pear grows abundant and wild, and when I visited the Salinas Valley in California, I was delighted to see acres upon acres of this cactus plant growing for commercial harvesting. The Mexican culture uses it in their cuisine, but I was especially happy to see a demand for it here in the States. When you find it nice and ripe in your market, buy it and make this simple and delicious granita with it.

SERVES 6 TO 8

10 prickly pears

Juice of 1 orange

Juice of 1 lemon

¼ cup sugar

Peel the skin from prickly pears (wear plastic gloves). Slice the flesh into pieces, then gently push the pear flesh through a medium-holed sieve, pressing the flesh and juice with a wooden spoon or spatula into a bowl, leaving the seeds behind in the sieve. You should have about 2 cups juice.

Mix the orange juice, lemon juice, and sugar into the prickly-pear juice in a bowl, stirring until the sugar dissolves. Pour the granita juice into an 8-inch square metal pan (or a similar size; you want the granita to be an inch deep or less).

Cover, and freeze the granita until crystals begin to form on the sides of the pan, about 30 minutes. Stir and scrape crystals and granita, breaking up any solid parts with a fork. Freeze until firm, scraping mixture with fork every 30 minutes to form icy crystals.

To serve, scrape granita into chilled serving glasses.

Prickly pears growing at Andy Boy Farms

# Spumoni

*Gelato a Tre Colori*

Spumoni is a delicious dessert made from three flavors of ice cream stuffed into a cup, and cut in four when frozen. The ice-cream colors reflect the colors of the Italian flag—red, white, and green—and spumoni has long been a big item on the menus of Italian American restaurants. Spumoni has its origins in a Neapolitan dessert, and supposedly came to America in 1905 with Salvatore Lezza. Lezza's spumoni can still be had on Chicago's Upper West Side. I filled many a cup with my own homemade ice cream in my early restaurant days, in the seventies, but spumoni is still delicious when made with good store-bought ice cream as well.

Here rum gives the spumoni an extra layer of flavor, but the juice of the sour cherries is a great alternative.

SERVES 8 OR MORE

1 pint pistachio ice cream

1 pint vanilla ice cream

1 pint strawberry ice cream

8 sheets chocolate graham crackers

¼ cup rum (or juice from sour cherries; see below)

¼ cup finely chopped unsalted pistachios

One 15-ounce can pitted sour cherries, drained, juice reserved if desired (see above), cherries roughly chopped

Remove the ice cream from the freezer about 10 to 15 minutes before beginning, to let it soften. Line a 9-by-5-inch loaf pan with plastic wrap, letting about 3 or 4 inches hang over each edge.

Put the graham crackers in the bowl of a food processor, and pulse to make fine crumbs. Pour the crumbs into a medium bowl, drizzle with the rum or cherry juice, and add the pistachios. Toss to combine and moisten the crumbs with the rum or juice.

Sprinkle about a third of the crumbs in an even layer in the bottom of the loaf pan. Spread the pistachio ice cream on top in a flat, even layer. Sprinkle with half of the chopped drained cherries, then layer on another third of the crumbs. Spread the vanilla ice cream on top of the crumbs in a flat, even layer. Sprinkle with the remaining crumbs, then the remaining cherries. Spread the strawberry ice cream on top in a flat, even layer. Cover the top of the ice cream with the overhanging plastic wrap, and freeze overnight, or until firm throughout.

To serve: Let the spumoni sit out of the freezer for about 5 minutes. Unwrap, and cut into slices with a serrated knife dipped in hot water.

# Chocolate Soup

*Zuppa al Cioccolato*

I guess you could call this silky chocolate milk, or luscious liquid chocolate pudding. I remember it as a very special treat when I was a child. It is simple and delicious, and, served with some Italian cookies, it becomes dessert.

Bring the milk just to a simmer in a sloped-sided medium pot (so the pudding will not stick in the corners of the pot). Ladle about ½ cup of the milk into a small bowl, and whisk in the flour to make a smooth paste. Whisk the flour paste back into the hot milk until smooth. Add the sugar, orange peel, butter, vanilla, and salt, and bring back to a simmer.

Pour the cocoa powder into a medium bowl. While whisking, gradually pour about 1 cup of the hot milk into the cocoa. Whisk until smooth, then whisk the cocoa and milk back into the pot. Bring the soup to a simmer, whisking constantly, and making sure you get into the corners of the pot. Let simmer until thickened, about 3 minutes. Strain through a sieve into a clean pot. Serve hot in bowls, with brioche or plain cookies for dipping.

SERVES 6

4 cups whole milk

¼ cup all-purpose flour

⅔ cup sugar

Peel of 1 orange, in thick strips

2 tablespoons unsalted butter

½ teaspoon vanilla extract

¼ teaspoon kosher salt

1 cup cocoa powder

Toasted brioche or plain cookies, for serving

# Limoncello

I am sure just about everyone who has traveled to Italy was offered limoncello at some point or other during the trip. This delightful lemon-flavored drink is a custom born in southern Italy, but now limoncello has crossed into not only all of Italy, but also across the Atlantic and into the United States. You can now make limoncello easily at home—no need to travel—and this recipe also works well with oranges. Limoncello is best served cold. Keep a bottle in the freezer for your guests.

MAKES 1½ QUARTS

Peel of 15 lemons
750-milliliter bottle of vodka
3½ cups water
2½ cups sugar

Wash and pat dry the lemons. Use a vegetable peeler to zest them, making sure to omit the white pith. (The pith would make the limoncello bitter.)

Stir the lemon peels into the vodka in a glass jar. Cover, and keep in a cool, dark place for 30 days. (There is no need to stir or mix the liquid.) When it is ready, the liquid will smell strongly of lemon rinds and be a deep-yellow color.

Bring water and sugar to a boil and boil for 5 to 7 minutes; let cool.

Add sugar syrup to the vodka and lemon zest, stir, and let rest for an additional 30 days, to let the flavors further mellow and blend with the sugar syrup.

Strain the limoncello through a moistened cheesecloth or coffee filters. Discard the lemon zest, pour the strained limoncello into your choice of bottle, and seal tightly.

# Italian Clubs and Organizations
# in the United States

There is an endless number of Italian clubs and organizations in the United States, and http://www.italian-american.com/italorg.htm lists many of them. But here are some of the iconic ones, and some with which I have been involved.

NIAF—www.niaf.org—The National Italian American Foundation is a nonprofit, non-partisan educational foundation that promotes Italian American culture and heritage. NIAF provides resources about the Italian American community and runs educational and youth programs, including scholarships, grants, heritage travel, and mentoring. NIAF is also the voice for Italian Americans in Washington, D.C., and works closely with the Italian American Congressional Delegation and the White House. NIAF's mission includes advancing U.S.–Italian business, political, and cultural relations and has a business council that promotes networking with corporate leaders. I attend every year the Anniversary Gala, which is held in October, and in 2009 proudly received the NIAF Special Achievement Award for Humanitarian Service.

The Columbus Citizens Foundation—www.columbuscitizensfd.org—is a nonprofit organization in New York City committed to fostering an appreciation of Italian American heritage and achievement. The foundation, through a broad range of philanthropic and cultural activities, provides opportunities for advancement to deserving Italian American students through various scholarship and grant programs. The foundation organizes New York City's annual Columbus Celebration and Columbus Day Parade, which has celebrated Italian American heritage on New York's Fifth Avenue since 1929. In 2007, I was honored to be the Grand Marshal and proudly led the parade down Fifth Avenue.

NOIAW—www.noiaw.org—The National Organization of Italian American Women is an organization for women of Italian heritage, committed to preserving Italian heritage, language, and culture by promoting and supporting the advancement of women of Italian ancestry. NOIAW serves its members through cultural programs and networking opportunities, and supports young women through nationally acclaimed scholarship, mentoring, and cultural-exchange programs. It is an organization formed of diverse women from varied professional backgrounds. Members include doctors, lawyers, artists, scientists, nurses, businesswomen, educators, writers, judges, and women working in the home. It is the only national membership organization exclusively for women of Italian ancestry. I have been involved with the organization since its foundation and was proud to be its Thirtieth Anniversary Gala honoree in 2010, being honored for outstanding contribution to Italian culture in the United States.

Sons of Italy—www.osia.org—is a national organization of men and women who represent the estimated twenty-six million Americans of Italian heritage, dedicated to promoting the Italian culture, traditions, language, legacy, and contributions to the United States and the world. "We exemplify the very best of what it is to be Italian American." The Order Sons of Italy in America (OSIA) is the largest and oldest national organization for men and women of Italian heritage in the United States. Founded in 1905 as a mutual-aid society for the early Italian immigrants, OSIA today has more than six hundred thousand members and supporters, and a network of more than 650 chapters coast to coast, making it the nation's leading service-and-advocacy organization for people of Italian descent. Its missions include encouraging the study of Italian language and culture in American schools and universities; preserving Italian American traditions, culture, history, and heritage; and promoting closer cultural relations between the United States and Italy.

Italian Cultural Society of Washington, D.C.—www.italianculturalsociety.org—was established in 1953, but an Italian Society was already in existence in Washington by the second half of the nineteenth century. The Italian Cultural Society of Washington was formed when a group of Americans and Italians was organized under the leadership of Professor Salvatore J. Castiglione, chairman of the Italian department of Georgetown University. The word "Cultural" was added in 1978 to reflect its broad objectives, and the organization was chartered as a nonprofit corporation.

UNICO—www.unico.org—states that its objectives are to "promote and enhance the Image of Italian Americans; for members to be of service to the community; to promote Italian heritage and culture; to promote, support and assist charitable, scientific, cultural, educational, and literary projects; to promote members' interest in public welfare; and, to cooperate with others in civic, social and cultural development."

# The Public Television Series of
## *Lidia's Italy in America*

Episodes from Season One of the Public Television Series of *Lidia's Italy in America*

# Index

# A Note About the Authors

Lidia Matticchio Bastianich was born in Pula, Istria, a peninsula that belonged to Italy at the time and is now part of Croatia. She came to the United States in 1958 and opened her first restaurant, Buonavia, in Queens, in 1971 and a second restaurant, Villa Secondo, shortly thereafter. A tremendous success, it inspired her to launch Felidia in 1981 in Manhattan, followed by Becco, Esca, Del Posto, and Eataly (also in New York), and Lidia's in Kansas City and Pittsburgh. With her daughter, Tanya, she has developed a line of Lidia's Pasta and Lidia's Sauces, and with her son, Joe, she produces Bastianich wines, all of which are available throughout the United States.

Lidia Bastianich is the author of six previous books, *La Cucina di Lidia, Lidia's Italian Table, Lidia's Italian-American Kitchen, Lidia's Family Table,* and *Lidia Cooks from the Heart of Italy* (with Tanya Bastianich Manuali). She has also been the host of several public-television series—*Lidia's Italian Table, Lidia's Italian-American Kitchen, Lidia's Family Table,* and *Lidia's Italy*—and she gives lectures on Italian cuisine across the country. Lidia also has developed a very interactive Web site, www.lidiasitaly.com, where she shares daily recipes, pictures, information about seasonal products, tips, and personal stories. Ms. Bastianich lives on Long Island.

Tanya Bastianich Manuali's visits to Italy as a child sparked her passion for the country's art and culture. She dedicated herself to the study of Italian Renaissance art during her college years at Georgetown and earned a master's degree from Syracuse University and a doctorate from Oxford University. Living and studying in many regions of Italy for seven years, she taught art history to American students in Florence, and also met her husband, Corrado Manuali, from Rome. In recent years, Tanya cocreated, with Shelly Burgess Nicotra, Experienze Italiane, a custom-tour company devoted to the discovery of Italian food, wine, and art. Tanya is integrally involved in the production of Lidia's public-television series and is active daily in the family restaurant business. She has also led the development of her mother's Web site, lidiasitaly.com, and related publications and merchandise lines of tabletop and cookware. Tanya has co-authored two previous books with her mother, *Lidia's Italy* and *Lidia Cooks from the Heart of Italy.* In 2010 Tanya co-authored *Reflections of the Breast: Breast Cancer in Art Through the Ages,* a social-art-historical look at breast cancer in art from Ancient Egypt to today. Tanya and Corrado live on Long Island with their children, Lorenzo and Julia.